CHRISTIANITY AND REVOLUTION

CHRISTIANITY AND REVOLUTION

The Lesson of Cuba

LESLIE DEWART

HERDER AND HERDER

1963
HERDER AND HERDER NEW YORK
232 Madison Avenue, New York 16, N.Y.

Library of Congress Catalog Card Number: 63–19832
© 1963, Herder and Herder, Incorporated
Printed in the United States of America

For the mission of Holy Church, that as a faithful witness she may preach the Gospel to the ends of the earth and be found irreproachable on the day of the Lord's coming, let us pray to the Lord.

—From the *Litany of Peace.*
(Adapted from the Byzantine Rite by Bryant Langmuir.)

CONTENTS

PREFATORY NOTE

Of all those Cuban friends, acquaintances, and relatives, both in exile and at home, from whom I have received assistance by way of information and documentation for this book, I should single out particularly Ramón Casas. As holder of the highest lay Catholic office in Cuba in 1960, the chairmanship of the National Council of *Acción Católica*, he was in an ideal position to observe the role played in the revolution by the Cuban Church. I have most specially depended upon him for advice in my evaluation of information received from other sources and in my colligation of divergencies and contradictions. He has helped me unstintingly all the more generously and kindly because, without exception, he disagrees with every one of my fundamental interpretations of the history and philosophy of Church-State relations in Cuba since 1959. Having entered its thirtieth year, however, our friendship can easily stand the strains of such disagreement.

I am obliged at least to mention the fact that most of the Cuban documentation I have used was supplied by Mrs. Mary Ricart Madera, of the Cuban National Archives. Since Mrs. Ricart's exile in 1961, Mrs. Leonila Duarte has fulfilled the same function with equal kindness. Mr. Alberto Boza and Mrs. Julia González, of the Cuban Ministry of Foreign Relations, have also provided me with some of my primary sources. Mrs. Hada D. de Ferrer, Mrs. Doris Delgado and

Mrs. Consuelo R. de Cruz have made available to me many valuable personal observations. The Reverends R. J. Moreyra, Oscar Méndez, Osvaldo Estenoz and, very specially, Fernando Faraldo, all of the Cuban province of the Society of Jesus, have given me the benefit of documentation and personal observations. The Reverend Charles-Eugène Ouellet, Vice-Superior General of the Société des Missions Étrangères de Québec has kindly answered several specific enquiries.

In relation to the broader political themes of this book I have profited greatly from discussions with Professor and Mrs. Karl Polanyi, and with Professors David Riesman, Kenneth McNaught, William Appleman Williams and Samuel Shapiro. Concerning certain theological topics I am similarly indebted to the Reverends Thomas Merton, OCSO, and Gregory Baum, OSA. It is hardly necessary to explain that in this volume I set down my views, not those of any of the persons mentioned above.

Justus George Lawler's editorial advice was as indispensable to me as it was generously extended by him. Englishing my manuscript was only the first way in which he gave me his profuse help.

To my wife I owe quite as much as any married person who writes owes to his or her spouse—for all the usual drudgery not any the less than for encouragement, consultation, and advice.

Finally, in addition to numerous clerical and lay persons everywhere to whom I have addressed specific enquiries, I must acknowledge my debt to my colleagues, in philosophy and in other disciplines, in Catholic and other circles, in Canada and in the United States, from whose willingness to listen as well as to criticize, I have learned much in speculative and practical matters. But very particularly is this true of my immediate colleagues at St. Michael's College in the University of Toronto who, disagreeing with me as often as not, have nonetheless never argued unfairly, nor ever in any way failed to do us all, and St. Michael's, the kindness of honoring both freedom and thought, and of cleaving to their faith in the value of rational enquiry and intellectual enterprise.

To all these persons (who will understand, however, if I do so with a special thought for my wife) and to those Cuban Catholics who after the events of 1960 and 1961 remained faithful to the Church as well as to those who did not, I wish very affectionately to dedicate this work.

A few portions of this essay were first published in one or more of the following periodicals: *Blackfriars*, the *Canadian Forum*, the *Canadian Register*, *The Catholic Messenger*, *Continuum*, *Council of Correspondence Newsletter*, the *Commonweal*, the *Nation*, the *Current*, *Liberation*, and the *Montreal Star*. I am indebted to their respective editors for permission to include those portions in this work.

This volume will reach the public well after Pope John XXIII's gift to the world, his encyclical *Pacem in terris*. It may be necessary, therefore, to explain all absence of reference to a document that is of obvious relevance to the topics here discussed with notice that my manuscript was completed and delivered before the publication of the encyclical. More important: a captious reader of Chapters 15 and 17 might conclude that certain passages are intended to contradict Pope John's doctrine. Such an inference would be quite incorrect—chronology alone makes it impossible. Intention aside, moreover, I believe that nothing which I state here does as a matter of fact conflict with *Pacem in terris*—though I have no doubt that if I were writing today I would express myself differently in a few instances and make certain stipulations which the reader, in any event, can probably make for himself in the light of these remarks.

A Note on Newspaper Sources

References to the *New York Times* are abbreviated as *NYT*, and to the *Toronto Globe and Mail* as *G&M*. The latter newspaper is a subscriber to the *New York Times* Service; therefore, the majority of its reports as quoted here are also to be found *verbatim* in the *New York Times* of the same date.

I make frequent reference also to the *Toronto Star* and to the *Canadian Register*. The first receives most of its foreign reports from the Associated Press, United Press-International, and Reuters news agencies. The second, which is the diocesan newspaper of all the Catholic dioceses of the Province of Ontario, subscribes to the NCWC news service. Similar if not identical reports, therefore, are likely to be found in most large-city newspapers in the United States and Canada for the same date, in the case of the first, and in most American and Canadian diocesan weeklies for approximately the same period, in the case of the second.

PROLOGUE

THE CUBAN PARADIGM

This is an essay in political philosophy. Its viewpoint is Christian, empirical, and existentialist. Its subject, in general, is the relation of twentieth-century Christianity to the world polity of today, to a world that is politically definable in terms of the thermonuclear confrontation of East and West. Its subject, in particular, is the relation of the Cuban Church to Castro's communist state.

The conflict between communism and the Church in Cuba was neither the first nor the most violent struggle between religion and social revolution: on the contrary, it was only a late and, relatively, rather peaceful one. But it has taken place under conditions that did not obtain at the time of the Mexican revolution or of the Spanish civil war or even as late as eastern Europe's communist revolutions of the post-war years. Cuba's revolution took place after the division of the world into Russian and American poles: This had an essential bearing on the policies and positions of the Cuban Church. The same reasons that have made Cuba a crucial battlefield of the cold war have also made it especially significant in the struggle of Christianity and communism. To guide our conduct wisely in that struggle we must learn the lessons of Cuba. To the Christian of today the relations of the Cuban Church to the revolution suggest an invaluable paradigm.

There is a second reason why the study of this subject may be profitable. It was in Cuba that, for the first time in the history of the West's relation to communism, the Church found itself challenged by a situation where its policy was a significant if not decisive factor in the course and the outcome of events. Elsewhere, even in Spain, that opportunity had never been available. In Cuba, choices were open and, hence, decisions of great moment were required. Today the Universal Christian Church finds itself, though on a larger space and time, challenged in an analogous way. We should analyze, therefore, the choices available to the Cuban Church and the decisions that it took. For the choices open to us are not essentially different nor is the urgency of our problem significantly less.

In a way the Cuban revolution's struggle with the Church was microcosmic. As in Cuba, the Universal Church is physically powerless and, spiritually, it is sapped by frailties and weakened by wounds. For all that, its moral force is the most powerful in existence, and could determine in great and, perhaps, decisive measure the course and outcome of world events. If we wish to repeat on a world scale the Cuban Church's policies we should do so with a full awareness of their nature and consequences. If we wish to do otherwise the history of Church-State relations in Cuba may suggest alternatives.

This enquiry, therefore, centers upon a description and interpretation of some relevant historical highlights of the Cuban revolution in its relation with the Church. However, before we proceed to attempt this, a preliminary survey is required to determine the political background against which the Church-State drama was played—in other words we shall have to account for the origin and causes of Cuba's communism.

Part III seeks to determine the nature of the critical problem that the Church experiences today in its confrontation with communism on a world scale. The final part examines some aspects of the world political situation in which the Church exists and, therefore, in which the Christian crisis takes place and in which the Church must act. The conclusion is—as is fitting in an ethical enquiry—moral: A certain role is proposed for contemporary Christianity in its relation to the political world of today.

I. THE ORIGIN AND CAUSES OF CUBA'S COMMUNISM

We would like to hope—and we prayerfully ask this favor from God—that, once the legitimate aspirations of people for liberty and independence have been satisfied, the richer will aid the poorer, the stronger support the weaker, the more advanced reach out a helping hand to the less developed, and, in the end, that all will feel themselves brothers, for all are sons of the same loving Father Who is in heaven.

—Pope John XXIII. (Allocution to Secret Consistory, January 16, 1961.)

It is unfortunate that the Cuban revolution and Castro have turned to communism. But what does Cuba's communism mean? Why and how did it come about? We do not know the exact answer to these questions. The first has to do with a process which is still at work for the ultimate nature and orientation of Cuba's and Castro's communism are yet to be determined. The second has to do with a process which is now closed, but one which is obscured by the scarcity of reliable documentation as well as by the passions it has excited among people everywhere. Nevertheless, it is possible to determine the broad limits within which the answers may lie. This is the question to which we shall now turn.

Since the thirteenth century an excessively Hellenized conception of Divine Providence has tended to make Christians see in God's presence in history little more than the stifling unfairness and the sapping inevitability of an intelligent and wise fate. They are prone to grant quite as much determinism to the development of history as orthodox Marxism does—and it makes little difference to the rigor of that determinism if hylomorphism is put in the place of dialectical materialism. One of the issues at stake in the Christian's consideration of the Cuban revolution involves the answer to the question whether or not it matters how Christians respond to their society with others, and how they create their history with them; whether it matters, that is, in relation to the finalities and responsibilities of Christianity and of the Church as such, and all this with specific reference to international politics in a political age dominated by the presence and reality of communism.

The Cuban revolution, like any other historical process, was not preordained or fated in advance. It was the result of an interaction of free and responsible men. If we understand this, not only in principle but as a matter of fact, then we may question the assumption that the truth and the rectitude of the Christian faith mean that for the Christian there are no genuine options in relation to communism, unless, perhaps, he is willing to betray his faith. It may be that one of the lessons of the Cuban revolution is the suggestion that *within* the alternatives open to the Christian faith there are both good and bad or better and worse possibilities, and that it is from among these possibilities rather than between the unique categories of belief and unbelief that the Christian is required to make a free choice.

CHAPTER 1

THE BASIC ASSUMPTIONS

Two extreme theories have been proposed to account for the Cuban revolution's turn toward communism. The first is that the Cuban revolution was a communist-master-minded plot from its inception. Among the numerous variations upon this, the least sophisticated is that Castro was a dedicated agent of international communism, groomed and trained by Moscow to do precisely as he later did. This view, which has been expounded at length in more than one book, remains quite unsupported by any kind of objective, documented evidence. Theodore Draper, with great charity, remarks that "those who insist that Castro has led a Communist revolution from the start have never thought through the implications of their position,"[1] and he finds himself "mildly amused that [Castro's] enemies on the farthest Right should attribute to him a political consistency and integrity that he has done little to deserve."[2]

Perhaps the most popular variation of the theory of Castro's antecedent communism, one particularly favored by the daily press, is that though Castro himself was not originally a communist he was either a dupe or a "captive"

[1] Theodore Draper, *Castro's Revolution: Myths and Realities* (New York, 1962), p. 75.
[2] *Ibid.,* p. 74.

of the communists. This hypothesis, too, can hardly be the product of serious thought. There never has been the slightest evidence that Castro's command of political and military forces in Cuba was less than total, thorough, and incontestable.[3]

Not to be confused with these theories is the rather widespread notion that Castro himself has stated that he was a

[3] The lengths to which some writers will go in order to support the idea that Castro has been captured by Cuban communists and is "not really in charge" may be illustrated by the following.

I shall refer below in detail to Castro's speech of December 1, 1961, in which he stated that "I believe absolutely in Marxism." On December 8, the New York Times published a report by Tad Szulc in which the suggestion was advanced that the Cuban communist party was beginning to bypass Castro. This was supported primarily by the allegation that Revolución had "censored" Castro's speech, probably because the direct admission of communism was an embarrassment to Russia at this time. Revolución's Saturday morning issue having been set while Castro was still speaking carried an understandably incomplete version, which broke off just before his remarks concerning his belief in Marxism; however, when Monday's edition came out, continued Mr. Szulc, specifying carefully that Revolución is not published on Sundays, the speech was conspicuously absent. The reason, obviously, was that the communists were trying to suppress Castro's ill-advised admission—all of which went to show who really determined what the Cuban people would or would not hear.

This web of speculation would never have been spun if Mr. Szulc had wondered about the practicality of censoring a speech that had already been delivered over a network of every radio and television station in Cuba—or if he had consulted another Havana daily, El Mundo, which carried the text in full. Or, in any event, if Mr. Szulc had learned that Revolución had a second, afternoon edition for December 2, 1961, which carried the text in full.

But the foregoing evidence was not sufficient to convince Mr. Szulc when it was called to his attention. He then claimed, this time privately, that Bohemia, at least, had expurgated the text. Now, Bohemia, a weekly magazine, usually prints only excerpts from Castro's speeches. Thus, it is not altogether surprising that the issue of December 10 did not carry the speech in full. Interestingly, the excerpts it did carry were precisely those which dealt with his belief in Communism.

communist before he came into power. This misapprehension comes from the fact that certain early reports of a speech made by Castro on the night of December 1 to December 2, 1961, proclaimed him to have said so. But later wire service reports correctly stated that "Castro did not give the specific date on his switch to Marxism,"[4] and that "he said that it was only after he came to power that he developed into a Marxist-Leninist."[5] As often happens the second reports never quite dispelled the impression created by the first. Moreover certain other publications, though evidently written on the basis of the full text of the speech, persisted in maintaining that "Premier Fidel Castro of Cuba has admitted that he concealed his long dedication to communism simply to deceive the world."[6] In reality, the only reasonable, informed conclusion to draw was that there was in Castro's speech "no convincing evidence to back up assertions in some U.S. quarters that Castro had always been a Communist or that the revolution, from its

[4] G&M, December 4, 1961 (Associated Press report). Another AP report in the Toronto Star, Dec. 2, 1961, made clear, against earlier despatches, that "he [Castro] said when he graduated from Havana University he was not a Marxist-Leninist."

[5] NYT, December 3, 1961.

[6] The Canadian Register, December 16, 1961 (NCWC report). Time went well beyond this. In its December 8, 1961, issue it fabricated a quotation out of four propositions which it attributed, in continuity, to Castro: "Ever since college I have been fundamentally influenced by Marxism. I believe absolutely in Marxism. I always believed Marxism was the correct doctrine. I am Marxist-Leninist and I will be Marxist-Leninist until I die." The second and the last propositions were uttered by Castro. The first was constructed by Time from words in a much longer proposition, part of which explained, on the contrary, that despite his studies of Marxism he had been prejudiced against it while in college and, indeed, had not been a Marxist at the time. The third proposition, as the published text of the speech shows, was invented in its totality by Time.

first days of power, was inevitably fated to slide down the Communist path."[7]

At the other extreme stands the view that the explanation of Castro's turn to communism is to be found simply and exclusively in American foreign policy, which "drove Castro into the arms of Communism." Here, too, there are variations which we need not isolate and catalogue. This alternative has the advantage that it rests upon many publicly known and well-documented facts. But, if nothing else, this sort of explanation is too simple. There were many more facets to the Cuban revolution than the Cuban-American dispute.

Theodore Draper is rare among the American critics of the Cuban revolution in his apparent opinion that extreme alternatives are often not quite as mutually exclusive as they may seem at first. For this reason alone he has a claim upon the attention of the serious student. He rejects the notion ("invented" by Guevara, he says) "that the United States was responsible for Castro's action or 'responses'."[8] In Draper's view "the Communists and Fidel walked toward each other, each with his eyes open, each filling a need in the other."[9] This, at least in a descriptive sense, is perfectly true. It is but a faithful summary of some facts.

Yet, Draper's theory is not unambiguous for all that. Who are "the communists" toward whom Fidel walked with his eyes open for the sake of a felt need, and *vice versa*? There are, in fact, three distinct communist components in that communism to which Castro and the revolution eventually turned, all of which are blanketed by any general reference

[7] G&M, December 9, 1961.
[8] Draper, p. 105.
[9] Draper, p. 107.

to "the communists." There is, first, the Cuban communists, the *Partido Socialista Popular* of Blás Roca, Lázaro Peña, Carlos Rafael Rodríguez, and Juan Marinello. This component is of least importance. It was not *their* help that Castro needed vitally; they are not underwriting Cuban economy or providing Cuba with arms; though, to be precise, as a party they did have certain assets that Castro badly needed at a certain point, principally discipline, organization, honesty, fiscal integrity, reliability, devotion to a revolutionary cause, commitment to change, even a sort of patriotism (according to their lights), and no disposition whatever to take the American side regardless of what the alternative might be. Castro obtained these things from them along with some disadvantages that he had to put up with but in no event did Castro turn to communism on that account. It was another component, Russia, that mattered most of all, though there is also a third, namely, Marxism-Leninism as a political philosophy. The reasons why he allied himself with the one are not the reasons why he adopted the other.

Similarly, Draper is in part correct when he states that "only the ingenuous can still believe that Fidel Castro walked into a communist trap or that he gave up the democratic road because the United States did not give him enough support in his early months in power."[10] Now, the first part of the statement is unqualifiedly true: the suggestion that Castro was hoodwinked by the Cuban communists into moves that he himself was originally incapable of making cannot be maintained. The second part, however, is ambiguous. Does it deny absolutely every connection between American diplomacy and the ultimate convergence of

[10] Draper, p. 107.

Castro and communist Russia, communist ideology, and Cuban Communists? Even a priori this would be unlikely. But Draper equivocates: the statement is true in the context of a polemic with "the ingenuous." For there has been misinformation and less than sound reasoning at all levels of American opinion, and some persons have written as if Castro had originally offered to lead a democratic revolution under American tutelage, and as if the United States had then turned down this implicit or explicit offer.

This is quite incorrect. There was no doubt from the outset that Castro wanted *full* independence from the United States in every respect, and that he never was disposed to entertain any sort of arrangement whereby in exchange for economic aid he would compromise in the slightest his freedom of action regarding either the nature of the domestic reform or the conduct of foreign affairs. Castro may or may not have wanted to seek help from the United States. Above all he wanted to be left alone to pursue his purposes. He never maintained or indicated otherwise, and it is naïve to think that Castro's purposes could have been bought off with a little or with much foreign aid; partnership, however, grounded upon full mutual respect and on a footing of political equality might have been something else again. But that was never expected by him nor entertained by the United States.

Draper himself borders on the naïve when he reasons that "a revolutionary leader does not betray the fundamental democratic character of his revolution because American oil companies refuse to refine Soviet oil or because the United States suspends a Cuban quota that has been attacked as 'a symbol of colonialism'."[11] If this means that there is no

[11] Draper, p. 106.

strict connection of mechanical causality between these events, then Mr. Draper's observation is as correct as it is irrelevant. But if he means that one could reasonably expect any government leader to subject his country's oil supply, or eighty per cent of his country's foreign income, to the whims of democratic businessmen in preference to commercial contracts with a totalitarian government, then Draper's militant anticommunism gets the better of his common sense.

There would be as little value in harping upon Theodore Draper's rare lapses from common sense as there would be in taking seriously the bulk of what has been written so far about Cuba. Quite the contrary, it is the strength of Draper's argument, its plausibility, its foundation in fact, its sophistication, its logic and its perceptiveness—all the good qualities that have made it emerge as the standard, certainly the moderate, interpretation of the revolution—it is all this that calls for criticism of his thesis, according to which American diplomacy neither determined nor hindered the Cuban revolution's "fusion" with communism; from which follows that the United States could not have profitably followed any policy essentially different from that which it devised, and that Cuba's communism justifies the basic objective of both Eisenhower and Kennedy, namely, the overthrow of Castro—though not necessarily the inept tactics to which they have had recourse.

Indeed it is because Draper's case is so well built that its failure to reach the truth is noteworthy; its excellence makes his work all the more misleading and fallacious. What, then, if neither fact nor logic, is the root of Draper's mistake? Whether consciously or not, Draper has assumed several principles which have not been generally questioned

—perhaps because they are widely shared. The following is a case in point.

Draper criticizes Claude Julien's account of the revolution in these terms: "the fundamental weakness in Julien's analysis lies in the fact that Castro's collaboration with the Communists was sealed in 1959, when the United States policy was based on a 'wait and see' attitude, and not in 1960, when the United States decided that Castro had gone too far in his collusion with the Communists to turn back."[12]

Now, Draper is well aware that "collaboration with the communists" in 1959 can only refer to Castro's acceptance of the not particularly effective and certainly not obligating support of the PSP, whereas "collusion with the communists" of the kind that had gone "too far" in 1960 must refer essentially to Russian economic and political support. Draper is also aware that the latter did not begin until February, 1960, and that by this time the opposition of the United States government had become positive, militant, and acerb. Thus, if Draper is able to bracket both terms together, collaboration in 1959 and collusion in 1960, the reason cannot be that he is badly informed but, apparently, that he considers their distinction irrelevant. Why should he find it so?

The transition from "collaboration" in Draper's first term to "collusion" in the second may provide a clue. It is unnecessary at this point to consider whether, in the first place, one should not distinguish a variety of communist ends and motives which should be evaluated differentially both as to degree and kind. Even if one grants the unqualified malevolence of all communism everywhere and at all times, the

[12] Draper, p. 161.

presupposition is questionable that to accept communist support is the same as to share each and every communist purpose, and constitutes, therefore, "collusion."

The point is not at all whether this betrays emotional bias on Draper's part. The point is that, whatever its origin, the foregoing confusion is willy-nilly bound to the assumption that both democracy and communism are absolute political forms with antithetical and absolute values. The democratic political theorist should be very circumspect at this juncture. It may be that one cannot totalize communism or conceive it as an undifferentiated, subsistent, ideal Form without performing the same disservice for democracy. Of course, Theodore Draper did not originate the idea that only absolute and total political choices are open to man. Many who do not share Draper's Cuban interpretation assume with him that one cannot develop a democratic political ethics except upon a Platonic or Aristotelian metaphysics, and that one cannot be democratic except one makes of democracy an ultimate reality which one can only unquestioningly serve as the master of society and man.

The democratic political philosopher might well ask himself whether this does not imply a totalitarianism no less oppressive for its democratic origins than false for its dialectical view of politics and its rationalist view of man. And since a *total* choice is, by definition, religious, the Christian might well also inquire whether Draper's premise does not similarly imply a sacralization and divinization of the political order which may conflict with the deepest meaning and the most basic tenets of the Christian faith.

Evidently, the matter is of crucial importance for one's interpretation of the Cuban revolution and indeed every other political event. Once Draper's assumptions are granted, it is impossible in good logic to disagree with his conclusions.

The basic assumptions made here are that a Christian political philosophy is better developed empirically and existentially, and that democracy, like any other political idea, is neither the measure of political truth nor an end which man either worships or serves but, on the contrary, a means to human ends and to man's worship of Being and Truth.

CHAPTER 2

THE POLITICAL LABYRINTHS

From Castro's stiff resistance to American economic pressure one should simply conclude that his determination to carry out his revolutionary policy was strong enough to count no costs and reckon no consequences. But this is hardly a penetrating or novel conclusion. His resoluteness was plain for all to see long before the conflict of wills became deadlocked. It should have been evident that his will and strength of character—indeed, a latent ruthlessness, as it turned out—were not to be trifled with. In that character and in that will we find the first, but only the first, of the forces that were brought to bear upon the Cuban revolution.

Castro has all the single-mindedness of the true revolutionary. This is the foundation of his heroic stature, as has become manifest, but it was also deducible from the first, when only an unusual singleness and strength of purpose could have brought him to power uncorrupted, uncommitted, and uncompromising under the conditions of extreme institutionalized disorder that were normal in Cuba. It makes little difference whether we call this single-mindedness the fanaticism of a crazed demagogue or the devotion of a patriot. What matters is that he has been guided from the outset by an unshakable faith in himself and by the final and immutable principle that absolutely nothing should stand in the way of his revolution. When it seemed to him, rightly or wrongly, that to cast his lot with Communism was the best, if not the only, means to save the revolution, an inner struggle was hardly necessary for his decision.

Teresa Casuso, who knows him well, has graphically vignetted those flaws in Castro's character which made him first trap himself in impossible alternatives and then resort to communism as a way out. She has illustrated both his virtues and his pathetic desire to please, his oversensitivity, his all-too-human pride. She has posed the dilemma created by his inadequacies, on the one hand, and his responsibilities, ambitions, and sincere desire for revolutionary reform, on the other. "Day by day," she writes, "I saw how Fidel, lost in the labyrinth of power, tangled everything by his clumsiness, then in desperation sought clattering solutions."[1]

What Miss Casuso seems to have neglected is the role that the Cuban people themselves and the Cuban culture played in the revolution and its ultimate course toward communism. It is inadequate to account for that course as if Castro had been the only Cuban to become a communist in recent times. All but a few of his senior advisors, administrators, and ministers are persons of undoubted non-communist background who have nevertheless agreed, more or less enthusiastically, to a Marxist-Leninist line for the revolution. Millions of people in Cuba followed Castro into communism.

The beginning of misunderstanding occurs precisely at

[1] Teresa Casuso, *Cuba and Castro* (New York, 1961), p. 164.

this point. Castro is thoroughly Cuban: To see him as aberrant in any substantial respect is to reveal either one's bias against Castro or one's ignorance of Cuba. Though Teresa Casuso, unlike most other close associates who broke with him, has written with a great deal of objectivity and candor, she writes as though Castro's unpunctuality, his garrulousness, his general oversensitivity, his inability to appreciate criticism, his pride, his thoughtlessness, his vanity, his volatility, and his improvidence were not painfully typical of the Cuban character, however much they may ordinarily be balanced by many and noble traits. But Fidel Castro is, indeed, in all basic respects a stock Cuban character, and one has seen a dozen like him, down to trivial detail, among revolution-struck University of Havana students. Castro's tragedy, which is also Cuba's, is that he exaggerated both the worst and the best of the Cuban psyche, and that to the common qualities he united an unusual strength of purpose, great courage, and an imprudent degree of resoluteness and inflexibility.

The point is that Castro adopted communism pragmatically—this is one reason why it was not fated beforehand. But to say "pragmatically" is not to say half-heartedly or with reservations; Castro adopted Marxism-Leninism sincerely and systematically, though to judge by his public utterances with only little more than a cursory acquaintance with its theoretical points and thus he continues in character even in this respect. For to Castro questions of detail have never been more problematic than those about the correctness of otherwise effective means: All he seems to care to debate is their efficiency.

This is not to suggest that he is really a crypto-democrat playing the game of communism. It is to suggest, however, that it is "hazardous to predict [Castro's] future career in the Communist movement," and that "further surprises cannot be ruled out."[2] Be that as it may, Castro did not adopt communism because he became convinced of its truth in the first place, a truth which he then sought to implement. On the contrary, having found it convenient and, more than convenient, practical, to apply communism, he became sincerely persuaded of its truth.

Why, then, did Castro's single-minded resolve have to result in his espousal of Communism? The answer is that it did not have to do so. Castro was subjected to a variety of pressures from a variety of sources, all of which combined to restrict the choices open to him in order to avoid failure. A greater man than he, a man with either enough personal experience in the art of politics or, more to the point, with enough of cultural background in diplomacy and statesmanship might have made a better effort at channeling his will more efficiently. Teresa Casuso's expression is difficult to improve upon: Castro became lost in the labyrinths of power. This does not make of him a victim of bewilderment. But it points up that it is both unfair and self-deceptive to pretend, as so many of Castro's critics pretend, that the labyrinths did not exist.

[2] Draper, p. 70.

Chapter 3

The Abettors Abroad

No amount of manipulation of the evidence publicly available can obviate the fact that Eisenhower's Cuban policy was unwisely, unduly, and, as Professor Samuel Shapiro has ironically pointed out, inefficiently geared to the protection of the American investment in Cuba. However, as with every other financial wrangle the dispute between Washington and Havana could always be prolonged by meeting every argument on each side with a more or less reasonable counterargument. If no other argument were available one could always have based one's contention on the need to redress a previous inequity. Exactly how far back did one have to go to determine no more than a fair starting point for the dispute? This question itself could have been interminably controverted. What we may note, simply as a matter of fact, is that the United States, on the whole, favored restricting the dispute to immediate questions, whereas Cuba, quite definitely, wished to take a wider view of the subjects of negotiation. Let us, with that prelude, merely try to indicate the sort of escalation pattern which was set from the start.

The Cuban revolution, as promised by Castro, was to have been grounded upon a badly needed redistribution of the land. The reasons why this had to be so are well known: The inequities of land distribution and the injustices of land misuse were so great in Cuba that land reform was the minimal measure that a genuine, thorough, and efficient social reform program could have undertaken. It struck at the basic social evil in Cuba. Had this been left uncorrected the revolution would have been a sham. Castro's first act upon assuming office was to begin to draft a detailed land reform law and to prepare its implementation. Three months later, in May, 1959, the law was proclaimed.

Within two weeks of the proclamation of the law the United States made official representations to the Cuban government in a diplomatic note dated June 11.[1] The note "recognized Cuba's right under international law to take property within its jurisdiction,"[2] but it added that "this right is coupled with the corresponding obligations for prompt, adequate and effective compensation."[3]

But exactly what was meant by "prompt, adequate and effective compensation"? The Land Reform Law did not provide for *immediate* cash compensation on the grounds that Cuba could not afford it, since the country had been left on the edge of bankruptcy by Batista. Instead, it provided for repayment in four and one-half per cent, twenty-year bonds. As for effectiveness, Cuba also claimed, on the same grounds, that it could pay interest and principal only in Cuban currency. As to adequacy, the law provided that the evaluation of the property to be taken over should be based on the declared tax value of the lands. Needless to explain, this last arrangement was prejudicial to the in-

[1] See NYT, June 12, 1959.
[2] The Wall Street Journal, June 12, 1959.
[3] Quoted by Time, June 22, 1959.

terests of all those who, in conspiracy with corrupt officials of the Batista regime, had defrauded the public.

For all its claims, the American note was couched in moderate and reasonable language. The Cuban reply, four days later, was itself not unreasonable. The Cuban government, it said, "conceded that the United States government had always been 'consistent and unequivocal' in its support of rural land reform in countries where it was long overdue."[4] Moreover, as the same account put it:

In her note of June 15 Cuba acknowledged that "it is true that the Constitution of 1940 and the basic law in force provide that the price of expropriations shall be paid in advance and in cash in the amount fixed by the courts." . . . Nevertheless, the note went on, Cuba was unable to do this for several reasons: the regime of former President Fulgencio Batista had systematically robbed the treasury and sent dollar resources into private accounts overseas; the economy was in a chaotic condition when Dr. Castro's revolutionary regime took over, and there had been an unfavorable balance of payments between Cuba and the United States amounting to more than $1,000,000,000 over the previous ten years.

Moreover, the Cuban note said, Japan, when she was under United States occupation, instituted a land-reform program with compensation in agrarian bonds earning 3½ per cent and payable in annual installments over twenty-five years.

Cuba, the note continued, did not ignore the fact that United States private investment had contributed to Cuba's economic growth. The Government would be "pleased," it said, if the United States Government "would induce United States investors affected by the agrarian reform to help further the overall development of the Cuban economy in accordance with the planned policy" [of Cuba].

The American note had put a case of undoubted *prima facie* validity: The United States was only asking for its due. On the other hand Cuba's answer, too, was not only

[4] *NYT*, January 10, 1960.

highly conciliatory[5]—indeed, it hoped the United States would "understand and appraise the powerful reasons which justify the form of payment of the indemnities"[6]—it was also irrefutably true.

It was so irrefutable, in fact, that no one has tried to argue the contrary, though the contrary has often been an unstated premise of many interpretations of the Cuban revolution. The United States government, in particular, never tried to rest its case on Cuba's financial ability to have offered substantially better terms than she proposed. Nevertheless, the United States pressed its claim. Later, on September 26, 1960, Castro was to suggest to the General Assembly of the United Nations that to the United States "prompt, effective and just payment meant payment right now, in United States dollars and at their own evaluation."[7] It seems that this statement was not altogether imprecise.

But this was still in the future. Indeed, the United States did not even reply to the Cuban note of June 15 until four months later, on October 12. By then conditions had changed somewhat. Yet, even before the text of the Cuban

[5] For example, it conceded to the United States a legal claim on the strength of both the 1940 Constitution and "the basic law in force." The Cuban government could have alleged that it was constituted not on the 1940 document, but upon a *Ley Fundamental*, approved by Miró Cardona's cabinet on February 7, 1959, ten days before Castro's accession to power. The *Ley* provided that "in cases of forcible expropriations pursuant to land reform . . . compensation in cash shall not be indispensable" (as it had been according to the 1940 Constitution), and that "the law can determine other means of repayment, provided they incorporate appropriate guarantees." See Antonio Núñez Jiménez, *Geografía de Cuba* (Havana, 1959), pp. 194–7. The Land Reform Law itself provided for cash compensation only upon movable property and not upon real estate.

[6] *NYT*, June 16, 1959. "Appraise" is a mistranslation of *apreciar*, which means both "to appraise" and "to appreciate."

[7] Text in *Obra Revolucionaria*, No. 26 (Fall, 1960).

note of June 15 became known "some Congressmen [had] threat[ened] to cut Cuba's [sugar] quota"[8]: It was an ill omen of a difficult summer ahead. It seems, in any event, that both sides were overconfident in two respects: first, as to the justice of their respective cases, second, as to their ability to make their views prevail. These are obviously the two circumstances which in conjunction usually generate the worst international conflicts.

When to these dispositions of the Cuban government are added the inefficiency, disorder, and high-handedness that had been perfectly normal for Cuba in the best of times, but which had become particularly exacerbated by the popular realization that a true revolution had arrived, it is totally unnecessary to ascribe secret intentions to Castro's cavalier treatment of United States business interests during that summer and fall. Even more, his treatment was in a sense provocative. But it is one thing to be provocative because one does not fear the consequences of one's behavior or disregards them or believes them avoidable; it is another to be provocative because one intends to elicit an aggressive response. It is the latter which is often ascribed to Castro.[9] But, on the contrary, every indication we have is that he thought that in his relations

---

[8] The Wall Street Journal, June 16, 1959; also idem, June 24, 1959.

[9] The United States government maintained in the General Assembly of the United Nations that Cuba "push[ed] the United States into a sugar embargo so that the Cuban regime could charge its neighbor with economic aggression," (the Boston Globe, October 14, 1960). The argument has been improved upon by others in more recent times: dupes and/or proto-communists in the State Department pressed Castro so that Castro would push the United States into economic retaliation so Castro could charge the United States with economic aggression.

with the United States government things would go not much further than they already had gone. Extremely ambitious plans were laid and predicated upon continued good relations between the two countries, for instance, "a four-year, $200,000,000 tourist development program."[10] And INRA, the government agency in charge of implementing land reform, invested huge amounts in American agricultural machinery—and, only a year later, when the American embargo on spare parts was applied, would Cuba regret this decision. At any rate, the land reform program, as the contemporary Cuban slogan had it, "went on."

One can only guess whether indeed things would have gone no further if the suspicion of communism had not been skillfully raised at this point. For obvious reasons, it is difficult to reconstruct exactly how this was done. We do know that from the beginning of Castro's regime the suspicions of at least two groups had been aroused for reasons otherwise as diverse as the groups themselves. One group, the Catholics within the 26 of July Movement, particularly those in the Agriculture Department, thought that Castro's neutralism was sufficient evidence of ideological error, when, at a later date, Castro did not reject domestic communist collaboration, their convictions became unshakable. For instance, they did not know what position to take on the Land Reform Law; more particularly, the project of establishing co-operative farms strained their faith, since the co-operatives might well turn out to be Chinese-style communes. As for the other group, the latifundistas, those domestic and foreign interests most directly and adversely affected by the land reform, it would not be idle to suppose that between the sincerely convinced and the insincerely persuaded few were left who were not ready to cavil at the

[10] The New York Herald Tribune, October 19, 1959.

danger of communism in Cuba. And, understandably, in view of the prevailing American climate, the rumors and suspicions fell as a spark among the tinder of American public opinion.

The role of a certain segment of the American press in fanning these fires is well remembered. *Time* magazine's in particular has become proverbial. As soon as Castro used unmistakable formulas expressing neutralism as his foreign policy *Time* suddenly adopted the sort of imprecise and insinuating vocabulary in connection with the revolution ("card carrier or sympathizers, . . . a leftist fellow-traveller network,"[11] "Red-liners . . . pro-Communist"[12]), which once, when used by Senator McCarthy, it had not dismissed lightly or condoned.

On June 22 *Time* discovered that Antonio Nuñez Jiménez, the Executive Director of INRA and architect of the land reform program, was "a longtime Communist-liner," and thereafter it systematically identified the danger of communism with what, from Cuba's point of view, could also have been described as Cuba's legitimate aspirations. Eventually *Time* descended to a direct charge of Marxism against Núñez Jiménez, the adduced evidence of which was as easy to check as it was demonstrably false.[13]

As far as can be determined, the most common opinion

[11] *Time*, April 20, 1959. The issue of May 11, 1959, stated that "fellow travellers work on the 'Commission for the Revision of Cuban History Books'." Angel del Cerro, a prominent Catholic layman who was a member of the Commission categorically denied the truth of the charge. See *Bohemia*, May 17, 1959.

[12] *Time*, May 4, 1959.

[13] "Antonio Núñez Jiménez . . . wrote a Marxist *Geography of Cuba* that is now a standard textbook in Cuban schools," *Time*, December 7, 1959. This was reasserted on January 4, 1960, and the *Boston Daily Globe* repeated it on February 23, 1960. There is no doctrine in the book that could be remotely called Marxist.

in the United States at this time was that Castro himself was not a communist, but that indirectly he constituted a grave communist threat to the safety of the United States. Relatively few would have gone as far as did Spruille Braden, former ambassador to Cuba and Assistant Secretary of State, who thought that "so grave is the situation, that I pray with all my heart, body and soul that the Communists and their most useful tool to date, Fidel Castro, may be ejected from their control of Cuba."[14] But, then, relatively few Americans would share many of Mr. Braden's other views on the danger of communism, particularly since his connection with the John Birch Society has become known: at the time, however, his words carried all the weight of his position.

What was the truth of the matter? No reasonable evidence has been adduced to contradict all the indications we have on this question, which General C. P. Cabell, Deputy CIA Director, summarized on November 5, 1959, for the United States Senate's Committee on the Judiciary:

> Our information shows that the Cuban Communists do not consider [Castro] a Communist party member, or even a pro-Communist [italics mine]. On the other hand, they are delighted with the nature of his government, which has allowed the Communists opportunity, free opportunity, to organize, to propagandize, and to infiltrate.
>
> We know that the Communists consider Castro as a representative of the bourgeoisie, and were unable to gain recognition or commitments from him during the course of the revolution.
>
> We know that the Communists were concerned when, at the time of his trip to the United States, he showed evidence of a friendly attitude toward the United States.
>
> We know also that it has been the assigned task of the Cuban

[14] Text of his testimony to the Comm. on the Judiciary, U.S. Senate, 86th Congress, 1st session, July 17, 1959. U.S. Doc. 2.449, p. 244.

Communist party to prevent Castro's revolution from going to the right, that is, from establishing friendly relations with the United States, or ending its tolerance of Communist activities.

Our conclusion, therefore, is that Fidel Castro is not a Communist; however, he certainly is not anti-Communist. His extreme policies, including confiscation of private property, lead him to take positions and make statements such as his violent anti-U.S. outbursts which are extremely useful to international communism and are being exploited by the Communists to the maximum extent.

He has delegated authority in key areas to persons known to be pro-Communists or who are susceptible to exploitation by Communists . . .

It is questionable whether the Communists desire to recruit Castro into the Communist Party, that they could do so if they wished, or that he would be susceptible to Communist discipline if he joined. As I say, that is subject to question.

The Communist viewpoint is that he represents leadership of a nationalistic, bourgeoise-democratic revolution which precedes a Communist rise to power . . .

Although it is evident that the Communists have been able to exploit Castro in his movement for their own benefit through these channels, as yet they do not appear to control him or his government. In terms of mass following they still represent a minority, though a very well organized one.

In certain areas, as in organized labor, there are experienced non-Communist leaders who form an obstacle to rapid Communist progress.

There are student and professional groups which are also non-Communist although firmly supporting Fidel, and within the 26th of July movement there is considerable evidence of opposition to communism.

As evidenced in recent demonstrations, however, these groups are prepared to rally to the defence of the regime.[15]

The exactness of General Cabell's statement, as of that time, has not been gainsaid to date except gratuitously: its unpleasant implications for an evaluation of American

[15] *Hearings of the Comm. on the Judiciary, U.S. Senate,* 86th Congress, 1st session, Nov. 5, 1959, pp. 162–164.

policy have sometimes been ignored. Note, most particularly, his concluding words.

The first summer of Castro's land reform, thus, passed without major discord, but by the early autumn the pressure of public opinion upon President Eisenhower to "do something" about Castro could not longer be ignored. Besides, the dust had settled: It had now become certain that unless it were tamed, Castro's revolution would achieve full independence for Cuba. On October 12 the United States government answered Cuba's note of four months earlier in the following terms[16]:

> Whatever the wrongdoings of the Batista regime, United States investors should not be penalized for actions in which they had no responsibility, nor did these actions provide the Castro government with a valid reason for ignoring international law and the basic law of Cuba.
>
> The Japanese agrarian bonds were used to pay Japanese landholders and not foreign owners.
>
> Encouraging private investment is not something the United States government can properly do, since such investment depends upon a confidence that only Cuba herself can create by her actions and attitude.

This, then, served notice that the United States intended to press its case.

But this was not all. In fact, by itself the reply amounted, diplomatically speaking, to an admission of weakness. The United States surely did not expect Cuba to create United States dollars out of the innocence—if such it was—of United States business concerning Cuba's political chaos. And the allegation concerning the dissimilarity between Japanese landowners and American foreign investors was sufficiently ingenuous to suggest Eisenhower's own hand.

[16] Summarized, *NYT*, January 10, 1960.

Nor was the veiled threat of economic pressure decisive at this time in changing the course of events. But on October 11, the day before the note was transmitted, the first concrete indication of the American government's basic opposition to the revolutionary government of Cuba became apparent. On that day the first of a winter-long series of bombing and incendiary raids was flown over a Cuban sugar mill.[17] We can realize in retrospect that this meant only that Eisenhower, after several months of indecision, had finally begun to heed Vice President Nixon's advice on how to deal with Castro.[18] The process leading to Eisenhower's eventual decision to "guatemalize" Cuba began its tortuous dialectic at this point.

By mid-October, 1959, however, as the events suggest, only a compromise between inaction and Nixon's recommendation was adopted, namely, to countenance the efforts of the Cuban counterrevolution rather than directly to mount an American one. No evidence has come to light to support the Cuban Government's charge (made only later) that the training of the bastistianos, or fully active co-operation with them, was undertaken by the United States government at this time—that was still three to four months away. All the collusion proved by evidence is that the batistianos were allowed a free hand and given no more than occasional assistance. But we should grasp the weight of this passive (though not purely passive) decision. Let us trace its development.

At the end of Batista's rule, the majority of his henchmen fled to Miami expecting, in the usual tradition, to return to

---

[17] NYT, October 14, 1959.
[18] As early as April, 1959, Nixon had officially urged training Cuban guerillas to overthrow Castro. See Draper, pp. 62–3.

Cuba before long. But they soon appreciated the meaning of Castro's revolution: the executions, for instance, demonstrated its unprecedented character only too well. Counterrevolutionary plotting would thus have to be undertaken on a relatively large and unified scale. The *White Rose* was the first counterrevolutionary society to be formed.

On August 9, 1959 an air invasion was launched from the Dominican Republic.[19] But the plot had been infiltrated by Cuban double agents and it was easily foiled. Only a month later, in September, 1959, did it become evident that the counterrevolutionary bases of operations had been transferred to Florida. For it was during that month that the Miami counterrevolution succeeded in establishing a small guerilla force in Pinar del Rio province headed by Manuel Beatón, a *batistiano* corporal against whom a murder charge was pending. Before the end of the month, however, Beatón's forces had been split. Among twenty guerillas captured were found two American pilots.[20] The band had been, and continued to be, supported from bases in Florida. Supplies were flown in "by night aboard small planes flying out of southern Florida."[21] The Cuban government lodged "an official protest in Washington over the use of the Florida fields by the anti-Castro rebels,"[22] which made it clear that it did not believe the United States government consciously implicated in such activities and expressed the hope that all that was required for Washington to act decisively was knowledge of what was taking place.

Now, up to this point both sides, despite an increasingly

[19] See *Bohemia*, August 16, August 23, and August 30, 1959.
[20] *Time*, October 26, 1959.
[21] *Ibid.*
[22] *Ibid.*

violent tone in their domestic pronouncements, had maintained all the diplomatic formalities and, as far the public record can show, had spoken to each other only within the limits of strict truth. But at this moment a different note was introduced in the proceedings. And it is necessary to admit that it was introduced by the United States government as it began to dissimulate and to adopt mental reservations all the less effective because they were transparent. For as the flights became more numerous and Cuba's protests correspondingly more pressing, the United States government insisted not only that it was unconnected with the raids, but it also asserted that it was doing all within its power to stop them. Not only was this untrue but, before long, the American government had begun to extend to the counter-revolutionaries its fairly active co-operation.

It seems, therefore, that by October 12th when the American government's note was delivered to the Cuban government, there was some reason on the part of the latter to wonder what the former's intentions were. The first air raid of October 11 was followed by another on October 19. Then, at dusk on October 21, 1959, Díaz Lanz flew his sortie over the city of Havana. This was the third raid within the ten-day period during which the United States had manifested its intention to press its opposition to Cuba's land reform. The events were, obviously, not unrelated. The summer of indecision had come to an abrupt and explosive end.

Pedro Díaz Lanz had fought in the Sierra beside Castro. After the victory he had been made chief of Cuba's remaining air force. According to the Cuban government he had been dismissed from his post on account of irregularities; according to him he had resigned in protest over

Castro's communism. Whatever the truth, he had fled to Miami. Now he had returned—at the controls of an American aircraft. The only fact about Díaz Lanz' raid on which there is unanimity is that two people were killed and about forty injured. The Cuban government maintained that Díaz Lanz had bombed Havana and asked the United States government to apprehend and prosecute him under United States law. The United States reported that Díaz Lanz had, indeed, flown a leaflet raid over Havana in a DC-3 (a commercial aircraft), but that it did not know the whereabouts of pilot or plane. Cuba asserted that it was a B-25 Mitchell bomber, that in addition to leaflets the aircraft had dropped explosives of some type and, possibly, strafed the streets, and it insisted that the United States Government's security services could not be as inefficient as was claimed. Cuba's allegations were bolstered by the fact that an enterprising correspondent-photographer team sent by *Bohemia* magazine located the aircraft at the Pompano Beach airport within forty-eight hours of their arrival in Florida: It was, indeed, a B-25. Ironically, it was an aircraft originally purchased from the United States by the Batista government, but it had never been handed over because of the late embargo declared by the United States in 1958. It also appeared that it had been delivered by the Dade County sheriff to a *batistiano* Air Force captain over the protests of the Cuban government.[23] Collusion, therefore, is inescapable. The United States government seems, in effect, to have provided Díaz Lanz with the aircraft he used in the raid. This, to repeat, was early October, 1959.

It would not be inexact to say that this was the Eisenhower government's rehearsal for the soon-to-come U-2

[23] See *Bohemia*, November 1, 1959.

affair. For the United States now had to admit, of course, that a B-25 had indeed been used to fly the raid. But it retrenched to a position so half-heartedly conceived and so hastily prepared that it was quite indefensible. The United States government now stated that though it had erred in claiming that the aircraft was not a military type nevertheless "it was impossible for it to drop bombs" (something to do with the mechanical intricacies of bomb racks, it appeared) and, moreover, that "an analysis of the available evidence . . . indicates that *many, if not all* [italics mine] of the persons injured received their wounds either from stray rounds from antiaircraft fire of the Cuban Armed forces or from hand grenades or bombs thrown from automobiles by terrorists."[24]

Cuba boggled at this qualification on the grounds that the directly implied admission, namely, that some casualties remained unaccounted for, plainly contradicted the substance of the claim made by the United States, namely, that there had been no aerial armed attack whatever on Cuba from American soil. Curiously, although the American government's attempt at exculpation was indefensible it managed to prevail. For the contradiction seemed to escape American public opinion, perhaps because in the first place it escaped the American press, which continued to report, on the basis of the American government's denial, that Cuba's allegations were a gratuitous fabrication which could only serve hostile purposes. Cuba's protests thenceforth were commonly construed as unwarranted "attacks" on the United States.

At a mass meeting on October 23, Castro accused the

[24] Statement issued by the U.S. State Department, *NYT*, November 10, 1959.

United States of allowing the raids and of passive complicity with the *White Rose*. On October 27, Ambassador Bonsal was received by President Dorticós, and delivered a note to the latter charging "deliberate and concerted efforts to replace traditional friendship with distrust and hostility," and rejected "with indignation" the suggestion that the United States government was countenancing the clandestine flights.[25] When Cuba tried to buy fighter aircraft in Great Britain, the move was blocked by the United States.[26]

At Eisenhower's press conference the same week a reporter asked: "What do you suppose, sir, is eating Castro? . . . bringing a telling hoot of laughter from the newsmen. Eisenhower could only express bewilderment: 'We are Cuba's best market, and you would think they would want good relationships. I don't know exactly what the difficulty is'."[27] If Eisenhower did not truly know exactly what the difficulty was, no doubt should have remained in his mind when Cuba answered the diplomatic note of October 27 with her own note of November 13. This note, in effect, stated in detail the policy of the Cuban government in all that pertained to Cuban-United States relations. Its earnestness is attested to by later events: It is basic to an understanding of Cuban-American relations.

The note outlined with great precision how the Cuban government perceived its past relations with the United States and how it proposed to modify them in the future, hoping that this might be achieved while furthering the desire of the Cuban government and the Cuban people "to live in peace and friendship and to increase their diplomatic

25 *Time*, November 9, 1959.
26 See *NYT*, December 3, 1959.
27 *Time*, November 9, 1959.

and economic relations on the basis of mutual respect and reciprocal benefit with the people and government of the United States of America." This, the note added "can be achieved with great ease if, on the one hand, the identification is not made between the financial interests of a restricted group of American citizens and the permanent interests that should rule the relations between two traditionally friendly countries who have been good and cordial neighbors; and if, on the other, a definitive stop is put to the counterrevolutionary activities of the Cuban war criminals who have taken shelter in United States territory, and if those Americans are rendered powerless who instigate and support those unlawful activities against Cuba."[28] Such a guarantee against direct or indirect aggression was an undertaking that the United States was not ready to give until after the Cuban missile-bases crisis of October 1962. It has now been given, although only by implication and not in a fully explicit form. It would be difficult to compute exactly how many lives it has cost.

The substance of the note made clear three important points. The first was that the United States should recognize the significance of the historical reality of the present revolution, in return for which Cuba would recognize the historical reality of the bonds of her historical past with the United States: This would permit the establishment of a commonly advantageous future. Second, the note made clear that the economic problems that endangered good relations between the two countries ranged well beyond the mere issue of land reform. Therefore fundamental revision

[28] Text of the note *En Defensa de la Soberanía Nacional,* Department of Public Relations, Ministry of External Affairs of the Republic of Cuba, November, 1959, p. 21.

of the total economic pattern between the two countries should be undertaken. In particular "it is of cardinal importance that . . . the sugar trade pattern be the object of a bilateral agreement."[29] Finally, the note stated (perhaps a little too candidly), what course Cuba intended to follow. "It is only logical [therefore], that Cuba try to resolve the growing deficits of her trade balance, without prejudice to the intensification of her economic relations with the United States, by increasing [Cuba's] foreign income by means of the diversification of production, the opening of new markets and the expansion of trade with all countries of the world."[30]

This was the turning point. The United States did not return an official answer, but it argued, unofficially, in the terminology of those days, that the United States government had abandoned all belief in Fidel Castro as a revolutionary idealist and now considered him a demagogue anxious to obtain power in the Caribbean by taking advantage of anti-American prejudice. This was, perhaps, a permissible reading of the Cuban note. It is equally permissible to see some significance in the sequence of Cuba's note and the State Department's disillusionment. Even if economic self-interest were not the only motive of the American government and even if, indeed, Cuba's economic independence would have been as advantageous to Russia as the United States claimed, the question can be asked whether it was reasonable to expect Cuba to sacrifice her aspirations on the altar of anticommunism. What is even more remarkable than the American expectation is that this question was soon to rage in Cuba itself, and that a veritable

[29] *Ibid.*, p. 12.
[30] *Ibid.*, p. 13.

division of the country took place along the lines of yeas and nays. Thus there originated in Cuba a dissension that developed to a point barely short of class war.

We need not remember in detail the intensification of the air raids during the winter of 1959–60, when more than sixty bombing and incendiary raids were flown, exclusive of the illegal transportation flights and supply drops to *batistiano* guerrillas. Gradually, as it became evident that the Cuban government would not be subverted by such means, the relatively passive co-operation of the United States government became more and more active, and, on March 17, 1960, mere active co-operation officially gave way to a complete take-over of the counterrevolutionary movement by the CIA, which, eventually led to the Pig's Bay invasion thirteen months later.[31]

Some time during the winter Cuba decided to implement her policy. But to implement that policy under the regnant conditions really meant to "radicalize" the revolution. Previously, in mid-June, as foreign and domestic opposition to the land reform law had been felt, Castro had dismissed five cabinet ministers,[32] including Humberto Sorí Marín who held the Agriculture portfolio. But on November 25 the break came with the last of the remaining "moderate" elements among his collaborators such as Felipe Pazos (to be replaced by Ché Guevara), Manuel Ray, Rufo López Fresquet, Faustino Pérez, and others who soon arrived in Miami, either to try their fortunes with the CIA or to preach a *Fidelismo sin Fidel* which the United States government was no more disposed to countenance (at least, at

[31] According to Eisenhower, on March 17, 1960, he gave Allen Dulles the order to proceed (*NYT*, June 13, 1961).
[32] *NYT*, June 12, 1959.

the time) than it was to allow Marxism without Russia or Communism without Stalin. There were, moreover, other internal pressures yet to come.

American pressure, too, continued to increase. At a press conference on December 10, Secretary of State Christian Herter "hinted at what the United States might do to the Cuban sugar quota here if Cuba doesn't calm down."[33] The cause of Castro's excitement, however, continued to be made exceedingly vague and gratuitous to the American mind. Castro, on his side, did not trouble to hide his by now pronounced hostility towards the United States government. Worse, he did not bother with formalities, legalities, or restraints such as might have earned him some good will or, at least, produced less resentment.[34] This was equally true in both foreign and domestic affairs. Thus, when on December 29 President Dorticós in a public statement "called again for better relations between the United States and Cuba to be worked out on the basis of a new trade agreement," and "emphasized the Castro regime's stand that Cuban sugar exports to the United States should be regulated by mutual

[33] The Wall Street Journal, December 11, 1959.

[34] It is true, as has often been adduced, that the bonds to pay for the expropriated lands were never printed or valuations made of all the seized land. Unlike Draper and others I cannot conclude from this that Castro never intended to pay: had he really been a dissembler nothing would have been easier than to make these inexpensive gestures and avoid honoring them at a later date. His cavalier disregard of sensibilities and legalities manifests his motivation rather than masks his intentions. In any event, it is in point of fact false that Castro never made any repayment for expropriated lands. For example, on December 19, 1959, INRA expropriated six sisal plantations for which it paid 50% cash, $1,300,000, and promised to pay the remainder in twenty-year bonds; see NYT, December 21, 1959. This strikes me as rather better evidence of good will than merely to have had the bonds printed immediately.

agreement,"[35] the sincerity of his offer to negotiate was not so unimpeachable as to be fully credible to those who may have harbored resentment and wounded pride. The United States, on the other hand, was not in a position to inspire confidence, but for a different reason. Though the final decision to "guatemalize" Cuba was eleven weeks away, it had already become evident that the United States was committed to subversive purposes. It was, above all, committed to opposing any radical revision of its neo-colonial relations with Cuba. In short, the United States did not intend to negotiate.

We do not know, of course, at exactly which point Cuba decided that her proposed bases of negotiation of November 13 were totally unacceptable to the United States, and that she must, therefore, attempt to present the United States with accomplished facts. We know that as late as mid-December, 1959, the Cuban government was turning for economic help to non-Communist sources. We also know that the United States government successfully pressed them to refuse it.[35a] Unless Cuba preferred to capitulate there was, of course, an obvious last recourse: Russia. But that was yet two months away. In the meantime, on January 11 the United States gave official reply[36] to the previous Cuban note: it simply reasserted American claims. On the next day, it was reported, "a spokesman for the Hershey Sugar Mill said that an unidentified plane dropped incendiary bombs on seven sugar cane fields northeast of Havana."[37]

[35] The Christian Science Monitor, December 29, 1959.
[35a] See below, note 46.
[36] See NYT, January 12, 1960.
[37] NYT, January 13, 1960.

On January 20, during a television broadcast which was destined to become famous because it featured Spanish Ambassador Lojendio's interruption demanding to be heard, Castro brought tension to a new high by reaffirming not only the complicity of Cuban and United States business interests in the counterrevolution (and, for the first time, the participation of Spanish clergy in Cuba in counterrevolutionary activities), but also the participation of Spanish and American embassy personnel in such activities as helping counterrevolutionary Cubans to leave the country illegally. We now know that this was so; it is general knowledge that the Guantánamo naval base was often used for this purpose as well as for its opposite, namely, to introduce CIA personnel into Cuba.

The United States government responded, indirectly, by recalling Ambassador Bonsal "apparently to stay [at home] as long as he [could not] live in Havana without insults."[38] It also responded, more directly, on January 26, by issuing a statement denying Cuban charges, affirming that the United States would not intervene in Cuba, and protesting that it found itself in "real sympathy" with Cuba's aspirations.[39]

Within twenty-four hours Cuba's President Dorticós replied in the following terms: Cuba gladly took note of Washington's non-interventionist intentions and appreciated "with satisfaction, that [her] full sovereignty has been recognized as a vested right and not as a grant."[40]

[38] Time, February 1, 1960.
[39] NYT, January 27, 1960.
[40] From the official text published by the Department of Public Relations, Ministry of External Affairs of the Republic of Cuba, 1960. Subsequent quotations from the note refer to the same source.

He expressed Cuba's worry, however, about "statements uttered by legislators of the United States . . . and by other high officials of the United States Government . . . [including] Vice President Nixon [who] on the sixteenth of this month [insinuated] the possibility of economic aggression against our country." He reiterated Cuba's willingness to consider complaints and claims by American business and promised that "no confiscation of foreign properties will take place, but only fully compensated expropriations made on the terms and through the means authorized by our constitutional provisions and to the extent permitted by our financial resources."

But there precisely was the rub—and there was also the test of American intentions. For if it was true, as Cuba claimed, that the extent of compensation permitted by her resources fell short of what, to the United States, was the minimum just claim, then the American insistence on foreclosure could have been interpreted only as a sign of American intention to deter Cuba's reforms. Cuba's wealth and hence her ability to repay could not have increased by American economic retaliation. It follows that the United States government's claim that it objected not to land reform itself, but to the terms of compensation was no more obviously sincere than the later claim that the sugar quota had to be cut because of Cuba's inability to guarantee an adequate supply.

Dorticós went on explicitly to call once again for negotiations, in the belief that "there [were] no obstacles of any sort preventing such negotiations through any of the channels and instruments traditionally used for such purposes." And he added: "It is worth pointing out . . . that Cuba is a small country, which neither militarily nor economically

can represent any risk or threat whatsoever to other countries, and much less to a nation as large and powerful as the
United States." He ended with the hope "that all the
presently existing differences may be dismissed through
natural channels of diplomatic negotiations conducted with
the full respect due to our sovereignty. This respect, and a
correct interpretation of the revolutionary process of
Cuba, are indispensable to the maintenance and improvement of the relations between the two governments." It
cannot be reasonably maintained that they were not. Of
course, Cuba too was required to respect and understand
the American stand. On the basis of the evidence reviewed
here so far, it is difficult to avoid the conclusion that mutual
respect and understanding were often dispensed with by
both sides.

On the other hand, it cannot be suggested that simply
because the policies of the two sides were reciprocally unwise
that they were also symmetrical in every respect. Mutual respect and understanding were lacking, but aggressivesness
was not evenly indulged in by both sides. The pressure was
being applied to Cuba by the United States, not the other
way about. And the existence of the United States as an independent, economically viable country was not being
threatened by Cuba, whereas that of Cuba was. In short, it
was the Cuban revolution that was in danger, not the
United States.

By the end of January the incendiary raids were daily oc-
curences. When Cuba had protested the raid on the Hershey
fields the State Department had issued a statement on January 13: "the United States Government looked into this
[allegation] on the basis of press reports and can say there
has been no indication that any plane from the United

States dropped incendiary bombs on Cuba."[41] On the same day Dorticós answered Eisenhower, an abortive incursion took place against another sugar mill. And the next day, the worst on record, incendiary flares were dropped on the town of Puerto Padre and fields of four sugar mills along a two-hundred-mile stretch of Cuba's north coast.[42]

It is not clear whether, as Cuba thought, more than one aircraft was used in this day's raids. But unlike earlier raids, when only small passenger aircraft of proportionally small range had been used, the raids of January 28 featured a B-25 bomber, the regulation markings of which, CN 325, had not been covered over with canvas. Again on the 29th two sugar mills were attacked, and fires were set in another by ground saboteurs. On the 30th the crops of four other sugar mills were set on fire from the air. By the end of the week, it was estimated, about 250,000 tons of sugar cane had burnt down. The offensive was only beginning to gather momentum.

Cuba, of course, protested once more, and once more the United States government claimed innocence and, indeed,

[41] Quoted in a later report, NYT, February 20, 1960. This assertion in no event could have been intended to refer to such flights in general, since as early as December 2, 1959, there had been official confirmation in the United States that the batistianos were, indeed, bombing Cuba. On that date the New York Times reported (from Washington) that five Cubans had been arrested in Florida while loading bombs aboard a small aircraft. The idea, evidently, was to demonstrate that the United States government did not approve of the batistiano operations; but the farcical nature of the arrest is shown by the fact that they were freed shortly afterwards and that at least one of them, Miguel Orozco, became a CIA agent a short time later. Orozco was captured in Cuba in November, 1962, while carrying out sabotage operations for the CIA. See Bohemia, November 16, 1962.

[42] Bohemia, February 7, 1960.

heavily hinted that it was all a fabrication of obviously sinister intent. Aircraft CN 325, the Civil Aeronautics Administration pointed out in this vein, was not an American
plane: It was of Moroccan registry. Washington officials,
however, explained to press correspondents that "the possibility that the plane belonged to a Moroccan living in the
United States or somewhere in the Caribbean was not ruled
out."[43] The Cuban government pointed out that it was
well aware that aircraft CN 325 was of Moroccan registra-
tion. It explained that the aircraft had been bought in
Morocco, thence flown through Canada to Buffalo, N.Y.,
and finally to Sarasota, Fla., where it had been consigned
to the name of a Mr. Jaffe who, as it so happened, was a
pilot in the employ of Rolando Masferrer.[44] The State Department did not reply.

It was under these circumstances that a few days later, on
February 5th, Anastas Mikoyan arrived in Havana, osten-
sibly to open a Soviet exposition that had been touring
Latin America. There was little doubt, however, that Mikoyan's real mission was to initiate previously non-existent
trade relations with Cuba. Diplomatic relations did not at
this time obtain between the two countries. Before his ten-
day visit had ended Mikoyan had promised a hundred
million dollar, low-interest long-term credit and had contracted to buy one million tons of sugar a year from Cuba
for the next five years.[45]

[43] *NYT*, January 30, 1960.
[44] *Bohemia*, February 7, 1960. Masferrer, a former *batistiano*
senator, had been one of Batista's most feared henchmen. He maintained a private army of 500, nicknamed *Masferrer's Tigers*.
[45] The United States Embassy in Havana immediately issued a
statement pointing out that whereas Russia would buy Cuban sugar
at world market prices, the United States bought three times as
much at premium prices, insinuating that the treaty was disadvan-

This was the signal among both American and Cuban opponents of Castro for proclaiming no further need of witnesses.[46] Catholic students had already rioted in Havana upon Mikoyan's arrival. Upon his leaving Cuba, Havana's *Diario de la Marina* wrote: "thank you, Señor Mikoyan. Your visit has clarified many things and defined the camps:

---

tageous to Cuba. This was a half-truth. The United States paid premium prices within a trade-restricting agreement that traditionally left Cuba with a huge sugar surplus. Russia's sugar purchase was not disadvantageous to Cuba, but it did threaten in the long run to disrupt the patterns of world trade in sugar. The case for the trade objectives of the Revolutionary government and its whole international trade policy is argued by Núñez Jiménez in a chapter of his *Geografía de Cuba*. He concludes: "our country must trade freely with all the countries of the world, including the new and growing markets of the Soviet Union, China and other socialist countries. A skillful barter policy would permit our selling that part of our sugar production which we otherwise cannot allocate, and to obtain industrial and agricultural machinery, raw materials, fuel and other products necessary to our economic development, without payment in hard currency," p. 307. This was, of course, the same point that had been made by the note of November 13. Moreover, it was the same policy that was being followed by Brazil respecting coffee trade with Russia, but with two differences: (a) whereas the Cuban agreement with Russia was not completed until February 13, 1960, the Brazilian agreement was completed in early December, 1959 (see *NYT*, December 10, 1959) and (b) whereas the Cuban agreement amounted to $100 million, the Brazilian agreement amounted to twice that amount, $200 million. The amounts are worth noting, because one of the grounds for scandal proferred by the State Department had to do not with Cuba's Russian trade as such, but with the "surprisingly large" and "staggering" amount involved. To put it quantitatively, what Cuba sold was about 20% of her average yearly sugar production, i.e., about 100% of her average yearly overproduction.

[46] A mere two months before Mikoyan arrived in Havana Antonio Núñez Jiménez had been in Europe trying to negotiate a loan for, coincidentally, $100 million from financial interests in the Netherlands, West Germany, and France. The United States brought pressure against these countries to refuse—which they did. See *NYT*, December 5, 1959.

on the one side the Communists and their knowing and un-
knowing accomplices; on the other side Cubans who want
to continue being free men in a free world."[47]

The United States government, in effect, seems to have
agreed with that estimate of the significance of Cuba's step:
"Herter described Cuba frankly as a 'deteriorating situation.' A flustered Congress, turning to the only weapon it
had, considered more than sixty bills designed to clip
Castro's wings"[48] by cutting the sugar quota. Since nothing
else had happened, the deterioration can only be attributed
to Cuba's establishment of commercial relations with Russia. On the same week a Florida-based aircraft was shot
down on a bombing run over a Cuban sugar mill killing its
two American pilots.

Cuba protested once more. Since it would have been impossible to claim that the corpses and documents produced
by the Cuban government were a fabrication, the United
States government for the first time acknowledged that
Florida-based aircraft had bombed Cuba, and Secretary of
State Christian Herter in a diplomatic note to the Cuban
government expressed regrets that "the plane managed to
escape the vigilance of our intensified airport patrols."[49]

[47] Quoted by Time, February 22, 1960.
[48] Time, February 29, 1960.
[49] Quoted by NYT, February 20, 1960. Note the ad hoc expression airport patrol, so easily confused with air patrol. Exactly what
was an airport patrol? The answer became known only later. "This
center [i.e., the flight information center at the Miami headquarters
of the Immigration and Naturalization Service], it was explained,
will receive voluntary [sic] information on proposed flights by privately operated planes to foreign countries from the southeastern
United States," NYT, March 24, 1960. The same newspaper, same
date, reported that "an estimated total of 60,000 tons of cane had
been destroyed in the last forty-eight hours. The sugar fields have
been fired with bombs dropped from small planes and from the
ground, it is reported."

Castro was reported to be "irate, but did not charge that the United States authorities knew about or consented to the clandestine flights. 'They had nothing to gain,' [he] said."[50]

The sincerity of the American government's words of regret became suspect within twenty-four hours. The note of apology was dated February 19. On the next day the United States government made clear to the American press that private flying was a very popular sport in Florida (sic); the number of private flights, therefore, was so large that the United States government could not be expected to keep track of them all: "Federal officials in charge of the expanded patrol force the Government has assigned to prevent unauthorized flights . . . conceded that they knew of no sure way to guard against the repetition of the flight,"[51] an assertion that went unchallenged by the press. So much for the suspicion. The proof took another twenty-four hours: on February 21 an unidentified B–25 bombed an oil refinery on the outskirts of the City of Havana.[52] This time the Cuban government did not take the trouble to protest.

On the contrary. On February 22, as "thoughts of Monroe and of intervention in Cuba were inevitably voiced in Washington"[53] Cuba forwarded a note to the United States government asking once again that the two countries enter into negotiation. And since Washington had met every previous Cuban proposal to negotiate with the assertion that they were not made in good faith, that Cuba would never actually engage in diplomatic talks, this time the Cuban government added what it considered reassuring evidence. It announced that it had already appointed an ad

[50] *Time*, February 29, 1960.
[51] NYT, February 21, 1960.
[52] NYT, February 22, 1960.
[53] *Time*, February 29, 1960.

hoc commission which was ready to travel to Washington. The members, moreover, had more than simply advisory capacity to the Cuban government; they had been fully empowered to settle the full range of differences in dispute. But the note specified: "The Revolutionary Government of Cuba wishes to make clear, however, that the renewal and subsequent development of the said negotiations must necessarily be subject to no measures being adopted by the Government or the Congress of your country, of a unilateral character which might prejudice the results of the aforementioned negotiations or cause harm to the Cuban economy and people."[54] Officials in Washington "said that this condition meant that the United States must undertake not to enact, during the negotiations a Sugar Act unacceptable to Cuba."[55]

Theodore Draper has written that "on Feb. 22 the Cuban Government for the first and only time in 1959 and 1960 offered to negotiate—but carefully attached a clearly unacceptable condition. It demanded that the United States bind itself to take no measures considered harmful to Cuba during the negotiations. This one-sided stipulation . . . left Cuba free to do as it pleased on top of all the accomplished facts in the very period when negotiations should have been conducted. . . ."[56] Apart from Draper's error of fact concerning the number of Cuba's offers to negotiate,[57] his reasoning

[54] From the text of the note, reproduced in *Obra Revolucionaria*, No. 26 (1961).

[55] *NYT*, February 24, 1960.

[56] *NYT*, November 16, 1962.

[57] The origin of the common opinion that Castro made no effort to negotiate was the State Department. In his press conference of December 10, 1959 (see *NYT*, Dec. 11), Herter said: "We have tried to discuss with the Cuban Government a number of the problems that have caused . . . deterioration [in mutual relations] and

on this point is a little difficult to follow. The matter of the sugar quota was very much in the air at the time; if the quota were to be cut negotiations would have been hardly necessary. Why should the United States have not wished to provide reassurances (which were not costly, and which left the United States free to take any course if the negotiation broke down) against what was a reasonable fear of a very real threat? Unless there lacked a reasonable foundation for Cuba's apprehensiveness, there was a reasonable purpose to Cuba's test of American intentions. Cuba had offered reassurances—would the United States offer corresponding reassurances in return? It is difficult to avoid the conclusion that Draper accepted too uncritically the version put out by the State Department in its domestic press background briefings. For to Cuba, indeed, the United States government's reply of February 29 offered a much more forthright explanation. It rejected the condition on the grounds that the United States "must remain free, *in the exercise of its sovereignty,* to take whatever steps it deems necessary."[58] The implications for political ethics of a rejection of conditions of negotiation on this basis shall not be extracted here.

---

have found that the present Cuban Government is not anxious to talk with us." What did this mean? The answer to the next question explained: "[Ambassador Bonsal] has made very little progress [in negotiating on the matter of compensation for expropriated land]. I think that the standard answer that he receives is that they do not have money and hence must make compensation in terms of long-range bonds." As it so happened, that very morning, just prior to Herter's press conference Raúl Roa had reiterated (*NYT*, same date), that although Cuba was unable to pay cash she "would be willing to discuss with the United States the amount of compensation."

[58] Text of the note, quoted by *NYT*, March 1, 1960. Italics mine.

Another year was to elapse before the next occasion arose
—at the Cuban government's initiative—to open up negotiations, specifically to include the question of compensation for expropriated American investment. And it took
another year after that for the next occasion to come up,
also at the initiative of the Cuban government. Both over-
tures were rejected by the United States.

The remainder of the story of United States–Cuban relations until January 3, 1961, when the United States broke
diplomatic relations between the two countries, is too well
known to bear repeating here. It is also the part that is most
often emphasized in many accounts, perhaps because it
shows clearly Castro's steady drift toward ever closer ties
with Russia, toward the adoption of ever more radical socialist measures and toward his espousal of communist
philosophy. But a few of the highlights may be noted. On
March 4 the ship *La Coubre* exploded in Havana harbor
while unloading explosives and small arms purchased in
Belgium. Castro voiced avowedly unproven suspicions that
the CIA had sabotaged it. The United States government
indignantly denied the charge. The truth of the matter remains obscure. On March 18 the day after Eisenhower's
order to implement the guatemalization plans, U.S. Ambassador Philip Bonsal returned to Havana. Before the end
of that month another aircraft with two American pilots
had been shot down. The *Time* magazine report, among
others in the United States, suggested the theory that "the
flight was faked to give Castro one more small-plane yarn to
howl about."[59] On May 8 diplomatic relations with Russia
were established with the arrival of Ambassador Kudriatsev

[59] *Time*, April 4, 1960.

in Havana. Shortly afterwards Castro sounded the alarm:
The United States was preparing to invade Cuba. "A wacky
obsession," was the comment made by *Time*—in the same
issue that reported another aircraft shot down over Cuba
with another American pilot at the controls.[60]

We do not know the first target date for the guatemalization of Cuba, but a number of unexpected developments
combined to prevent the early execution of the plan, until
finally it was attempted thirteen months later, in April
1961. But among the first of these unexpected developments was the fact that the United States executive power
soon lost almost all control of its dealings with Cuba. The
oil crisis of that summer, leading to the sugar quota cancel-
lations and Castro's expropriation of all United States property in Cuba was not precipitated, it appears, by any United
States government design, but by the oil industry acting on
its own.[61] This fact deserves some attention.

As early as May 23, the Cuban government had approached two United States- and one English-owned oil refineries in Cuba and notified them that in pursuance of the
treaty of the previous February, Russian oil would soon begin to arrive in Cuba, and to plan thenceforth to refine Russian crude to supply about twenty per cent of Cuba's con-
sumption. The refineries first demurred and finally refused
to comply. They were threatened with administrative seizure
(but not with nationalization). Late in June the Russian
crude began to arrive. The refineries refused to take delivery,
and on the 29th and 30th all three were put under government direction. In an all-night session lasting till dawn of
July 4, the United States Congress cut the remainder of

[60] *Time*, May 23, 1960.
[61] Sidney Lens, "Which way Cuba?," *Fellowship*, March, 1961.

1960's Cuban sugar quota. On July 6, Castro received cabinet consent to expropriate American property in Cuba.

It is—in retrospect—easy to see that in the escalating rounds of mutual reprisals involving these measures both sides were manifesting more pique than prudence. Castro might have gotten away with token retaliation—on the other hand, how much difference would that have made at this late stage? And, of course, it could be argued that the United States had not yet cut off the sugar quota permanently, but only for the remainder of 1960. However, could Castro have reasonably counted on a resumption of sugar purchases in 1961 unless he capitulated to the United States? Of course, it is fair to point out that when Castro struck he struck with all his might: it is also true that he did not strike back incontinently. Castro's immediate reaction to the American sugar embargo was to appeal to the Security Council of the United Nations and charge the United States with economic aggression in violation of the United Nations Charter and of bilateral and regional agreements.

The United States alleged that the matter could be settled more adequately within the Western Hemisphere family of nations. In view of the recalcitrant opposition of the American representative to have the charges aired, on July 19 the Security Council which, as is well known, can act only by unanimous decision, agreed to the only viable solution, namely, to act upon the American submission and refer the dispute to the Organization of American States. There was no doubt in anyone's mind, of course, that this meant the end of the Cuban complaint. Then, and only then, did Russia step into the breach. Before the end of July she had bought the sugar embargoed by the United

States. And it was only on August 6, three weeks after the decision of the Security Council, that the Cuban government began to expropriate American business interests in Cuba.

On that date twenty-six American firms, including Cuba's major utilities, were nationalized, as were the American oil refineries thus far only under administrative seizure; the British-owned Shell refinery continues to date under seizure only. Repayment was provided for, with not unintended irony, out of a special fund to be created from future United States sugar purchases over and above the 1960 quota. Other United States investments were similarly expropriated throughout the month of September, and before the end of the month the first among the sizable Cuban firms was also nationalized. On October 14 almost 400 firms, virtually all Cuban big business, were wiped out.

If the expropriations of August and September had been more than a token, the United States' pride had been wounded much too deeply to countenance them without further reprisals. On October 19 it adopted a measure aimed directly at the survival of Cuba's economy: it placed an embargo on all exports to Cuba (except food and medicine). Spare machine parts, of course, were the main object of the prohibition. Its effects were not to be felt immediately, but they would be grave. In avowed retaliation, Cuba countered on October 25 by taking over 167 American firms, the remainder of American interest in Cuba. Eisenhower's last gesture, in December 1960, was to extend the sugar quota cut into 1961: it was hardly more than the symbolic formalization of the already accomplished total break between the two states. Not quite four months into the new year Castro proclaimed the "socialist" character of the revolution, and on the following 26th of July speech he announced not only an economic policy of total state possession and control of the means of production and distribution, but also the formation of a United Party (built around the core of the old communist party of Cuba, the PSP), as the political instrument of the proletarian dictatorship. Though Cuba's relations to Russia were yet to be worked out, and though Cuba's role in the international Communist movement remained, as it remains to date, rather imprecise and vague, one thing at least had become finally settled: in less than two-and-a-half years of American diplomacy and Castro's premiership, Cuba, though in no sense a satellite, had become in every sense a communist state.

CHAPTER 4

THE DETERMINANTS WITHIN

It is not unreasonable, then, to suggest that there is some connection between the events here recounted and the increasing rapprochement between Cuba and Russia. But it does not warrant the conclusion, therefore, that communism was forced upon Castro by American policy. Here we must distinguish. It is one thing to be forced into economic and even political alliance with Russia: it is another to have adopted the ideology of Marxism-Leninism. This is especially important because though Cuba's dependence upon Russia was to become much greater than, e.g., Egypt's, there is no reason to believe that Cuba was forbidden the possibility of pursuing an internal policy of more or less democratic socialism, perhaps even doctrinaire socialism, without the need to institute orthodox Marxism, and to impose it precisely as an orthodoxy. There is, indeed, not even a reasonable suspicion that Russia put undue pressure on Castro, to which Cuba had to yield as to a lesser evil. In this sense, therefore, it is true that Castro adopted communism by his own free choice.

On the other hand, his adoption of communism appears rather less than gratuitous if we remember that, in addition to the pressures from without, a number of domestic developments were taking place at the same time. Understandably the foreign press has reported domestic Cuban events only under the light of the United States–Cuban impasse. But during this period there was a greater political and social struggle within Cuba than foreigners were apt to realize: It may even be that Castro was subject to greater pressure from within than from without.

We have already noted the conspiracy of August, 1959, which involved Cuban *latifundistas* affected by land reform. Earlier, in late June, Castro had produced documentary evidence to show that before the land reform had been approved, indeed while it was still being discussed in cabinet, the Cattlemen's Association had voted a $500,000 fund to influence Havana newspaper editors to present the news in a light favorable to the landowners.[1] Of course, the near universal venality of the Cuban press was hardly a recent development in Cuba—in fact, this is the reason why, throughout the harshest dictatorships, the Cuban press had rarely been suppressed: it had usually been bought.

Soon after Castro's accession to power it became apparent that the *batistiano* threat of counterrevolution was less grave than the militant opposition from certain domestic vested interests. This term does not refer exclusively or even principally to commercial interests though these, of course, were the first to react and to give body to the brew of discontent. The term refers to a much larger group—those who had in

---

[1] Ample photostatic evidence was reproduced by *Revolución* at the time, notably a report of the meeting at which the fund was voted, written by a representative of the Francisco Sugar Company, which left no doubt whatever that the funds were to be paid to editors for the purpose of anti-land reform propaganda. The bribery was reported as an advertising campaign fund in *NYT*, June 24, 1959, and in *Time*, July 6, 1959.

a great variety of ways traditionally benefited from, contributed to, and made possible the perpetuation of the social and political chaos in which tyrannies such as Batista's could sporadically appear. Anyone who is aware of the traditional social and political problems of Cuba will not reject lightly the suggestion that Batista, like Machado before him, was but a symptom of a deeper and more pervasive malady which could be described as social and political disintegration of the very culture itself. The worst side of this cultural problem was that through a number of historico-social processes, from which we must here abstract, the disintegration and disorder of Cuba had become in great measure institutionalized. That is, not only they had become perfectly bearable, they had become an integral part of the social fabric itself. Cuba had adjusted to those otherwise abnormal conditions so efficiently that they had actually become fully normal. That is why, in a way, the criticism leveled at Castro by many exiles today—that regardless of his reforms the country is much worse off today than in Batista's time—contains at least this element of truth: the revolution *has* upset the normality of the worst Cuban times.

It is true that this normalization of the abnormal, this self-inoculation, had to be paid for at a high price. The peasantry in particular paid long and dearly in the coin of hunger and poverty. But the whole nation was ultimately to suffer. Those conditions gradually produced a deep estrangement between the city and the country which in turn eventually made a class war possible. Estrangement need not mean enmity, but simple alienation or mutual ignorance and the petrification of class into caste. The urban Cuban rarely saw the country, and few seemed to care about the abject conditions of the peasant. The peasant, in turn, was unaware of the city, and lacked all consciousness of the injustice of his condition. Now, unlike that of Latin America in general, Cuba's peasantry is a minority of slightly under fifty per cent of the population. Since Cuba is not highly industrialized, the labor class is relatively small. Therefore, close to half the Cuban population constituted a sort of highly anomalous middle class, with about half concentrated in Havana, a metropolis of one and one-half million citizens. This group was middle class only in the sense that it was neither proletarian nor peasant on the one hand, nor high bourgeois on the other. But it was an atypical petty bourgeoisie in that economically and socially it ranged very widely, from the professional and the middle-size independent businessman down to the part-time or unemployed clerk, the ward heeler, the economically precarious fruit peddler, and the totally dispossessed newspaper vendor or shoe-shine boy. Social class in Cuba was largely a frame of mind. Perhaps the greatest anomaly of all was that though this urban mass was thoroughly stratified into classes and subclasses separated by clear-cut distinctions and numerous status symbols, a surprisingly high degree of social mobility within the urban classes was allowed and even encouraged by the culture. This culture developed in an environment of disorder: The result was not only a highly competitive society, but one in which civic immorality had become a way of life. Muted disorder was one of the elements that helped preserve a certain ecological balance by ensuring that the fight for spoils that were very scarce did not become such a mortal struggle that no one could make a living.

There is a popular superstition, created in the first instance by an uninformed American press, to the effect that

Fidel Castro led a great popular revolution against Batista. Nothing could be further from the truth. Castro had a famous reputation and much sympathy, but very little active following until after his victory. Nor did the significance of Castro lie in the fact that after his victory he was hailed by several million people who, though they had not hailed Batista in 1952, had elected him in 1940. It lay in the fact that having come to power with the moral strength given him by his proven incorruptibility, Castro gave good reason, even to the more cynical observers, to believe that he might inspire the people of Cuba to overcome their collective, nearly universal social and political immorality. Since the very beginning of Castro's government this was the real problem that he faced, and his most challenging task was to inspire a sufficiently large majority of the Cuban people to distill a spirit of civic virtue out of their meager character reserves.[2]

Before the revolution was a year old there were many signs that the newly found Cuban integrity had taken less firm hold than the Cubans themselves might have thought. Yet, one could explain away the senseless treason of a Díaz Lanz as an isolated instance, an exception, symptomatic of nothing. And one could misunderstand completely the case of Hubert Matos, another well-known defector. But perhaps the misunderstanding was unavoidable, since it could not have been known at the time, as it is now, that by the autumn of 1959 an extensive counterrevolutionary network, later to become famous as the MRR, had infiltrated various government departments. Nor did one know until much later that the plotting had actually begun as early as March,

---

[2] Cf. my article on "Cuba: the moral of the story," *The Canadian Forum*, XL, 481 (February, 1961), pp. 242–3.

1959—that is, in the second month of Castro's regime—by a group of Catholics within the Rebel Army under the direction of Manuel Artime, who was destined to become famous two years later as the field commander of CIA's Pig's Bay invasion force.

The point is that too many people who were united with Castro in opposing Batista were now unwilling to agree with Castro on the course of the revolution, a difficulty that was made all the greater by the original lack of any but the most superficial and amateurish ideology in the Twenty-sixth of July Movement. Therefore, it was not only the few who were disgruntled because the spoils of victory were not as great as they had anticipated, or those who, at the other end of the spectrum, wanted revolution but did not want to share their land; it was all those who were insecure by reason of having to readjust to new socio-economic patterns, and those who, rightly or wrongly, had something to protect from change: it was they who became disillusioned with the revolution. It would be inexact to say that they turned against Castro, though they provided the reservoir whence his later conterrevolutionary opposition has been drawn. Few of them would have fought for anything, even the *status quo ante* for which they so yearned. Relatively few have conspired against Castro—no more than they did against Batista. They have no more than quietly compounded chaos, their predominant political emotion being outrage, their instinctive reaction being to leave Cuba in protest—until the United States government saw the inherent possibilities, and drastically restricted the flow of "refugees."

We have seen how, for external reasons, it became necessary by the end of November, 1959 to make some resolute decisions concerning the future of the revolution. For internal reasons, some radicalization became imperative at this time. This caused a sharp division at the highest levels of government. On November 26 Manuel Ray and Faustino Pérez resigned their portfolios and Felipe Pazos resigned the chairmanship of the National Bank: As we have noted, Guevara was immediately appointed in his place. Before the middle of 1960 all three had joined the counterrevolution and gone underground or to Miami. More significant was the fact that a radical shift in the basis of Castro's support began to take place at this time. Labor's support, which had been rather less than unconditional (in a small part through communist influence), became very strong; and the peasantry's, which had been strong, became enthusiastic and even fanatic in the wake of a number of social measures adopted by the regime. Correspondingly, the middle classes became first, cool, then skeptical, and finally hostile, disgruntled, and divided—often within the family itself, often along the lines of age. By December, 1959 the signs reading *Gracias, Fidel,* which had until recently dotted Havana, had almost entirely disappeared.

The Urban Reform law proclaimed on October 15, 1960 —significantly, the day after the nationalization of Cuban big business—was an attempt to cater to the *Habaneros* and, particularly, to the lower bourgeois. It attacked grave social evils in the Cuban housing situation, but though it did much good it also served to compound the disorder— and it provided a powerful incentive for people to inform on each other, often falsely, in order to occupy the homes of those who had been taken away to jail. This was not, therefore, a contest between the good and the bad. The increasingly sharp division more often brought out the worst in all rather than the good, as crises sometimes will. The *fidelista* majority particularly found in these events an occasion to luxuriate in an intolerance that Cubans legitimately inherit from their Iberian forefathers, but which in their case was reinforced by a recently acquired self-righteousness which was all the more ill-worn for its superficiality and pride, (were they not honest, genuine social reformers?). In the six months between December, 1959 and May, 1960 the Cuban revolution became a full-fledged class struggle. Had it been physically possible it would have become a civil war.

Though it would be some time yet (one estimates) before Castro was to adopt Marxism-Leninism as a matter of a conviction, he appears to have become conscious during this period that the ultimate choice might lay between two extremes: either to allow the middle classes to wreck the revolution, or to institute a dictatorship of the proletariat. One may safely conjecture that, given Castro's commitment to reform, the choice was never in doubt.

But was no moderate solution possible? Though one may disagree with Castro as to whether he made the right choice —as one should if one believes that people cannot be made to enjoy freedom nor be given justice unless they themselves choose the one and deserve the other—there cannot be much doubt that only increasingly extreme alternatives were open to him. Perhaps another man might have found a way to evade them. But we have already seen how American policy limited his options. The United States pressed Castro to face the reality of a possible failure. Again, the suggestion is not that Castro was forced. There is a distinction between the basic decision to protect the revolution of the lowly many, even at the cost of crushing the faithless few, and the decision to adopt Marxism-Leninism as a framework on which to hang future policy. We have accounted for the first. The latter was yet to come.

Since we have to do here with a deep psychological process and an inner dialogue, we can be sure that there is no one moment which we can mark as the point at which Castro's decision took place. What we can try to ascertain is the fundamental motivation at work and the basic human traits that were called into play. Naturally, one can never be sure of what passes through a man's mind; but if one goes back over Castro's speeches searching for this process, one can detect an increasing and finally ill-concealed, deep feeling of disappointment by reason of all the foregoing events, both internal and external. Castro, for all his faults, has a paradoxical streak of personal humility about him; one can trace in his words the lengthening of a certain shadow of self-blame, a sort of shame even, at not having been wiser and more sophisticated in the beginning. One cannot very well read his speeches and doubt the fact that he has never been perfectly satisfied with himself. I hazard the interpretation, for what it may be worth toward understanding the events, that a strong sense of inadequacy at not having foreseen accurately the course of the revolution played a large role in this process. In later speeches he has practically confessed as much and has almost apologized for having taken such a long time to discover a "scientific" explanation and a revolutionary theory "based on scientific laws, with a long historical experience,"[3] namely Marxism-Leninism.

This is not quite to say that he made an act of faith in Marxism—Castro already had another religion, namely, his revolution. It is to suggest that this was a highly convenient

[3] *Revolución*, September 20, 1961.

short cut to a political philosophy that would serve his own executive needs, and, quite as important, one that would provide a stable, systematic, well-thought-out conceptual framework according to which he could undertake the political formation of a politically illiterate people who— partly in virtue of Democracy's aggressiveness—desperately needed to acquire two generation's worth of political skills overnight.

Marxism, as far as his limited, unique purposes were concerned, did work. It was perhaps as simple as that.

CHAPTER 5

THE PHANTOM DISJUNCTIVES

In conclusion: Why and how did the communism of the Cuban revolution come about? Was it avoidable? Might history's course have been otherwise?

The dimension of improvisation and unpremeditation of the Cuban revolution is well illustrated by a commonly neglected fact. Castro did not assume political office upon his military victory on December 31, 1958. Those who say today that "Castro promised one revolution and then made another" do not realize how true this proposition is. More exactly, Castro undertook one revolution and, having achieved it, then made another revolution he had neither promised nor planned for. For Castro had always pledged that once he defeated Batista he would not seek power for himself. On January 2, according to announced intention, he installed Manuel Urrutia as Provisional President at a public meeting in Céspedes Park in Santiago, the capital of Oriente province. There was no doubt that Urrutia was quite uncommitted to Castro, and when Urrutia asked José Miró Cardona to form a government the latter did so with a free hand. Miró himself has never denied this, not even after having become the leader of the anti-Castro forces in the United States.

Miró's government was unworkable. The people, perhaps because they instinctively felt the need for a leader who could inspire rather than for possibly competent and honest but uninspired, uncreative administrators who had next to nothing to administer and much to create, simply ignored the government and constantly recurred to Castro. Fidel could be trusted. Fidel knew what was wrong with Cuba. Fidel was certain to command assent, respect and co-operation. Hardly anyone in Cuba thought otherwise. Miró Cardona himself agreed. For it was Miró who on February 15, 1959, with the advice of his Council of Ministers and with the consent of President Urrutia, asked Castro to assume the Prime Ministry. (Indeed, the Council had also amended the *Ley Fundamental* lowering the presidential age requirement so Castro could become President if he wished). Castro accepted the premiership on February 17.[1] The liberating revolution which he had promised had ended in fulfilment six weeks before. The reconstruction for which he, as he has admitted, was ill-prepared, began on that precise date.

If it is true, on the other hand, that American diplomacy

---

[1] In an interview filmed for French Television in April, 1961, Castro explained: "I must admit that we really believed, for a time, that it would be possible to leave the power to others: we were a little . . . utopian. In the first days after victory we kept away from the government altogether, and took no part in the decisions of the Council of Ministers. We had no doubt that the people responsible in power would take the elementary measures that the people were expecting and that seemed to us to be the ABC's of the whole revolution." Quoted by Hervé Chaigne, OFM, in "La Révolution Cubaine: miroir de notre temps," *Frères du Monde,* No. 3, 1962 (Martin Corbin's translation). Note that in his public appearances Castro usually refers to himself in the first person plural. This should help the reader surmount some ambiguities in quotations presented below.

did not force Castro's will, the reason may be that the disjunction between being compelled and being free is not only false but radically misleading. It can be posed only if one assumes that freedom is ahistorical, unconditioned by time—which we often do, so that we can seek the intelligible necessities of events elsewhere than in man (for his will is free). And yet, it is doubtful whether freedom is really safeguarded when it is made to consist in man's ability to choose regardless of history and as if he did not exist in situation, for if the explanation of history is not found in human nature then history can only be either omnipotently engineered by a devil or fiendishly fated by a god.

American diplomacy did not force Castro into either ideology or policy. What American diplomacy did manage was to impose upon the Cuban revolution the definition of "communist." But, malevolently or not, to have succeeded in this was to have succeeded in casting a self-fulfilling horoscope—for to the same degree that American policy permitted no relations except on the basis of the assumed Cuban "pro-communism" or communism every move of the revolution tended to coincide with what a communist revolution should have intended aforethought. Castro's conversion to communism, like that of so many other Cubans, took place when it finally dawned on him that, from its point of view, the United States was correct after all in defining the revolution as communist.[2] Castro's fault lay in having allowed himself to be deceived by the line of argumentation unanimously insisted upon by foreign and do-

[2] Castro's introspective speech of December 1, 1961, in which he accounted for his conversion (see above, Chapter 1), documents this point profusely. It describes the stages of experience through which he came to believe that unknown to himself he had been a communist long before he consciously became one.

mestic enemies as well as, presumably, his communist supporters: the absolute antithesis of capitalist democracy and
communism. But once he adopted that point of view, while
retaining his original motivation, there was little he could
intelligibly have done except as he did: the conjunction of
the two necessitated his voluntary political regeneration.

If so, Castro's was no ordinary conversion. He underwent
that peculiar mental inflexion, so dramatically analyzed by
Arthur Koestler, by which a man becomes persuaded for
the sake of his own motives that he ought to affirm the
contrary of what follows from them. This is quite the opposite of compulsion, as when "a certain type of accused
. . . confesses under pressure, [for] . . . the political utility
of [this kind of] . . . confession . . . lie[s] in its voluntary
character.[3] Its voluntariness must be absolutely genuine.

The psychological means, particularly the communication
techniques, whereby this process can be artificially induced,
are a modern discovery. They are a communist invention.
The Chinese have coined a term that graphically underlines
the voluntary (as distinct from the spontaneous) character
of the results. They call it brainwashing. In the strict sense
of this word, then, it is possible to conclude that American
diplomacy brainwashed Castro into communism.

Before the year 1960 had ended, just as Castro's economic
dependence upon the communist bloc had become almost
complete, his reliance upon the relatively efficient, sophisticated, dedicated Communist Party at home had become a
vital need. Little purpose would be served by trying to de-
limit more exactly when his mind was made up about
Marxism-Leninism; but a highly significant milestone may

[3] Arthur Koestler, *Darkness at Noon* (New York, 1955), p. 157
(paperbound reprint).

be discerned in an interview granted in January, 1961, to a correspondent from an Italian communist newspaper, in which he stated:

> . . . not only did we destroy a tyrannical system. We also destroyed the philoimperialistic bourgeois state apparatus, the bureaucracy, the police, and the mercenary army. We abolished privilege, annihilated the great landowners, threw out the foreign monopolies for good, nationalized almost every industry, and collectivized the land. We are fighting now to liquidate once and for all the exploitation of man over man, and to build a completely new society, with a new class content. The Americans and the priests say that this is Communism. We know very well that it is not. At any rate the word does not frighten us. . . . Yet, if such a great welfare conquest—which can be seen by my own eyes—is Communism, then you can even call me a Communist. [And then, asked what he thought of the Cuban Communist Party:] It is the only Cuban party which has consistently called for a radical change of social structures and relations. It is true that at the beginning the Communists distrusted me and the rebels . . . [but] then, we met each other, we understood one another, and started to work together. . . . At present we continue to work together in a loyal and brotherly way.[4]

Less than three months later, on the eve of the Pig's Bay invasion, Castro proclaimed the "patriotic, democratic and socialist" character of the revolution. The term socialist was to be taken in this context in the sense given to it by Marxists.

There is no reason to suppose that the invasion accelerated Castro's conversion to communism. It was complete by then. It is, therefore, ironic that a considerable segment of public opinion outside the United States has finally and probably irrevocably chosen for its interpretation of the Cuban revolution the fractional truth that the United

[4] *Unità*, February 1, 1961, quoted in translation by Wyatt Mac-Gaffey et al., *Cuba: Its People, Its Society, Its Culture* (New Haven, 1962), p. 261.

States forced Cuba into communism; for somewhat illogically what swayed them was the invasion attempt. Without the invasion world opinion might well have continued to give the United States some support for a less radical anti-Castro stand.

The period since the official adoption of communism in Cuba has been dominated by the fact that communism, though passively espoused by most and tolerated by many, sits very badly with a sizable minority. There are no indications that there are any masses in Cuba eagerly awaiting the call to rise up in arms. However, though relatively few much mind communism, most Cubans still dislike the communist old guard. Even Castro himself makes fun of the local communists, "those satellites here" who as soon as Khrushchev criticizes abstract art "ask me to ban abstract art. But I tell them that my enemies are capitalism and imperialism, not abstract art."[5] And the lower classes once excepted there remain too many in Cuba who are, perhaps not unintelligibly, put out by the uncertainties and the insecurities and the numerous hardships and inconveniences of the times. Lastly, many who, to be sure, would rather another invasion did not come, are simply not, as once for a fleeting moment they were, willing to risk their lives for an ideal which they may or may not too well understand but for which they have clearly ambivalent feelings. To put it harshly, except among the dispossessed patriotism in Cuba has ceased to be in vogue.

Fleeing to Miami, on the other hand, is not only an act of protest and, often, an economic advantage, it is also a great frolic. It provides and outlet for anomy at the same

[5] Interview with Claude Julien, Le Devoir (Montreal), March 27, 1963.

time that it pampers rebellion. But the exiles do not find themselves at home in the United States; they are much too Cuban for that, and what they really want cannot be found where they came to, but only in the irretrievable past. If and when the Cuban situation becomes stable and a prosperous economy encourages it, they may very well flock back to Havana, communism or not. Or better conversely: if and when they return to Cuba we shall then know that Castro's victory, though communist, shall have become complete.

II. THE REVOLUTION AND THE CHURCH

That man is a Catholic who opens himself to all . . . He is a Catholic who . . . becomes . . . overwhelmed by distress, whatever form that distress may take. He is a Catholic who instinctively rejects everything that is a source of division, who cannot meet anyone without tirelessly seeking out an area of agreement. He is a Catholic who sees in each man not . . . the label which is applied to him, of unbeliever, or Protestant or Jew or Communist, but the brother for whom Christ died, and who has been placed in his path in order to receive his love.

—Bishop Huyghe, of Arras, Boulogne and St. Omer. (Pastoral letter of May 14, 1962.)

Fidel Castro's was only the second social and political reconstruction ever undertaken in Cuba. For those who remember the first, and Antonio Guiteras' defiance of Cuban and American economic interests in 1933 and 1934, the events of 1959 and 1960 have been shrouded in the uncomfortable aura of the *déjà vu*. In some respects the parallel is amazingly exact.

In the wake of Gerardo Machado's downfall in 1933, Guiteras' social reforms—the eight-hour day, minimum wage, social security, confiscation of ill-gotten wealth, and others—culminated in the order to the American-owned power monopoly, the Cuban Electric Company, to lower its consumer rates. The Company, which had resisted the earlier measures, now refused to comply. On January 14, 1934,

Guiteras personally delivered to the Company a decree of administrative seizure: units of the United States fleet lay at anchor in Havana harbor. But American diplomacy under Franklin D. Roosevelt's Secretary of State Cordell Hull would not accept the recommendations of such conservatives as Ambassador Sumner Welles, who had proposed the traditional course of armed intervention. The more liberal Good Neighbor policy, executed by Ambassador Jefferson Caffery, shunned direct intervention and the use of external forces; it preferred to work through a "chosen instrument" within Cuba herself. On January 15, 1934, Army Chief Fulgencio Batista toppled the Government and ordered Guiteras' arrest. (Guiteras escaped, but was assassinated a year later.)

Unlike Guiteras, Castro was not only a radical reformer who could not be manipulated; he also was in effective and total control of military power in Cuba. Therefore, Christian Herter's early use of the *batistiano* and other damaged Cuban interests was only an anemic copy of Hull's policy: even with American help they did not have the effective power within Cuba that Batista had in 1934. But just as Cordell Hull once discovered the strategy of the "strong man," Herter gradually discovered a new if rather more complex force within Castro's redoubt which he could impress into the service of his ends. That force was an abstraction. Its name was anticommunism.

I say its name was anticommunism because in reality the motivation of the counterrevolution was ideological only in part. But sincere anticommunism was both the seed from which it grew and the garb it always wore.

Thus, American diplomacy would not have been viable except under certain conditions. Those conditions were pro-

duced mostly by the majority of lay and clerical Cuban
Catholics and passively tolerated, at first—later, increasingly
participated in—by the Cuban hierarchy. The conditions already obtained before the Cuban-American conflict arose.
They were created, in fact, within the first six weeks of
Castro's premiership. In this sense, therefore, the Cuban
Church was one of the parties responsible for having helped
bring communism to Cuba—rather more so, perhaps, than
any other single cause.

Of course, to ascertain the degree and nature of the
Cuban Church's contribution to that effect is not the same
as to allot its share of guilt. One should note the understandable fears, the apprehensions, the indecisions, the human
fallibilities of the persons involved. It may be to one's advantage, however, to attempt to understand what their
actual role in the revolutionary process was.

CHAPTER 6

FROM COLONIAL ESTABLISHMENT
TO LAY STATE

Much of the world's understanding of the Cuban revolution has suffered from a general absence of historical perspective and from insufficient knowledge of Cuba's historical background. This is especially true with regard to the
conditions of the Church in Cuba before the revolution.
Though many have recently discovered that indifference
to the institutions of religion is the norm among Cubans
who are Catholic by inertia and custom, deeply devout in
an instinctive way, and in communion with the Church
only through the desiccated umbilical cord of cultural tradition,[1] we are not as likely to know that the profound alienation between the people and the clergy, (hence between the
people and the sacraments and the liturgy), began well over
a century ago. As Cuba began to acquire a national consciousness and stir from her long colonial lethargy, the
Cuban hierarchy and clergy, who had always remained more
closely identified with the mother country than with the

[1] Angel del Cerro, in "¿Ha comenzado la persecución religiosa?"
Cuba, 1961 (Paris, 1961; supplement to Cuadernos, No. 47,
March–April, 1961), p. 25, estimates that 10% of the Cuban population practices the Catholic religion to some degree, and that about
80% would accept it nominally.

masses, chose to remain faithful to Spain. This, of course, does not differentiate Cuba from dozens of other colonies, Spanish and otherwise. The process is well known and one need only mention it in order to mark the origin of the cleavage between the people and their pastors, who in Cuba as elsewhere since early modern times had increasingly thought of themselves alone as "the Church." The peculiar effect that this had for the Spanish colonial Church, and nowhere more markedly than in Cuba where the independence movement was more protracted, was that it tended to preserve the clergy and hierarchy in an outlook characteristic of Spanish Catholicism: The breath of modern times, thus, had vivified Cuba no more than it had Spain.

To say that the outlook of the Cuban Church had remained Spanish is no more than to say that it had remained medieval. Medieval is not of itself a pejorative term. There was a time when to be medieval was to be progressive and abreast of the times. But that was seven centuries ago, and time has since gone on. If an institution is medieval today then it is by definition anachronic, and perhaps it should be otherwise. The Spanishness of the Cuban clergy and hierarchy is one of the factors that must be understood if one is to appreciate the concept of State-Church relations that the Cuban Church tended to regard as an ideal.

The wars of Independence saw the Church lined up solidly and militantly, though not very effectively, against the Cuban patriots. In 1898, on the eve of the defeat of Spain, the Bishop of Havana wrote a pastoral letter "for civilization, against barbarism," that is, for colonial rule rather than independence. The effects of such a teaching may be easily deduced. Protestantism, however, was too for-

eign to Cuba, and so the advantage fell to freemasonry as it
chose to identify itself with the cause of independence.
Some historians have argued, indeed, that freemasonry's
co-operation made Cuban independence from Spain possible. It is unimportant whether the claim is correct: It is
widely believed. What is certain is that many events of
French history were repeated in Cuba before the end of the
19th century. By 1898, when Spain was vanquished, the
Catholic Church was discredited; it was also so powerless
that active anticlericalism was not, and has never been until
very recent times, a problem.

The Church and the clergy became figures of fun. If one
thought of them at all, they were to be ridiculed, but to
be neither feared nor hated: the feeling remains in Cuba to
this day that organized religion is a matter for women and
young children. The same Cuban who would as likely as
not openly wear a medal around his neck (Castro wore one
as late as 1960), would not wish to be seen speaking civilly
to a priest or entering a Church on Sunday, so heavily
taxed might he be with the charge of effeminacy and un-
virility. The depth of this feeling can perhaps best be
gauged from the fact that clerical concubinage (which is
probably not as frequent as elsewhere in Latin America)
is frowned upon by Catholics, but is one of the few ways
in which Cuban priests can hope to earn a modicum of respect from other Cuban men.

Since the turn of the century the Church seemed gradually to have become uneasily and unstably acquiescent in
conditions it could not change. Its isolation brought about
its involution, partly checked only by a religious revival of
ambitious proportions among the urban middle classes beginning in the late 30's and continuing into the 40's. But

the complexion of the clerical face of the Church did not appreciably change. The Spanish clergy still predominated in proportions of about four or five to one. Most of these belonged to religious orders, relatively few of which were engaged in pastoral work. The majority of the Cubans among the clergy were secular. A small number of Canadians and a very few American priests had arrived since the end of World War II.

As an illustration, one can note the national composition of the Cuban hierarchy. As late as March, 1960, out of six Cuban dioceses one was vacant, two were headed by Spaniards, and three by Cubans. Since then the vacant diocese has been filled by a Cuban, and a number of Cubans have been appointed auxiliary bishops. However, when another diocese fell vacant through death in November, 1960, it was filled, even at this late date, by a Spaniard. As of this writing, then, out of Cuba's nine bishops only three are Spanish but these three head half the Cuban dioceses.[2] It goes without saying that only the suspicious could see in this traditional sort of national configuration anything sinister. But perhaps only the imprudent could rejoice in it, and one imagines that only the unsophisticated could think that it is irrelevant to an understanding of Cuban events.

Immemorially, then, the Church in Cuba thought of itself, correctly, as impotent, as barely surviving under duress, as threatened by secularism, indifference, freemasonry and, in the last twenty years or so by Protestantism as well. To the Cuban high and low clergy this was especially humiliating in view of the privileged position of the Church in Spain. They knew that Cuba would never realize the Spanish ideal, yet this ideal, being a matter of Christian

[2] See *Bohemia*, May 21, 1961.

principle, as they thought, was never to be given up in intention. The Church, thus, was caught in a vicious circle: it was discontent with the here and now, but it saw no other solution than trying to hold on to the past. This was the sort of posture that, by its own implications, could not but confirm the stagnation from which the Church suffered.

The problem of the shortage of priests may provide an enlightening instance of how the vicious circle went. For two generations the shortage was made up, as far as it was ever made up, by the massive importation of Spanish regulars. It is relatively unimportant that the heavy dependence upon regular clergy appears to have reduced appreciably the influence of the dioceses, though this condition may have tended further to increase the reaction of involution of the hierarchy. It is more important that the Spanish as a whole have not yet become quite reconciled to the reality of having lost their Empire, and most especially Cuba. Many still entertain, and voice, thoughts of a possible reversal of history. The Spanish clergy's militant Spanishness toward the former colony, no less than their conception of what the relations between clergy and people should be, operated generally only to the disadvantage of the Church and tended to diminish the appeal that the priestly ministry might have had for Cuban Catholics.

Naturally, with few native vocations the congregations could not very well maintain seminaries and houses of study in Cuba, so Cuban candidates were sent abroad. Until recently that meant, of course, Spain: Thus, even the native clergy became hispanicized. One should not misconstrue this disadvantage of a Spanish clergy as due to xenophobia, from which Cuba is fortunately almost totally free. The difficulty was specifically Spanish. For example, Canadian priests were sufficiently liberal, and up-to-date to earn respect and admiration. And what was probably the most powerful single agency in the Catholic revival of Cuba's middle classes, namely, the Christian Brothers—who established their first Cuban foundation at the turn of the century—was until very recent times almost entirely French in composition. It should be added that, unlike the Spanish clergy, the Christian Brothers usually became Cuban nationals. In time they attracted native vocations in great numbers. They were also unique in having had a native Cuban provincial. Their contribution to the modernization of the Church in Cuba was as magnificent as it was unemulated.

Further to compound the sinuosity of the circle, since early Republican times the Church had concentrated its resources in education work for the upper-middle and upper classes, a condition that prevailed without exception until after World War II, when a few schools for the poor began to appear. The hierarchy seem to have reasoned logically, but not necessarily perspicaciously, that the faith of these classes could be built up most easily and quickly, and that once this was accomplished the middle classes would constitute a sort of élite that would help carry the Gospel to the humble and the poor. The plan was successful enough in the first respect, but certain side effects were not foreseen. They may well have been unforeseeable. For instance, the Church lay itself open to the charge that it was neglecting the poor and courting the rich. Worse, it also lay itself open to the temptation of actually doing so. It seems, indeed, that to some extent it did so: And, upon occasion it did so extravagantly and even unnecessarily. For instance, despite the traditional policy of the Cuban Church to avoid taking sides in temporal matters, "in view," as the formula went, "of the spiritual mission of the Church," Batista's last regime, after his *coup d'état* in 1952, enjoyed an unprecedented degree of episcopal benison during six and a half of its not quite seven years. Some Cubans thought that this departure from custom was not totally unrelated to the justly famous largess of Batista's second wife—a largess which was itself a departure from Cuban type. Since Batista's first wife was still living, Marta Fernández de Batista's generosity was, justly or unjustly, suspect and was widely commented upon unfavorably.

However, the Cuban Church's consortium with the rich was never so much a compromising reality as a tempting thought to be delighted in morosely. But the Church by its own choice did depend especially upon certain classes for whatever native clergy could be recruited. Would vocations come out of this middle- and upper-class elite? This was, of course, the objective of the policy: Otherwise, the problem could not be solved.

The answer, as it turned out, was disappointing. There were many vocations, of course, but in general the distance between the Spanish clergy and the Cuban people proved too much, even under these conditions, to be bridged very rapidly. The hope of a native clergy simply did not materialize. Moreover, what vocations there were went largely to the religious orders. Two reasons can be given for this: First, the Catholic schools were owned, directed, and staffed without exception by regulars and, consequently, vocations normally went to them; second, only the religious orders could offer the opportunities for work and advancement (e.g., positions in Spanish seminaries, education abroad, advanced training, employment in Cuban schools) that would attract the elite. Relatively few city dwellers in Cuba had as much as seen the Cuban countryside—and to be well educated in Cuba was to belong to a certain class. The possibility of living away from the city did not easily and naturally occur to what was, literally, the Cuban bourgeoisie. Thus, because pastoral work was being neglected, even in the city, vocations from the sort of people who would ordinarily have considered going to remote and backward country parishes simply were not forthcoming in sufficient numbers.

It can be said in all sincerity that this reluctance was more than understandable. Only those who have actually chosen to go to the most inhospitable lands could possibly cast the first stone of criticism in their direction. For if the Cuban Church as a whole was poor, the country parishes were indigent. A country pastor would have starved if he had had to depend upon the parishioners' support. The peasants themselves were not only so needy, but generally so indifferent that only a few would have given even if they had been able. Since the end of World War II the situation was alleviated in part when a few sugar mills began to relieve the diocesan burden by paying pastors' salaries and ordinary parochial expenses. On occasion they built little chapels. The hierarchy appears to have thought that if the Church in Spain was justified in receiving a subsidy from the State, how much more justified was the Cuban Church in accepting the benefaction of private enterprise.[3]

[3] It goes without saying that the Cuban Church has never received a state subsidy since colonial times. Least of all did it receive one in July, 1961, when an American diocesan weekly published a document supposedly proceeding from the secret files of the Cuban government and purporting to be a directive "regarding measures to be taken against the Catholic Church" which included the establishment of a schismatic, national Church; the directive recommended

Recently, since the break between Castro and the Church, the Cuban hierarchy has maintained that to make too much of such arrangements was an unfair attack upon the prestige of the Church, and it has defended its action on the grounds that the clergy was entitled to take such salaries, and that no conflict of interests influenced the priests unduly. "We do not know . . . of a single case of a priest in a sugar cane plantation or refinery who acted as an instrument of exploitation . . . [whereas we know of] many cases in which the priests defended the rights of the workers, putting themselves on their side in cases of strikes."[4] It is quite unnecessary to stipulate that the clergy were, indeed, entitled to take such salaries, and that Castro's criticism of the Church in this particular respect was grossly unfair. As to the question of the interests thus vested, there is not the slightest reason to believe that the Cuban bishops deviated in the least from the truth in the foregoing declaration. Compromising situations, however, can be entered into in the best as in the worst of faith, and wittingly as well as not. The dependence of the rural Cuban Church upon the fringe benefits of the companies owned by American and Cuban millionaires was, however unavoidable, only an immediate palliative and an eventual millstone. It did not really bring the Church close to the people. Native vocations did not thereby increase, though no one can say of course what might have been the case if the system had endured ten decades instead of only one. But, as with other

---

that the Church's "financial subsidy by the state" be reduced. I would deduce, therefore, that the document was not forged by a Cuban, who would have known better.

[4] Open letter from the Cuban hierarchy to Fidel Castro, dated December 4, 1960. Reproduced in translation by Warren Miller, *Ninety Miles from Home* (Boston, 1961), pp. 43–4.

measures, the chasm between the Church and the destitute masses, far from being bridged, was ultimately deepened by this.

It is easy to be wise after the event. Perhaps none of the consequences of these palpable realities were actually foreseeable. In any event, they went unchecked. The point is not that the hierarchy did anything wrong, but that it operated exclusively within the set of assumptions defined by the almost total acceptance of the social and political conditions of Cuba, not as desirable, but as irremediable. The Church did not plan for change, but for stability; when revolution finally came, it was the last thing the hierarchy was prepared for.

Now, one may well suppose that just as individuals must sometimes suffer a dark night of the soul, Churches too may have to go through ages in which, like Christ on the cross, they experience the total forlornness of being abandoned by all, even, seemingly, by God. This constitutes a great trial: It conjures up the temptation of infidelity to one's call. Yet, it is also the anvil on which the metal of ordinary virtue can be forged into the sword of heroic strength. Not the least among the paradoxes hid in this darkness is the fact that even after the call to heroism is issued, that is, once we are required to exercise our freedom by heeding or refusing that call, we may persist in pretending that we do not need to chose at all, as if in these circumstances mediocrity were a genuine possibility. On the contrary, since the object of God's temptation is precisely to excise mediocrity, mediocrity is the worst possible choice, because it is the least decisive and because it does not proceed from the conquest of our autonomy but from the renunciation of our freedom and, indeed, from our attempt to escape its responsibilities.

That is why the option for mediocrity would also be the least likely, but for our wasted tenacity clinging to the discomforts of inertia and ease. Ordinary behavior tends, *ex hypothesi*, to be excluded by extraordinary times.

The greatest trial of the Cuban Church as the first half of the twentieth century was drawing to a close was caused not so much by its truly pitiful condition, or by the dimness of its prospects, or by the mountainous height of its immemorial problems, but by its pedestrian and natural desire above all to survive the perils of the times. It is difficult to take risks, as sometimes one must, or to take them wisely, when concern for security is dominant.

CHAPTER 7

FROM COUP D'ÉTAT TO CIVIL WAR

It has been said of late that the Catholic Church in Cuba supported Castro's revolution during its struggle against Batista, and that its opposition began only more recently, say, in 1960, when the revolution's true color began to show. The reality is rather more complex.[1]

The proposition that Catholics supported the revolution during the Sierra days applies without major qualification to the laity, whose contribution to the revolution, both individually and through all the Catholic Action organizations, was second to that of no other Cuban group. This was the first time in Cuba's history that Catholics as such had actively and effectively demonstrated their patriotism. Their prestige was accordingly enhanced, especially since, by all accounts, their devotion and courage allowed only admiration and praise. Among the clergy, however, though many

[1] See the article "La Cruz y el Diablo," *Bohemia,* January 18, 1959, prepared by the editorial staff of the magazine. Unless otherwise noted this is the main source of my account of the Church's participation in the revolution prior to January 1, 1959. I have checked all the essential facts related by the article with Cuban Catholics, lay and clerical, who have invariably confirmed the accuracy of the article as to its general tenor, though disagreeing with it (and with each other) on minor details. The only exception to this shall be noted below.

instances of courageous and patriotic collaboration were to be recorded, a certain division could have been more easily noticed. This division tended to follow, though very irregularly, national lines and, therefore, tended to coincide with a division along the regular-secular line. It is understandable that many among the Spanish clergy felt less engaged than their Cuban confrères. On the other hand, many among the anti-Franco, Basque clergy[2] were decidedly and actively against Batista. The superiors of religious orders were generally reluctant to court hardship. But the pattern varied from one community to another and from one diocese to the next.

The great majority of the predominantly Cuban secular clergy, however, had no hesitation as to where their duty and their sympathies lay. Most of them were at one time or another molested by the *batistianos*; many were arrested and interrogated; several were tortured. At one point despite his earlier collaboration, Manuel Cardinal Arteaga, an ailing, elderly man was struck by the brother of Batista's Chief of Police, who searched the Cardinal's residence while looking for documents incriminating the rebels. (Having found none he took $30,000 in diocesan property instead.) The incident was glossed over when Batista's wife called the next day and apologized on her husband's behalf.[3]

If the clergy's support of the rebellion was mixed, the hierarchy's is even less easily categorized. Besides, its relations to the regime did not remain static throughout the dictatorship. The Archbishop of Santiago, Msgr. Enrique

[2] The Basques constituted a good proportion of one congregation in particular, the Franciscans. It is widely known, I suppose, that for historical reasons the province of Vizcaya sided with the Republic almost to a man during the Spanish civil war.

[3] Claude Julien, *La Révolution Cubaine* (Paris, 1961), pp. 39–40.

Pérez Serantes had consistently opposed Batista since March 10, 1952, the date of the coup d'état. Msgr. Alberto Martín Villaverde of Matanzas was probably the most outspoken opponent of Batista among the hierarchy. Cardinal Manuel Arteaga, of Havana, on the other hand, preferred "having recourse to diplomacy rather than to militant action."[4] He congratulated Batista upon taking power and was photographed with him on many ceremonial occasions. The diocese of Pinar del Río was at this time vacant: its Apostolic Administrator was Msgr. Evelio Díaz who, being also Cardinal Arteaga's Auxiliary understandably did not allow his feelings to show until the Cardinal began to withdraw from active direction of the diocese. Of the remaining two diocese, that of Camaguey was occupied by a Spaniard, Msgr. Carlos Riu Angles, who is known to have thought that the Church should not oppose Batista on the grounds that it was not the Church's business to do so. The titular of the last diocese, Cienfuegos, whose name need not be recorded here, completed the spectrum: all the more irritatingly to Cubans because he was a Cuban himself, he was sufficiently incriminated in certain business transactions to have found it advisable on January 1, 1959, after Batista's downfall suddenly to resign his diocese and flee to the United States along with other high ranking batistianos. An Apostolic Administrator was then appointed in his place.

When Batista's coup was not yet a week old, Fr. Julián Bastarrica, a Franciscan, made a public statement: ". . . legitimate government cannot issue from guns."[5] Not long afterwards Andrés Valdespino, then president of the Juventud Católica, one of the oldest and most influential Catholic

[4] Ibid., p. 40.
[5] Quoted by Bohemia, January 18, 1959.

Action groups in Cuba, published a similar statement in
Bohemia; so also did other Catholic lay leaders, including
Angel del Cerro, another well-known intellectual whose
luminous assessment of the Catholic problem in confrontation with the Cuban revolution we shall consider in some
detail. It was the first time in Cuba's history that Catholic
opinion as such, on matters of political philosophy was being publicly expressed, and its influence felt, and thus the
first time in Cuba's history that Catholics as such began to
feel the weight of political tyranny. Thus in June, 1952, a
Catholic meeting in Guanajay was broken up by Batista's
soldiers and several persons were wounded, a few being arrested. This was only the first of a long series of increasingly
grave incidents. As the tyranny became more and more oppressive, and as its record of murder and torture became
equaled only by the refinements of its systematic looting
and piracy, Catholic opposition became proportionately
irate and strong.

On the 26th of July, 1953, an obscure lawyer called Fidel
Castro unsuccessfully attacked the Moncada Army barracks
in Santiago. When those few of his raiders who escaped
were being hunted down and shot on sight, Msgr. Pérez
Serantes intervened and so aroused public opinion that he
obtained the promise of a trial for the survivors still at large.
Castro was apprehended shortly after. His defence plea has
become famous under the title of its final line: "History
shall absolve me." Condemned to a prison term, of which
he served only a few months before being amnestied, Castro
thus owes his life to Msgr. Pérez' intervention.

The participation of the Worker's Catholic Action in an
anti-government strike in 1955 resulted in a police raid on
their headquarters. Their chaplain, Fr. Enrique Orlé, was

accused by the Government of being "a Communist priest," and the movement was called "red." By this time Batista, eager to co-operate with the United States, had outlawed communism in Cuba, thus providing himself with an excellent blind behind which to persecute the most varied opposition. One of his most ferocious repressive corps was called the Bureau for the Repression of Communist Activities. Many Catholics fell victim to it: The accusation of communism became but a thin euphemism for anti-government opinion.[6] Later that year the National Council of Acción Católica, the supreme lay Catholic authority in Cuba, made known its views on the government's repeated violation of the rights to freedom, justice, and life. Toward the end of 1956 an unprecedented sort of violence against Catholics was introduced when Fr. Ramón O'Farrill, a parish priest in the diocese of Havana, was arrested and charged with having given asylum to eight revolutionaries. Fr. O'Farrill was ordered to inform. He refused. He was released only after four days of torture, bleeding through the ears and with several ribs fractured. Some among the clergy asked for the excommunication of those responsible—a meaningless penalty, of course, except as a gesture of protest. The petition was not granted. Shortly afterwards, on December 2, 1956, Castro landed at Playa Colorada, at the foot of the Sierra Maestra: His forces soon decimated to twelve men, he began to wage guerrilla warfare against Batista. The 26th of July Movement, along with other revolutionary organizations, began to organize an extensive underground.

Fr. Antonio Albizu, the pastor of Manzanillo, became an early and trusted contact point for Castro's couriers. Three

[6] See Angel del Cerro, "La Iglesia tiene que resuscitar," *Bohemia*, April 5, 1959.

Santiago priests, Fathers Antonio Rivas, Francisco Beris-
taín, and José Chabebe, joined the Movement. Rectories
often stocked weapons which were en route to the Sierra.
In Holguín, Fr. Chelala became the treasurer of the local
branch of the Movement. The national treasurer Enrique
Canto, was likewise a Catholic, indeed, he was a well-known
lay leader. Fr. Chabebe, who had a scheduled program over
the local radio station in Santiago arranged to transmit to
Raúl Castro, who by this time had organized a second guerrilla band in the Sierra Cristal, coded messages inserted as
parts of his religious broadcast. Then, in mid-1957 Fr. Guillermo Sardiñas, with Msgr. Evelio Díaz' permission,
climbed the Sierra Maestra to become chaplain to the
rebels.[7] Fr. Rivas was performing the same function in Raúl
Castro's group, and Fr. Manzanedo in a third that had been
formed under the command of Major Juan Almeida.
Toward the end of the year a member of Acción Católica in
Matanzas was murdered by the police. A funeral procession
was organized. The bishop tried to lead it, but the ceremonies were stopped and the congregation dispersed by the
police. "A pastoral letter, greatly praising the victim and
citing his attitude as an example of clear and courageous
patriotism, protested at once against the violence of the
police."[8]

Otherwise the hierarchy had remained silent since Msgr.
Pérez' plea for mercy in 1953. But the clergy, or at least that
part of it whose concern could not be contained, became
increasingly vocal. On February 10, 1958 (a patriotic date),
Fr. Angel Gaztelu, pastor of the Church of the Holy Spirit

[7] At least one Protestant clergyman also undertook chaplain duties
at the Sierra.
[8] Julien, La Rév. Cub., p. 43.

in Havana, preached a sermon destined to become famous
—condemning the regime openly and in the harshest terms.
It was followed on the next day by a statement issued by
Acción Católica. At about the same time Fr. Ignacio Biaín,
the Franciscan editor of La Quincena, Cuba's most distinguished Catholic magazine, began a vigorous, incisive campaign that did not let up until the defeat of the dictatorship.

At this juncture a very important event took place.
Toward the end of February, 1958, Msgr. Pérez called a
secret conference of the Cuban hierarchy in Santiago. Msgr.
Pérez' proposal was unprecedented in Cuban history. He
moved that the Cuban hierarchy issue at once a unanimous
statement asking Batista to resign. Msgrs. Martín of Matanzas, and Díaz, of Havana, agreed with the motion; Msgr.
Riu, of Camaguey, and the bishop of Cienfuegos, were opposed. Cardinal Arteaga, backed by Msgr. Alfredo Muller,
his Auxiliary, proposed a compromise which, after some
deliberation, appeared agreeable to all. The precise nature
of the compromise proposal, however, is not easy to ascertain. For, as it turned out, the bishops were sufficiently unaware of those subtleties of human relations which make
efficient procedure advisable even in what pertains to public
pastoral statements. It appears, from later events, that the
agreement of the bishops to the Cardinal Primate's proposal
was secured not on the basis of an actual draft, but only
upon a verbal statement of the general lines that the document should take. Nor were provisions made for checking
back with each bishop after the document was drafted but
before it was issued. It was all left in the hands of the proponents of the compromise.

It is not generally known who actually drafted the statement.[9] What is certain is that when it was published, on February 25, it caused a stir. "We exhort all those who militate in antagonistic camps," it said, "to desist from using violence, and that they search as soon as possible for effective solutions such as might allow our country to return to the physical and moral peace of which we stand in such great need. To that end, we do not doubt, those who truly love Cuba shall know how to gain merit before God and before history by not refusing to make whatever sacrifice may be required to obtain the establishment of a Government of National Unity which might prepare the way for our country's return to peaceful and normal political life."[10] It was proposed that a conciliation commission be formed to bring together Castro and Batista in order to work out the details of the union government. There is reason to suspect that, had Castro come down from the mountains in order to confer with Batista, the latter's most solemn guarantees of safe conduct might not have prevented an "accident": this had often happened with Batista before. More conclusively,

[9] The implication of *Bohemia*'s article on this question is that Cardinal Arteaga, either alone or in collaboration with Msgr. Muller was probably responsible for the draft that was issued. Here is where my sources differ. According to persons who were in a position to know, the Cardinal, who was already suffering from arteriosclerosis and became easily confused, left the matter in charge of two persons (neither of them a bishop), who in fear of the consequences of a strong stand, chose to reinterpret the proposal along the lines that were to become public. This rings true except perhaps for the motivation of the two persons concerned. But since I have no personal knowledge either of their character or of the terms of the compromise they were actually instructed to draft, I cannot decide whether honest misunderstanding is or is not enough to account for their part in the affair. Most persons in Cuba at the time assumed that Cardinal Arteaga was personally responsible for the tenor of the document. The circumstances of his earlier association with Batista lent added credibility to this impression.

[10] Quoted by *Bohemia*, January 18, 1959.

the bishops' proposal was unrealistic and naïve in every respect. Batista, of course, promptly agreed to its terms.

Msgr. Pérez Serantes was the next to speak out. In the direct and outspoken manner for which he is celebrated he said: "I did not couch my proposals in such vague and ambiguous terms, nor did I mention any 'national unity cabinet,' as it is now made out. I asked for a change of government: what this means is that Batista should go."[11]

As for Castro, his written reply followed a few days later: "We wish to state to the people of Cuba: first, that the Cuban episcopate ought to define what is . . . a National Unity Government; second, that [they] . . . ought to make clear to the country whether they consider it possible for any self-respecting and honorable Cuban to be disposed to sit in a Council of Ministers under the chairmanship of Fulgencio Batista." This was, of course, a telling point, and at a later date the bishops were to be reminded that they once had made this suggestion.[12] On the other hand, Castro's reply also implicitly acknowledged the good intentions of the bishops. It stated: ". . . third, that [the] lack of precision on the part of the episcopate facilitates the dictatorship's efforts to channel [the bishops'] intentions into a surrender and a counterrevolutionary maneuver." In sum, as the reply put it, "the *26th of July Movement* flatly refuses to enter into any contact with the Conciliation Commission."

[11] Quoted *ibid.*
[12] Castro's letter, dated March 9, 1958, was photostatically reproduced in *Revolución* on July 26, 1962, from which these quotations are taken. The bishops' proposal was now being resurrected in order to show (one-sidedly, to be sure) the sort of stand they had once taken regarding the revolution. Msgr. Pérez Serantes' own comments on the collective proposal were not as easily remembered.

Msgr. Martín's own despairing reaction was to act unilaterally and privately—robbing the gesture of the force that
Msgr. Pérez proposal would have had. He went to Batista
and appealed to his conscience to resign. The result of his
journey may be easily surmised. Indeed, after the failure of
the "conciliation" attempt, Batista openly turned upon
Catholics, and, notwithstanding the non-ideological character of his motives, the repression assumed the proportions of
persecution. It is regrettable that the American Catholic
press did not discover it, or the American secular press capi-
talize upon its latent news value: The course of history
might have been radically altered if they had.

Only a few days after these happenings the police apprehended a Catholic labor leader, Sergio González, whose
piety had earned him the nickname "the little priest." Msgr.
Muller interceded on his behalf and obtained official guarantees that González would be brought to trial. "The little
priest," like so many other Batista prisoners before him, was
shortly found dead in a back street: he had been tortured
and then shot. The general strike call issued by Castro for
early April was heeded by the Catholic labor organizations.
When the strike failed, partly because it was sabotaged by
the communists, two Catholic labor leaders fled to the
United States, hunted by the police in the reprisals that followed the strike attempt. Two priests, Father Enrique Orlé
and Salvador Freixado, had to follow them into exile.

But not all escaped. Three Catholic youths were arrested
by the police on April 9. A few days later they were found
shot. The initiative of two Havana priests was aroused by
this event, and on April 14 Fathers Madrigal and Eduardo
Boza—the latter, at this moment, only 22 months away
from the episcopacy—drafted a letter of strong protest to

Batista and asked every pastor of the diocese to subscribe to
it. Not all signed, but many did. It may be significant that
the letter was not delivered by any of the bishops of the diocese, but by Msgr. Luis Centoz, the Papal Nuncio. Or,
rather, the attempt to deliver it was made. Batista did not
receive the Nuncio. He already knew the burden of the
communication, he said, and it were better left undelivered,
otherwise there would be "grave prejudice to the Church."[13]

Fr. Boza's church henceforth became "the principal
centre of conspiracy in the capital."[14] Fr. Madrigal became
the treasurer of the 26th of July Movement's Havana
branch: not long afterwards he had to flee to the United
States, his life in danger. Lay Catholic leaders continued to
be tortured and shot. They were invariably described as
communists involved in anti-democratic subversion who
had fired upon the police or who had been killed accidentally while evading or resisting arrest. That fall, Castro decided that the time had come for bolder action. The guerrilla forces were beginning to gain recruits in greater numbers for previously their number (no two estimates agree)
had been exceedingly small.[15] The end was drawing close.

One more episode before the overthrow of the Batista
government deserves to be recorded. By early December it
had become clear that Batista would not last long. Fr. Be-
larmino García drafted a letter addressed to the Cuban
bishops asking them to take energetic action in the form of
a pastoral letter. Fr. García's letter was energetic enough in
its own right. "The [Cuban] ecclesiastical hierarchy," it

---

[13] Quoted by *Bohemia*, January 18, 1959.
[14] *Ibid.*
[15] See the exchange between Herbert Matthews and Theodore
Draper on this question; Draper, pp. 185 ff.

read, "has left the Catholic community undefended, and it has even insinuated an accusation of indiscipline and rebellion by reason of the attitude taken by its best priests and by the laity in the face of the grave dangers to the country. The high ecclesiastical dignitaries have either professed or publicly simulated an inconceivable indifference to the nefarious deeds perpetuated by repressive forces, encouraged and rewarded by the supreme might of the *de facto* ruler, who has ostentatiously boasted of outrages and cruelties that insult human dignity and sacrilegiously offend the Christian conscience in its most basic moral feeling."[16]

The letter, however, was not submitted directly to the episcopal authorities. It was taken by Fathers Rodríguez Rozas, Manuel Colmena, Angel Gaztelu, and Ignacio Biaín to the Papal Nuncio. The Nuncio approved. Indeed, he "asked" that the letter be delivered to the addressees " 'in order that in a worthy manner and without any possibility of [later] impugnations,' the prestige of the Church might be saved."[17] The letter was delivered. The bishops took its suggestions under consideration. It was believed that a pastoral letter would be issued on Christmas day, but Christmas day came and went and the only hope it brought was in the form of rumors that the General Staff was about to turn against Batista.

As we now know, the rumor was true. Representing the Army, on December 24 Eulogio Cantillo had secretly met with Castro to offer him the usual bargain: That the revolution assume power with Army support. Castro refused to consider any offer but surrender. Still, no pastoral was issued. It may be, of course, that it was being prepared. But

16 *Bohemia*, January 18, 1959.
17 *Ibid.*

we are not likely ever to know even that with certainty. On December 31, his forces routed or demoralized or plotting against him, Batista fled Cuba. The revolution's first stage, the civil war, had come to an end.

Shortly after his victory, Fidel Castro was asked about the role of the Catholic Church in the revolution's armed struggle. Mindful, no doubt, of the distinctions that needed to be made and, with unconscious theological wisdom not mistaking the hierarchy for the Church, he replied: "The Catholics of Cuba have lent their most decided co-operation to the cause of liberty."[18] This was, after all, only a fair and truthful statement of the facts.

[18] Quoted *ibid.*

CHAPTER 8

FROM OPPORTUNITY FEARED
TO PERPLEXITY INDULGED

As long as the armed struggle between Castro and Batista remained unresolved, Church-State relations in Cuba had had two distinct sides: a Church-Batista side and a Church-Castro side. During that period, of course, it was the first aspect that predominated: Batista was in power, and Castro's victory had been highly problematic until quite late in 1958. Few among the clergy, apparently only one among the hierarchy, and possibly none among the laity could have traced their attitude toward Batista—whether indifference, passive acquiescence, or active collaboration—to any desire to oppose Castro as such.

Very few Cubans had actually been taken in by Batista's routine charge that Castro was a communist. But the accusation of communism, even when unbelievable, and actually unbelieved, usually leaves behind embers of fearful suspicion. The Cuban bishops, evidently, did not really believe Batista's charge, but they were made uneasy by it; they craved reassurance. Ridiculously little, a word, would have satisfied them.[1] But by the time they obtained a word, a

---

[1] "Castro . . . [while] in the Sierra Maestra . . . refused an unofficial request formulated by Msgr. Pérez Serantes that in one of his

whole formula had become their minimum demand, and when that came, positive action was required: Eventually, they conditioned their collaboration upon an identity of purposes between Castro and themselves.

Such was the basic process by which an original benevolence, only faintly marred by a shadow of distrust, produced a crisis of conscience. The attitude toward Batista was diametrically opposite: None, not even his episcopal collaborator from Cienfuegos, approved of him. But some Catholics had this good word to say about him: At least he fought communism—to many Americans this expression will have a familiar ring. In brief, when upon Castro's victory the question of the Church's attitude toward him suddenly loomed up, the hierarchy's indecisiveness of the past no longer mattered, but their perplexity concerning Castro was something else again. Cuban communists, on the other hand, were well prepared for the change of regime. They knew exactly what to do: They immediately declared their total and unqualified support of the revolutionary government and of Castro.

It had not always been so. Early communist attempts to join forces with Castro against Batista had foundered on Castro's "intransigence."[2] Moreover, at the very moment when Castro's star began to rise the communists actually began to oppose him more or less openly—with particular

---

speeches or statements he mention the name of God, in order to clear up certain misgivings," Angel del Cerro, art. cit., Cuba, 1961, p. 27.

[2] This is by Carlos Rodríguez' own admission; he is one of the three or four leading Communists in Cuba. See Julien, La Rév. Cub., p. 83. For the Communists' appraisal of Castro at even earlier times, see Herbert Matthews' letter from Juan Marinello, in The Cuban Story (New York, 1961), pp. 51–2.

effectiveness, as we have seen, in connection with the April attempt of a general strike. Francisco Parés, a Spanish intellectual who had taken refuge in Cuba from Franco, and whose unconditional anti-Communism is matched only by his political perceptiveness, has explained that the co-operation of communists in the general strike was not extended to Castro because it had been conditioned upon "delivering the leadership of the revolutionary movement to the super-technicians of the Communist Party."[3] It is almost amusing to note another reason for the opposition of the Cuban communists: They believed that Castro was much too anti-American and, thus, unlikely to obtain the co-operation of all the other Cuban opposition groups and revolutionary organizations without which, as the communists thought, Castro could not overcome Batista.[4] Indeed, as late as June, 1958, they thought that no force existed in Cuba "capable of defeating Batista and of putting in power a progressive and anti-imperialist government."[5] But the time came, presumably some time that next fall, when "one did not have to have the eyesight of a lynx to grasp that the rebel victory was not far off. Not until then did the communist Party's stand become flexible, nor was a common front [with Castro] hinted at. Evidently, had they not pragmatically submitted to the fidelista leadership the communists would have found themselves in a bad position at the moment of victory."[6] Of course, their sudden move did not deceive

[3] Francisco Parés, "La estrategia communista en la revolución cubana," Bohemia, February 8, 1959. Parés, now a Miami exile, currently edits the Boletín published by Miró Cardona's Revolutionary Council.

[4] Also admitted by Rodríguez; see Julien, La Rév. Cub., p. 83.

[5] Letter from Carlos Rafael Rodríguez to Claude Julien, op. cit., p. 84.

[6] Parés, art. cit.

anyone. Indeed, it did not even "surprise anyone, for the simple reason that in Cuba since January 1, [1959] everybody is a fidelista."[7] Why, then, as it turned out, was this such a decisive event?

We must understand that what worried the Catholics above all was that Castro did not immediately repudiate and reject the support volunteered by the communists. He *did* repeatedly state his non-communism, but that was not enough. He was required to be positively anticommunist, while the best he could say was this sort of thing: "sometimes it has been made to appear in this country that whoever is not sold to the Americans, or is not abjectly and unconditionally for them, is a Communist. Well, I am not a Communist, but I do not surrender to the Americans either."[8] But to understand why this disturbed Cuban Catholics we must understand, in turn, how they seem to have perceived this situation and how they conceived their role in it.

Let us first note that the communist party's support of Castro was a more adroit and consequential move than appears at first sight. One of Castro's earlier acts, in order to enlist massive political participation and support after the failure of the April general strike, had been to call for a boycott of the elections that Batista had announced for the fall—under conditions that led everyone to suspect their genuine democratic value. Castro asked not only that the electorate abstain from voting in protest but, having by this

[7] *Ibid.* The weight of Parés' affirmation is twofold. It states not only that Castro's support was nearly universal in Cuba but also that such support became nearly universal only after the victory.

[8] Speech to the Havana Rotary Club, January 15, 1959; in Emilio Roig de Leuchsenring, (ed.), *Discursos del Dr. Fidel Castro Ruz* (Havana, 1959), p. 135.

time constituted his guerrilla command into a provisional, revolutionary government-in-arms legally claiming the constitutional right to allegiance, he issued a decree: Anyone who participated in the elections as candidate, under any party or independently, would, upon the victory of the 26th of July, find himself barred from active political life in Cuba and from every public office for a period of thirty years. For good measure he also decreed that not only the *batistianos*, but all those who had occupied public office under Batista would be required to make restitution of any monies which they might be found to have misappropriated. And, regardless of party, any candidate *elected* at the next election in defiance of the decree would, in addition to the foregoing, also be required to return to the national treasury the salary of his period in office.

Now, the communists were the only party who did not participate in the election. We shall never know, of course, whether they would have participated had they been free to do so: As we have seen, the party had been banned by Batista. The result was that the communist party emerged unscathed at a time when every other political party, *batistiano* or not, had in effect disappeared from Cuban political life in all but name.[9] The only part of the decree that could

[9] No action was taken against the parties themselves. Non-*batistiano* political leaders, like Ramón Grau San Martín and Carlos Prío Socarrás either returned from exile or remained in Cuba. They all retained their freedom of action and expression. But they were totally discredited and without influence: in that sense, it is true, they were destroyed. This precision should be insisted upon, because it has been made out that Castro suppressed all parties but the communist when he came into power. Draper, p. 116, equivocates when he says that despite Castro's pledge "to uphold the 'right' of political parties, even during the provisional government, to present their programs before the people, organize the citizenry, and participate in general elections . . . after he took power, nothing of the sort

have touched them was that concerning malfeasance, for they had occupied office, including cabinet positions. But, on the whole, they had been unusually if not scrupulously honest. They and they alone among political parties had nothing to fear from good government: Their honesty now began to pay. However, the legal measures against politicians taken by Castro's government-in-arms were not the *sine qua non* of the crumbling of the political parties. Upon the institution of honest government they would have collapsed from the dead weight of their own corruption in any event. So much was generally granted at the time—by Catholics as well. "It matters little that the disappearance of the traditional parties, *batistiano* or opposition, results from the law: their disappearance is imposed by a historical reality of such weight that it determines the actual annihilation of any political force [in Cuba] outside *fidelismo*."[10] But for Catholics especially the important consequence was that "the elimination [of the parties] is not complete: one party, and one alone, remains afloat, the [Communist] one. And it floats because from the first moment it behaves cynically: it declares itself more democratic and *fidelista* than even the 26th of July."

---

happened. With the exception of the P.S.P. [communist party] none of the former parties reorganized and no new parties emerged." It is literally true, of course, that "nothing of the sort happened," but not that the parties' right to do so was denied. Castro can be blamed for not having created, to whatever extent it might have been in his power to do so, the conditions of a healthy, democratic political life in Cuba. As with freedom of the press, it does not mean that he can be blamed for having destroyed what, in fact, did not exist. But the implication that special privileges were granted to the PSP or any discrimination made against the other, the "democratic" parties, or that the latter were suppressed, is false.

[10] Parés, art. cit. Subsequent quotations refer to the same source.

Consequently, few, if any, Catholics harbored suspicions about Castro at this point simply by reason of the emergence of the communist party as the only effective one in the Cuban political forum: They all realized that it could not have been otherwise. What they did consider sinister was the very existence of the communist party as a legal political force in a virtually empty political arena. For the 26th of July had never been a political party but, rather, an underground conspiratorial network supporting three guerrilla bands, with no more of a program than had been presented by Castro in his judicial defence. The danger came, Catholics thought, from the fact that the communist party was now active and free, with no other check upon it than could come from as weak a champion of anticommunism as Castro himself. Parés frankly explained:

The 26th of July[11] is an organization whose ideals are distinctly radical, democratic, leftist. Well, the secret, congenital weakness of the democratic left in all countries consists in ignoring that the democratic field is, for the Communists, but one among many battlefields; and that within the liberal left the Communists move with greater liberty than . . . within the right. . . . The right, . . . precisely because it is not ideologically committed to democratic postulates usually knows how to oppose Communist infiltration with a better strategy. But the left, bound to an abstract democratic concept, prefers, sometimes unconsciously, the abstract victory of principle, even though in the concrete the enemies of principle destroy democracy.

It would have been a misleading commentary on this position to remark that it implied lack of faith in democracy, for Parés was also careful to point out that the right

[11] In view, perhaps, of the unconditional and even intolerant worship of Castro at this time by the majority of Cubans, Parés does not refer in this article to Castro directly, but only to The 26th of July, to the revolution, or to fidelismo. It is clear from the context, however, that throughout he has Fidel Castro specifically in mind.

could be democratic too or, at least, that "the right, of course, need not include dictatorship." It may have been a little more important to note that this position was sufficiently pragmatic to make the choice between the right and the left depend upon practical success rather than the "abstract victory of principle." In any event, Parés then proceeded prophetically to outline the strategy that Cuban communists were likely to follow in order to exploit to maximum advantage their political fortune, and thus capture the revolution and turn it to their own ends. It is relevant, in tribute to the depth of Parés' political insight, to remark that his observations were written before the end of January, 1959. Castro's trip to the United States was still almost three months away.

The specific objective of the communists at this time, as they themselves made clear,[12] was to institute a popular front, whether in the formal sense or in the sense of making common cause with Castro. In order to achieve this, says Parés, "they have only one ally: the ingenuousness of some fidelistas. The danger will cease only when fidelismo learns the truth of Communism: it always cheats; when it pretends to play a certain political game it really also plays a different one." Parés then pointed out that since the communist contribution to the triumph of the revolution, exception being made of some "Communists who individually fought the tyranny," had been brief and late, they could not hope to exact considerations from Castro on that title. But they could nevertheless find a secure position for themselves in a Popular Front if they followed their twofold plan:

[12] Particularly in a "Thesis on the present situation," *Hoy*, January 11, 1959, which seems to have been very much in Parés' mind when he wrote this article.

On the international plane their first objective consists in putting emmity between Cuba and the United States. To do so it is enough to exacerbate the indignation caused in the Cuban people by some lamentable acts of the American Government. These feelings are shared by the *26th of July Movement* in some measure. It is only legitimate and human that it be so. There is no need to coat the pill: the State Department's behavior during the Cuban period that begins on March 10, [1952] and ends on January 1, [1959], is *completely absurd*, [italics his]. It persisted in the traditional course, fatal for both the United States and Latin America, of systematically defending dictatorship. It was grounded, apparently, on the suicidal belief that the "latins" are not ready for democracy. At bottom it covered, perhaps unconsciously, a bad faith: in point of fact, dictatorships are always more amenable to the economic requirements of the United States.

Fidelismo is, of course, nationalistic, insofar as it is a historic reply . . . to the myopic American traditional policy. But for the *26th of July* this reply is posed in precisely these terms, as required by sociological, geographic and economic considerations: *revision of Cuban-American relations within the framework of higher conditions defined by the legitimate interplay of interests of the two countries* [italics mine]. The Communist strategy . . . goes well beyond this: it is based on an intentional confusion between American political responsibility by omission and criminal responsibility by action. Thus, fostering the confusion between two reasonably unmistakable terms, Communism tries to pose the question of Cuban resentment on a demagogic, clearly emotional plane, hoping to drag the *26th of July* into extreme positions and to force Washington, in reaction thereto, into policies of rejection and of oversensitiveness, whose natural consequence, of course, would be *the progressive poisoning of relations between the two countries* [italics his].

Parés' clairvoyance did not come to an end with this insight. He went on to explain that, domestically, the communist strategy was likely to develop in two directions. First, toward trying to convert key personalities in Castro's Movement who might be receptive to communist views.

But, second, communism would work for "the radicalization of the policies of the Revolutionary Government under the pretext that in order to survive the revolution must become more revolutionary." In respect to the first move, Parés thought that the communists' arsenal of psychological techniques was "prodigious." Once they "select a target" they surround him with their "pawns" and then "praise him publicly and privately" and so manipulate him that eventually, "unawares, he becomes a satellite. But, of course, the Communists do not ask him to renounce democracy: on the contrary, they make use of the genuine democratic feelings of their chosen one . . . There is no question of complicity [on his part] . . . and that makes it all the more dangerous: the chosen ones believe that they *continue to think as democrats whereas in reality they act as Communists* [italics his]."

It is, of course, quite true that these things may happen. In fact, Parés merely described here part of the process that was to unfold in Cuba during the two years ahead, and I have already observed that Castro himself would one day agree that what he had always thought of as essential to democracy was convertible with communism. It may be pertinent to remark, however, that many persons aware of this sort of strategy, seemingly Parés included, unconsciously grant its success an inevitability that it cannot be reasonably said to have. It is at this point that experts in communist techniques glide from knowledge to superstition; one receives the impression that these techniques are supposed to work somewhat as spells and hexes do, and can be resisted only by a resolve not to listen, by chasing the tempter away with a firebrand. Castro was, of course, ingenuous and susceptible to flattery. But probably not less so than to reason (sophistical as well as wise). Catholics required him, not only to listen, but to be other than he was; they demanded, in effect, that he share all their views or risk their wrath. Castro did not mind risking their wrath. Indeed, their wrath may even have aroused his opposition all the more.

Parés believed, moreover, that "it is always easy to find a few ideas to serve as the key" wherewith to "open the consciousness of the weak: fascism, in Europe, was one of these pretext-ideas," though in reality communism did not seek the final elimination of fascism but, rather, "the disintegration of the democratic society, which is the sociological preface to the Communist revolution." What were the corresponding ideas in the Cuban situation? "Rancor against the United States, the equivocal conduct of certain prelates, the collaboration of certain newspapers with [Batista], the thesis that the only natural and disinterested ally of the 26 of July is the Communist Party." But why are these pretexts? Parés answers: "the Communists know perfectly well that not the slightest social revolution is possible in Cuba. No; that is not what they seek . . . [but, rather] the moral destruction of the traditional seats of the Cuban society . . . the destruction of the arches that support the capitalist, Christian and democratic Cuban society . . . [The communists] fool no one—except those democrats who, unwittingly, play the role of spearheads of Communism."

Parés' cynical dismissal of the possibility of revolution in Cuba is more understandable if one has seen Cuban politics than if one has only heard of it. For all that, his despair went beyond realism—it was actually misanthropic. This helps explain why for him as for many other Cubans who also despaired of politics it was more important to make the revolution anticommunist than to make it successful. Moreover, there is the question whether communism essentially wishes to achieve the negative goal that consists in the destruction of every type of society, rather than the positive one of establishing a different human order of its own device. It would not be directly relevant at this point to take exception to Parés' answer, unless to suggest that the failure to make this distinction works neither to communist advantage nor to one's own. The more relevant consideration is that, even granted Parés' assumption, one can still question the wisdom of the policy which he tangentially suggests, namely, to press Castro to choose between communism and anticommunism.

Finally, there can be little doubt that Parés was correct to think that the strategy of Cuban communism could only intend "the progressive poisoning of relations between the two countries." But Parés placed upon Castro all the responsibility for avoiding this and none upon the United States, which "in reaction" to Castro's emotions would be forced "into policies of rejection." Was this reasonable?

Should it have been necessary for Castro to adopt the principle that the supreme diplomatic principle of his foreign policy must have been that of safeguarding, above all, the friendship of the United States and Cuba? If so, why was it not necessary for the United States to adopt the same principle and thus be prepared ultimately to acquiesce, if necessary, in whatever demands Castro might have made? Obviously, this would have been self-injustice on the part of the United States. But, if so, the adoption of Parés' proposal would have been self-injustice on the part of Cuba as well. It may be that the principle reasonably to be recommended to both sides should have been that they

adhere to mutual justice. To have proposed that the claims
of justice must be conditioned by the need to foil communism could not have earned Castro's respect: It certainly could not have earned his agreement.

The communist strategy which Parés predicted began to
materialize almost immediately—as did the Catholic reaction
recommended by him. But Parés, and with him all the lay
and clerical Catholics of like mind failed to take into account that their own reaction to the Communists and to
Castro was a dynamic factor in the emerging political pattern. They do not seem to have realized that, contrary to
their best intentions, their contribution to Cuban political
life at this moment, by word, by action, and by omission,
began to facilitate the success of the communist strategy.
Parés, therefore, was wrong at one crucial point: the communists did not have only one ally, but two. One was
Castro's ingenuousness. The other was the unconditional
anticommunism of the Cuban Church.

If it was easier for many Catholics than it was for Castro
to subordinate the revolution to anticommunism, the reason may have had to do with the feeling (rather extreme
in Parés' case, who in this respect did not speak as the voice
of Cuba), that a genuine revolution was not possible in
Cuba. True, Cuban Catholics disapproved of the excesses of
Batista and many others, but it seems that for them mere
reform was enough. Many of them believe so to this very
day. In a way, therefore, it is not quite correct to say, as
Parés does, that no one was being deceived by the latter-day
support of Castro by the communists. Less by communist
wile than by their own dialectics, many Catholics were deceived by it—all the more naïvely because they knew and
confessed that the communist protestations had no claim

upon Castro or upon public opinion. By requiring that communist support be not only ineffective, but also repudiated, disallowed, and annihilated, they presented to Castro an ultimatum that was as unnecessary as it was unlikely to succeed.

Parés' views were perhaps most extreme of all in what respected capitalism. Few Cuban Catholic scholars would feel bound to defend capitalism on doctrinal grounds: In fact, most of them would tend to oppose it to some degree. In the heated debate that had thus been engendered by the Catholic opposition to the communists' declarations of support, it was rather voices like those of Andrés Valdespino that predominated at first. Parés' position, however, remained in the background, as a prepared stronghold on which to fall back in case of retreat.

Valdespino, one of the best known Cuban Catholic intellectuals,[13] introduced a badly needed note of realism into the debate by reminding Catholics that if communism had any force in Cuba at that time it was because of the *soidisant* anticommunism of Batista which Catholics had been so ready to praise and which they were now beginning wistfully to long for.[14] Valdespino reminded Catholics, that, first of all, it had been during Batista's legal tenure

[13] He was at this time a professor of Penal Law at the University of Havana. He was a past president of the *Juventud Católica* (FJCC), which was one of the two Catholic Action groups to which Catholic intellectuals tended to gravitate (the other was the Agrupación Católica). Valdespino was a ministerial undersecretary in Castro's government until early 1960. He is strongly criticized in certain Cuban Catholic circles today for having defended Castro in the beginning and having collaborated in the government until a relatively recent date.

[14] Andrés Valdespino, "La revolución no necesita del comunismo," *Bohemia*, February 22, 1959. Subsequent quotations refer to the same source.

in the presidency that the communist party had been officially recognized and indeed allowed to participate in a coalition government and to control labor unions. But "after [the coup of] March 10, tactical reasons on both sides made their separation advisable. [For Batista,] who had become the shameless lap dog of the State Department, it was convenient to adopt an anti-Communist posture that would . . . [yield] him the backing of the sort of 'democracy' that could be hypocritically shocked by the tragedy of the Hungarian people, but which could criminally ignore the agony of the Cuban people. [The communists,] on their part, . . . found that opposition to the detested [regime] was the propitious occasion to recover the popular influence that they had lost much before the [coup]." Moreover, notes Valdespino, a large contribution to the purposes of Cuban communism was made by Batista's effort to "underline his anti-Communist character." He and his followers "were the best propaganda agents of Cuban Communism. [They] qualified as Communist each and every action against the regime: . . . all those efforts to which the people were sympathetic, since they contributed to the conquest of their liberty, were [called] Communist. The Communist participation in the liberating struggle was given an importance that it never remotely had . . . Now [the communists] can present themselves as co-redeemers of the Fatherland, and as [having acted] on behalf of a revolution in which their participation was in fact minuscule."

Valdespino thought that Catholics should not oppose the freedom of the communists to make their proposals and to engage in legitimate political action; he suggested this not only on the grounds that freedom of expression for all must be respected, but also because "the public light" would expose Communism and "make it known in its true dimensions." On the other hand, he thought, the danger was that the revolutionary government might "fall in the trap that Communism sagaciously prepares for it, taking advantage of the freedom that Cuba now enjoys, in order to penetrate vital sectors of the nation and to frustrate in the end the revolutionary task." Unlike Parés he was convinced that a radical revolution was both requisite and possible, though he recognized the obstacles in its path:

The Revolutionary Government has given its commitment to the people to initiate the great social and economic transformation that the country has been crying for since the very foundation of the Republic. If it does not do this, Communism could rightly criticize it. But to do it, Communism's help is not needed. It is true that Cuba's unproductive *latifundios* must be abolished, that the abuses of an exploiting capitalism must be stopped, that the peasantry must be guaranteed decent conditions of life, that the iniquitous privileges granted to monopolies and to foreign and domestic interests must be suppressed, that the land must return to Cubans—and many other things besides. But to do all this, which perforce shall meet with opposition from conservative and reactionary interests, the revolution does not need the help of Communism.

Valdespino's recommendations, therefore, were twofold: Catholics and others "should not forget that the danger of communism does not reside, as capitalists believe, in the economic and social reforms it advocates (most of which have Christian roots), but in the materialist and totalitarian ideology that animates and inspires the system. . . . On the other hand, fear of Communism cannot under any conditions brake the progressive and reformative work of the Cuban revolution. This is, of course, what vested interests would desire as, crouching in the dark, they await only an opportune moment in order to make the revolution fail under the pretext of Communist penetration."

Valdespino's position had at that time quite a few adherents among lay Catholics, very particularly among the intellectuals. But it did not gain acceptance among the increasingly suspicious majority of the clergy, who had so far remained aloof from all these discussions, or among the hierarchy, whose lines of division at this point remain rather unclear. And in any event, Valdespino's thesis suffered from two defects. The first was that it remained too negative. It criticized aptly the excesses of such as Parés. It laid down sound advice concerning what the government should avoid, namely, communist co-operation. But it did not offer Catholic co-operation in its place. It did not urge the Church to help, as best and most wisely it could, the same revolution that the communists were trying to espouse. Worst of all, it offered no recommendation on what to do about the clearly foreseen clash between the revolution and the "vested interests." Parés, whether he posed the disjunctive correctly or not, at least had no doubt concerning which side to take if a choice had to be made. Valdespino seemed to believe that no choice need be made. In fact, such would not be the case. Thus, after much hesitation, and largely by default, the choice went to the extreme viewpoint represented by Parés.

At the other extreme was Angel del Cerro, another prominent Catholic intellectual.[15] He thought, in effect, that the Church was in no position to make demands of the government, and that the danger posed by communism could be fought only if the Cuban Church first sided with the revolution. In a brilliant article, unprecedented in the his-

[15] He, too, had been a president of the *Juventud Católica*, and a professor at the Christian Brothers' *Colegio De La Salle* in El Vedado, Havana. He had conspired against Batista, and was appointed to the directorship of the government's Institute of Fine Arts, an office he occupied until June, 1960, when he went into exile.

tory of Cuban Catholicism, Del Cerro tried to show that the problem of Catholics in Cuba was not unrelated to the history of the Cuban Church. At the time of Batista's coup, he said, at least two alternatives were open: "to acquiesce in the accomplished fact on the grounds that order must be kept and that the new order was in effective control of authority, or to denounce it vigorously as the usurpation of . . . a legitimately constituted authority. But to have gone to the extreme of discussing the legitimacy of Dr. Carlos Prío Socarrás' authority[16] on the grounds that our elec-

[16] This allusion may require some background. After his collaboration with the State Department began in 1934, Batista ruled through a succession of puppets until 1940 when, having learned the strategy of adaptation by apparent liberalization, he allowed a constitutional assembly to draft a Constitution, under which he called for elections and became President—through fraud at the polls. But the elections showed he commanded an unexpected amount of support from the middle classes, which, in their anxiety, were prepared to sacrifice for the sake of stability every other kind of political order. But Batista overestimated his strength. In 1944 he allowed honest elections and therefore lost to Ramón Grau San Martín, who rode into office on his 1933 record when as Provisional President he had sanctioned Guiteras' reforms. In the absence of Guiteras, Grau's inertia, ineptness, and ultimate venality soon became apparent. Nevertheless he allowed free elections in 1948: Carlos Prío Socarrás was elected on a reform platform. But the remedy proved worse than the disease. Prío, a drug addict, graduated from the traditional simple larceny and fraud to armed robbery and extortion. Public disorder and semi-political, semi-criminal gangsterism and racketeering reached new heights. Assassinations were commonplace. The people, agreeing that rebellion would jeopardize constitutional rule, waited to oust Prío at the polls. Now, Batista who, fearing prosecution under Grau, had been in Miami exile earlier, had returned to Cuba when Prío guaranteed him immunity—and a share in the spoils. But elections were due in July, 1952, and Prío was certain to lose to the Ortodoxo Party (under which Fidel Castro was a congressional candidate). On May 10, with the pretext of restoring order, Batista deposed Prío, repealed the Constitution, and prepared to take over where he had left off. The United States promptly recognized his government. Cardinal Arteaga travelled to the Presidential Palace and offered his congratulations.

toral system facilitated vote-buying, and by other [arguments] of that sort . . . was to assume a dialectical attitude similar to that of the decadent scholastics."[17] Del Cerro specified that there had been two different tendencies within the Church. Indeed, he said, the "internal debate" had reached great intensity towards the end of Batista's rule —we have seen some of the events that he probably had in mind at this point. But, he added, the question of the concrete past or future policies of the hierarchy and of Acción Católica was only at the surface of the real problem, "which was deeper and older: it was rooted in the clash of the traditional conformist attitude with the new, non-conformist attitude in the Church."

Del Cerro then explained the nature of these two legitimate attitudes but made it clear that in his opinion the second should prevail as more in keeping with the needs of the Church today, which particularly in Cuba, "must recognize two irrefutable facts: first, the existence of other, non-Christian religions, both anterior and posterior to Christianity, which unite millions of human beings: second, the dissidence that emerged in the 16th century, which is the origin of diverse non-Catholic Christian Confessions." When one remembered other historical developments such as the emergence of the idea of separation of Church and State, and philosophical and scientific concepts of later times, one could only conclude that the Church must adjust to radically new conditions:

More than to uphold the truth of which she is the depositary, she must accept the duty to go and expound, preach and defend her Truth to a world that is not quite sure of it.

Confronting this irrefutable historical reality, the two po-

17 Angel del Cerro, "La Iglesia tiene que resuscitar," *Bohemia,* April 5, 1959. Subsequent quotations refer to this source.

sitions emerge. Some, with passive nostalgia, cleave to old privileges and try to combat with arguments that may be quite true,
but which in the practical order turn out to be inoperative.
Others, adjusting to the new conditions, endeavor to give to the
Christian teaching a modern sense, alive and efficacious. In
other words, facing the reality of a world revolution, the momentum of which has not been checked after four centuries,
they want to give to the Church a *revolutionary* significance. . . .
To illustrate, . . . The first believe that excommunication and
interdict can yield better results today in *the temporal* order
than the press and television.

These thoughts sound moderate today, but del Cerro
wrote long before John XXIII's opening address to the
Second Vatican Council. In any event, as if the allusions
had not been sufficiently clear, del Cerro added: "the first
[attitude] is typical of those countries in which the Church
has maintained longer her old rights: Spain, for example."
He then recalled that although during colonial times Catholicism had been the officially established religion in
Cuba, the Republic had always been a lay state. Therefore,
he reminded Catholics, it was a non-official, insecure
Church, weighted down by her fears and her guilt, that now
had to face the present. Thus, the first reality Catholics
should recognize was that Spain's "political colonialism
gave place to [American] economic colonialism," a colonialism so culturally oppressive that Cuba had become demoralized. Castro, "with the crushing weight of his tremendous
moral authority," was trying to achieve not only an inner
social and political reform, but also economic emancipation
from the United States and, in the first place, a "psychological emancipation." Consequently, "it is understandable
that [Castro] should assume the risks of waging such a
battle [with the United States] even if we take into account
the dangerous complexities of the international situation

... The Church must, therefore, integrally confront the fact that *there is a genuine revolution* in Cuba ... the first true revolution, and that she must play an important role therein or resign herself to losing an appreciable amount of social influence."

The alternative was rather understated. Del Cerro added that there could be no doubt that the problem facing the Cuban Church was very grave and that it needed careful study.

There is a fact that confers a special character upon an analysis of the present scene. Our psychological emancipation from colonialism takes place at the very moment when the cold war between Russia and the United States reaches its most tense and dangerous point.

This means that Cuba needs to stand erect in the full right of her adulthood and with a redeemed sovereign dignity, at the moment in which the world has two orbits of daily increasing greater definition and greater concrete force: the orbit of Russia and the orbit of United States.

Thus, the emergence of Communism as a legal force in Cuba, (I say as a legal force, because as a clandestine force [during Batista's time] it never ceased to be in force, though the contrary was affirmed and supposedly believed by our undying ostriches), poses a most delicate problem to those of us who belong to the opposite camp, namely, that of democratic theism. What, then, must the Church do? To take scandal and thus play the game of the powerful league of interests that has effectively begun to mobilize a sordid and misguided counterrevolution? To become overwhelmed by her own complexes; ... by the old-fashioned mentality of old-fashioned (if young) people; by vested interests? Hysterically to demand the indiscriminate persecution of Communists, thereby failing to realize what the Church's own historical experience has demonstrated, namely, that ideas cannot be destroyed by fire?

Not at all. The Church must prepare herself for her historic role ... She must ... heal her structures and prepare men who can assume the new tasks demanded by the times ... Courageously, honestly, the Church must recognize her errors, human errors, and, taking her place within the revolution, allow passage to the renovating force thereof.

I write this on Easter Sunday [March 29, 1959], . . . The Church cannot remain bound to social or political cadavers, or weakly remain undecided in the darkness of old sepulchres. This is the hour of Resurrection and of Light.

It cannot very well be said that the future was not clearly delineated for the Cuban Church. Later events may have surprised observers elsewhere, but not Cubans.

Del Cerro's argument, however, did not convince many. Catholic writers, noticeably those among the Spanish clergy, who now began to enter the debate, tended more and more to subscribe to Parés' opinion. It soon became evident that they would countenance no compromise or collaboration with communism—even at the cost of the revolution's success. And they made it quite obvious that their stance was required of them in strict conscience. Thus, a matter of strict conscience began the conflict between the revolution and the Church.

CHAPTER 9

FROM PRUDENT SILENCE
TO BATTLE OF WORDS

The hierarchy's initial stand in relation to the Revolutionary government can only be described, in Claude Julien's words, as "withdrawing into a prudent silence, broken on rare occasions by rather unimportant statements."[1] Early in February, while Castro was still a hero to most Americans, Richard Cardinal Cushing, of Boston, was reported as having accused the Cuban government of seizing property of the Cuban Church. Msgr. Evelio Díaz promptly issued a denial, but as usually happens in these matters the denial did not fully undo the damage.[2] The incident was trivial, of course. But it served to mark the beginning of the American Catholic contribution to the formation of American opinion on the revolution.

[1] Claude Julien, "Church and State in Cuba: Development of a conflict," *Cross Currents*, XI, 2 (Spring, 1961), p. 186.

[2] Cardinal Cushing was once again reported a few months later as having said that "the Cuban Government had impounded 'the funds of the Church' and that Premier Fidel Castro was acting like a Communist," *NYT*, November 23, 1959. Msgr. Díaz again issued a denial. Cardinal Cushing, neither denying that he had been reported correctly nor explaining what was it he had meant, stated that "my extemporaneous remarks have led to considerable misinterpretation . . . the truth is I do not have any special information on what is going on there," *NYT*, November 25, 1959.

For instance, only a few days after the previous incident "a second complaint came from American Catholics, indignant at the execution of the killers and torturers of the previous regime."[3] One need not be a political reactionary in order to abhor the death penalty—in fact, it is more often liberals who object to it. And it would have been fair to point out that the legal provisions of justice in Cuba at this time, though strictly adhered to by the revolution, were no less harsh than they had been throughout republican and colonial times.[4] On the other hand, the indignation of Americans, Catholic and otherwise, now began to blur the distinction between political opponents and those convicted of torture and murder. In any event, Msgr. Pérez Serantes— who, more than anyone else in Cuba or abroad, was entitled to appeal to the revolution for clemency—did so in a pastoral letter in which, however, he reaffirmed his belief in the justice of the executions. The pastoral clarified the fact that *prima facie* cases of atrocities and "vile" murder against the accused had been amply substantiated.[5] These qualifications were hardly needed in Cuba, since everybody already thought so. Abroad, they were useless: no one believed them. It might have been different if Castro had been mollified by Msgr. Pérez. But, much to the detraction of his

[3] Julien, art. cit., p. 186.

[4] The only respect in which the legality of the executions might have been in reasonable doubt was on the grounds that the 1940 Constitution had abolished the death penalty. As we have seen, the 1940 Constitution had been set aside by Batista. The revolutionary government acted under a *Ley Fundamental*. Moreover, the death penalty had been restored by Castro's government-in-arms well before his victory, its legal basis having been worked out by his Judge Advocate General, Humberto Sorí Marín, a Catholic lawyer.

[5] This was reported in *The Boston Pilot*, February 7, 1959. See also Julien, art. cit., p. 187.

American image, Castro was not. American public opinion would never forgive him for having shown himself to be so rigorous.

The maladroitness of the Cuban hierarchy and its decreasingly realistic outlook in the face of the debate which raged in Cuba at this time over the Communist support of the revolution, were brought to light only in March, on the occasion of an educational reform law proposed by the revolutionary Minister of Education. As had always been the case in Cuba since the advent of the Republic, the law reaffirmed that the lay character of the public schools forbade the inclusion of religious instruction in any official way. The hierarchy, however, took exception to these provisions and moreover demanded the unprecedented introduction of instruction in the Catholic faith in public schools, partly on the grounds that Cuba was a Catholic country. To insist on this concession was, of course, their privilege. But it was hopeless, and one wonders why they did it.

One reason was that they had taken too much to heart a remark made by Castro shortly before he entered Havana, to the effect that he favored religious instruction in public schools.[6] It was amply evident, however, that the Minister of Education, Armando Hart, shared the more common

[6] Angel del Cerro, art. cit. in *Cuba, 1961*, p. 27. When del Cerro wrote this article (December, 1960), he had already found it impossible to continue to collaborate with the revolution and, moreover, had changed his mind about the adequacy of his original analyses. He now believed, as the majority of Cuban Catholics do, that the turn toward communism had been planned by Castro from the beginning. Consequently, he thought that Castro's remarks about religious instructions had been "a trap," and that "it is entirely possible that Castro himself was the initiator of this sinister strategy," *ibid.*, p. 27. Del Cerro has not explained his change of heart.

view and meant it to prevail. "Msgr. Pérez Serantes and some [lay] Catholic leaders tried to initiate immediately a campaign to reach [their] purposes."[7] To put it bluntly, they tried to pressure the government into adopting a measure that had traditionally been and quite obviously still was disapproved of by the immense majority of the Cuban people. Angel del Cerro remarked:

We are facing a very grave question: whether we have or do not have faith in democracy . . . There are minority groups, however, who often try to fish in the troubled waters that result from the complete upset occasioned by the victorious revolutionary process, in order to gain advantageous positions and to impose upon others, by means of calumny, intrigue, effrontery or any violent means[8] their determinate ideology. Let us take two examples, the Catholics and the Communists.

Though Cubans are vaguely religious, it is false to say that this is a Catholic country—or, at least, it is a delusion worth of being inscribed in pink characters upon the walls of vestries. And what of the Communists? They are even fewer than the militant Catholics. It would be effrontery, then, if we Catholics tried to take advantage of our fellows who died in the struggle, of the priests who conspired, of the militant Catholics who are revolutionary, and availed ourselves of the fact that the normal legislative bodies are not functioning, in order to impose Catholic education in schools; or in order to impose, by means of intrigues or the activities of goon squads of the *Young Catholic Workers*, our control upon labor unions . . . All such cliques which would impose themselves, be they clerical or Marxist, are also obstacles to the consolidation of [the revolution].[9]

[7] *Ibid.*

[8] Some clashes had already taken place between communist and Catholic labor unions. As is usual with these things, it is difficult to ascertain where the blame lay. It seems that Catholics did start some of the frays, but whether in retaliation for earlier ones or not, I do not know.

[9] Angel del Cerro, "Cuarenta casos de injusticia social," *Bohemia*, April 26, 1959.

It seems, then, that Cuban Catholics were fast becoming captivated by the view that their first if not their only duty toward the revolution was to oppose communism. They were beginning to enjoy the feeling, moreover, that they had a clearly defined obligation of conscience in this respect: that to oppose whatever might be sought by the communists was a good in itself and a duty to be fulfilled regardless of consequences. It was, in other words, the feeling which in the most literal and ancient sense of the term is called enthusiasm.

If such it was, then perhaps the concession made by the government at this point only served to whet their ambitions. For in deference to the hierarchy the government agreed to allow, for the first time in republican Cuba's history, religious instruction in public schools, provided the same facilities be made available to all creeds and provided the interested denominations supply the teachers.[10] American Catholics are in a particularly advantageous position to judge whether or not such a concession may have been significant. The matter, in any event, was amicably settled. The question of land reform now began to occupy the attention of all.

We have already remarked upon the range of Catholic opinion in Cuba on the subject of land reform. A spirited and unconditional defense of the right to private property can be composed very easily out of judiciously selected texts

[10] Julien, art. cit., p. 187. Julien's account of this matter, however, ambiguously refers to the suppression of religious teaching in schools, leaving himself open to misinterpretation as if religious instruction in schools had once been allowed. The permission to allow it now was, at any rate, meaningless: it could not have been taken advantage of, and never was, in the absence of the necessary resources.

from Papal encyclicals. The relatively few Catholic advocates of land reform had, of course, a more difficult task, since they had to avail themselves of distinctions and qualifications which only added to the complexity of arguments that were unpopular. A certain section of the regular clergy soon began to emerge as the decided adversaries of the law. The fact that the circles of the militant Catholics and of the *latifundistas* overlapped considerably served further to lend a distinctly religious character to the opposition.

For obvious reasons, little documentation is available for reconstructing this aspect of the role of Catholics in recent Cuban history. We do know, however, that a considerable number of lay Catholic leaders, particularly younger intellectuals and university students, have since been implicated in counterrevolutionary activities. In fact, one Catholic Action organization in particular, the Agrupación Católica, became the focal point of a Catholic counterrevolutionary underground.[11] Much of the avowedly Christian motivation claimed *de rigueur* in the pamphlets which emanate from Miami can be discounted, but the statements made by those whose militant Catholicism had been publicly professed prior to the revolution are obviously sincere. It is certain, moreover, that the specifically Catholic and religiously motivated conspiring began extremely early: it began as soon as Castro declared his intention to pursue a foreign policy of non-alignment and refused to ban Cuban communism.[12] In fact, though the MRR, the Movimiento

[11] See Tad Szulc and Karl B. Meyer, *The Cuban Invasion* (New York, 1962), p. 55 (in the paperbound edition).

[12] In his *Political Testament*, written shortly before he sailed at the head of the Pig's Bay expedition, Manuel Artime has explained his political motivation in detail. Essentially, it is that "Neutrality

de Recuperación Revolucionaria, would be formally founded only in December, 1959, its origins go back to an underground network that began to be laid as early as March, 1959, by Manuel Artime and another young Catholic, Rogelio González Corzo, who mobilized the Catholic element within the 26th of July Movement.[13]

Artime, at 29, was the older of the two. He was a physician. González was an agricultural engineer. Veterans of the fighting days of the insurrection, upon Castro's victory they were appointed to high positions in the Ministry of Agriculture. The Minister was Humberto Sorí Marín. Sorí put Artime in charge of the Rural Commandos, an organization created for the purpose of overseeing in the field the application of agricultural measures. González was appointed Director of Agriculture. In March, 1959, having become convinced of the imminent danger that the communists would capture the revolution either with Castro's connivance or through his inaction, they "began to conspire." Artime and González were joined, also in March, 1959, by Carlos Rodríguez Santana, who "travelled throughout the Island making contacts." It is not clear at what moment Sorí Marín began to conspire. It is public knowledge that he was opposed to the Land Reform Law from

_____

is hypocritical . . . [it] is one other disguise of the Red Beast, another triumph of Communism . . . The United States, with all its faults, is the only power efficacious enough to conquer [sic] the Communist world." Full text in *El Mundo* (Miami exile edition), April 29, 1961. Abridged English translation in *Our Sunday Visitor*, May 28, 1961.

[13] A brief, undated, mimeographed account of the origins of the MRR was published by that organization in Miami shortly after the Cuban invasion under the title *Dos Héroes y Un Ideal*. Unless otherwise noted this is the source of the facts about the MRR and of the quotations used here.

the outset, and that he was dismissed from his cabinet post by Castro on that account in June, 1959. Judging that it was "Castro's plan to organize the agricultural co-operatives following the model of Communist China,"[14] Sorí "escaped to Miami in a small boat," shortly to return under CIA auspices to Cuba where he was active in sabotage work until his capture in early 1961. He was executed by a firing squad on April 20, 1961.

It is not clear what connection there may have been between the MRR and Hubert Matos, who became famous for having been the first among Castro's followers to have been sent to jail. I know of no positive indications that he joined the conspiracy, but it seems likely that he knew of it because, in the MRR's own words, Artime "found it indispensable to return to underground life when Major Huber Matos was arrested."[15] When, in the fall, Cuban–United

[14] *El Mundo* (Miami exile edition), April 29, 1961.
[15] My own conjecture, in the light of this and of the few available facts (see *Bohemia*, November 1, 1959) is that Hubert Matos (*Hubert* is the correct spelling) was contacted by Artime's underground, which by October must have been extensive, and convinced him of the danger of communism in Cuba, but not of the need to conspire, in view of the generally granted fact at the time that Castro was not himself a communist. But, to judge by the terms of his resignation, Matos thought that Castro's inaction against communism was a matter of naïveté rather than of policy, as in fact it was, and that by provoking a public scandal he would force Castro to take action. If this is correct, Matos was the only naïve person involved in this affair. Under the circumstances, Castro's perception of the resignation as "disloyal" and "ungrateful" was not difficult to predict. Neither Artime nor any of his followers were under any misapprehension on this score, convinced though they were of Castro's non-communism. He and González Corzo had the good sense to resign only after they had gone underground. Thus, Matos may well have been a victim of his ingenuous moderation in a climate in which moderation became increasingly dangerous day by day—but there cannot be any doubt that he was at least dallying with the counterrevolution.

States relations became strained, the conspiracy gained momentum, and Catholic university students began to join in number. Two of the best known were Alberto Muller, a nephew of Bishop Muller, the Apostolic Administrator of Cienfuegos, and Juan Manuel Salvat.[16] Early in 1960 the MRR became one of the key exile groups to work under the CIA. As is well known, Artime was appointed by the CIA as the field commander of the invasion forces, and was captured when the invasion collapsed. Before that, González Corzo had returned to Cuba clandestinely and "initiated the wave of sabotage that began in November, 1960."[17] He was apprehended shortly after and executed. The MRR affirms that González' last words in front of the firing squad were: "Long live free Cuba! Long Live Christ the King!" At the time of his death he was 26.

Artime and González Corzo represent only one extreme of the spectrum of Catholic opinion, though one toward which increasing numbers of Catholics tended before the end of 1959, and toward which almost all had gravitated before the end of the following year. But in March, 1959, few had gone as far as Artime. Indeed, though some type of land reform was generally anticipated, its actual provisions remained unknown for several weeks at that time.

The Land Reform Law was promulgated on May 17, 1959. Its terms were even worse than the *latifundistas* had

[16] Muller and Salvat later broke with the MRR in order to form their own organization, the *Directorio Estudiantil Revolucionario*, which became best known for its shelling of a hotel in suburban Havana in the boat raid of August 24, 1962. *Alpha 66*, in turn, split off from the *Directorio*. I am unaware of the significance of the number, but I understand that the symbolism of the Greek letter resides in the group's hope to be the first to land in Cuba when invasion day arrives.

[17] *Dos Héroes y Un Ideal.*

expected. It raised "a storm of protest"[18] and within three weeks it had caused "a major [cabinet] split in the Cuban revolution."[19] Within two weeks of its enactment, however, on May 29, Msgr. Evelio Díaz made a public statement:

Our present Land Reform, in its noble purpose, fully enters into the spirit and sense of Christian social justice, so clearly stated and defined by the Roman pontiffs ... The Land Reform, in its just intentions and its necessary application in our Fatherland, is fundamentally in accordance with the mind of the Church regarding the principle of social justice. Its implementation binds the conscience of every Christian who, as such, leaving aside all personal and selfish interests, must contribute to the interests of the common good generously and peacefully.[20]

This was, of course, the sort of teaching that Catholics such as Angel del Cerro were hoping for. Unfortunately, it soon became apparent that Msgr. Díaz' statement was insufficient to still the mounting Catholic opposition to land reform,[21] even among the clergy of his own diocese. For instance, Fr. Luis González Posada, writing a column in the *Diario de la Marina* under the graphic pseudonym, Vulcan, repeatedly questioned the correctness of Msgr. Díaz' views and, indeed, went so far as to insinuate suspicions regarding their orthodoxy.[22]

By mid-summer Catholic opinion was as sharply divided over Castro as it once had been over Batista. The lines of division were by no means quite the same, but that was un-

[18] *Time*, June 22, 1959.
[19] *Ibid.*
[20] The full text is reproduced in *Bohemia*, May 31, 1959.
[21] Claude Julien, *La Rév. Cub.*, p. 185, says that Msgr. Pérez Serantes "made certain contradictory statements which disturbed the minds of some faithful." I am unaware of any statements by Msgr. Pérez either for or against or about the Land Reform Law earlier than the end of June, 1959, when he spoke favorably.
[22] See *Bohemia*, July 5, 1959.

important: what mattered was that in Batista's time it was the minority faction that was intensely vocal and active in opposing him. This time it was the majority which was in opposition to Castro and which both spoke and acted. It made the role of the bishops all the more difficult and, therefore, all the more in need of decisiveness. However, before the end of June Msgr. Pérez had openly sided with Msgr. Díaz, and a few days later Msgr. Martín, of Matanzas, also stated his support for land reform.[23] But Msgr. Martín's defense, though categorical, did not exclude an impolitic note. "Indentured labor," he said, "is not immoral in itself, but only in its application." This may well have been true: it was also the beginning of the emphasis on the principle that justice must obtain impartially both for the rich and for the poor. This, too, was undoubtedly true. But under irrefutable Cuban conditions and in the face of the unimpressive record of the Cuban hierarchy in defence of the poor, this was bound to seem hypocritical to many. In reality the bishops' fault was not hypocrisy but, rather, a sort of rationalistic Christian unrealism which made them tend to have greater concern for rights to property, for instance, than for its just distribution—a tendency motivated presumably by the fear that though economic injustice obtains in fact everywhere and is thus politically neutral, property rights are theoretically jeopardized only by communism.

Numerous lay Catholic organizations also voiced their support of the revolution and of the Land Reform Law and denounced the attempts of many to claim orthodoxy for themselves alone. But the opposition also closed its ranks. Before the end of June "a secret meeting" was held at Belén College with 62 representatives of the religious con-

[23] The text is reproduced in *Bohemia*, July 5, 1959.

gregations of Cuba inconclusively debating the questions of land reform and communism in Cuba.[24] This was the first instance of such conclaves; but it was not the last; nor were later ones similarly inconclusive. For all that, the hopes of pro-revolutionary Catholics were high: "in well informed circles it [was] being said that the definitive stroke [against the *latifundista* opposition] would be a document already being prepared by the episcopate."[25] This was ominously like the report circulated only the previous December in relation to Batista. The outcome was also the same: The document never appeared.[26]

Though less spectacularly than in December, the opportunity for decisive action was soon gone. For it was at this point, as related in Part One, that the problem of United States–Cuban relations arose. By the end of fall there were several indications that, whatever might have been their earlier doubts, the Cuban bishops now perceptibly inclined towards the opposition. The grounds were manifest: The Cuban government's foreign policy, by risking a rift with the United States was also courting communism. Neutralism, the bishops thought—and later said—is incompatible with the Christian faith.

It will be remembered that in mid-October Díaz Lanz' raid on Havana took place and almost concurrently the United States began to oppose Cuba seriously on the question of land reform. It was on November 13 that the Cuban government defined its foreign policy in Raúl Roa's note. On November 28 and 29 a National Catholic Convention or-

[24] *Bohemia*, July 5, 1959.
[25] *Ibid.*
[26] Claude Julien, *La Rév. Cub.*, p. 186, says that Msgr. Díaz' statement of May 29 was issued "on behalf of the episcopate." This is incorrect. The statement was signed by Msgr. Díaz only.

ganized by America Penichet on behalf of the National Council of Catholic Action met in Havana. One million people attended—about double the estimated number
of practicing Cuban Catholics.[27] It also brought together
every Cuban bishop and every Catholic lay leader of note.
Msgrs. Evelio Díaz, Pérez Serantes, and Martín spoke. They
avoided political themes other than "vows . . . for peace
and concord in the nation."[28] Msgr. Díaz added, however,
that "never has a [Cuban] government during the time we
have been a prelate extended as many facilities to the
Church."[29] But the lay speakers struck a more political
note. Divergences among them were evident: "The Christian must exercise constructive criticism, and not only point
out defects but also offer alternatives," said Mateo Jover,
the incoming president of *Juventud Católica*.[30] "Social
justice, yes; Communism, no," said José Ignacio Lasaga, a
professor at the Catholic University of Villanova.[31] News of
the attendance of Fidel Castro, of Osvaldo Dorticós, and
other government dignitaries at some of the functions was
practically suppressed in some quarters.[32]

A more direct form of political opposition was soon
offered by another noted Catholic, José Ignacio Rasco, who

[27] A week earlier it had been reported that "many Cubans tend
to regard [the forthcoming] meeting as a rally against Communist
influence in Premier Fidel Castro's regime," *NYT*, November 23,
1959.
[28] *Diario de la Marina*, November 29, 1959.
[29] *Bohemia*, December 6, 1959.
[30] *Prensa Libre*, December 1, 1959.
[31] *Ibid.*
[32] See Julien, *La Rév. Cub.*, p. 189. The rotogravure sections of
the *Diario de la Marina* for November 29 and December 1 contain
a combined total of fifty-two pictures covering the event. Not one of
them shows either Castro or any other government official. *Bohemia's* coverage was normal.

founded a political party, the Christian Democratic Movement on a non-capitalistic, democratic, Christian, anticommunist platform. This movement never was officially connected with the Cuban Church. Indeed, all executive members of Catholic Action organizations were forbidden to take part in it, on the grounds that it should be made clear that the Church did not participate in partisan politics. For all that, Rasco did represent a certain segment of Catholic opinion, even if his membership depended heavily upon non-Catholic numbers. He affirmed: "I hate liberal and individualist capitalism as well as dialectical materialism . . . [I stand for] a third force towards a better world . . . This does not mean a fence-sitting position between the Western world, essentially Christian despite its lapses, and the Eastern world, basically pagan . . . If, in case of political conflict a choice must be made between Washington and Moscow, between Lincoln and Lenin, we must decide, despite risks, for the world where liberty does not perish."[33] Rasco spoke at this time only for himself, but he merely anticipated the official position that the hierarchy would take a few months later.

The Christian Democratic Movement was short-lived. Within five months of its foundation, in May, 1960, as commercial relations were being established with Russia, Rasco decided that peaceful political action would not be as effective as revolt and, therefore, "took refuge in the United States and insisted that Cuba was in the process of becoming Communist."[34] In Miami, the movement became

[33] *Bohemia*, December 6, 1959.

[34] Julien, *La Rév. Cub.*, p. 188. Like that of many others, Rasco's "taking refuge" contained an ambiguity which proved a potent propaganda device. The legal status of most Cuban exiles in the United States is that of "refugees," because they have not been ad-

one of the five most important counterrevolutionary groups which, under the CIA in June, 1960, integrated the Democratic Revolutionary Front (FRD).[35]

In any event, the foundation of Rasco's movement in December did not create nearly the sensation that was caused a few days later by the action of two priests who unexpectedly appeared in Miami with a story that could not help but be extremely alarming to Catholics everywhere. It was particularly alarming to many Cuban Catholics, because they knew well the two priests' record of anti-Batista activities, which gave extraordinary weight to their testimony[36]: they were Fathers Eduardo Aguirre and Ramón O'Farrill. Their story, as reported by the NCWC news service,[37] which supplies over one hundred diocesan newspapers in North

mitted as tourists, residents, landed imigrants or under any other normal provision of the immigration laws of the United States. It is not necessary that an applicant be persecuted in order that asylum be granted to him. Most of the refugees, however pressed they may have been economically or otherwise enjoyed normal civil freedom until the last moment of their departure from Cuba, which they usually effected openly and by regularly scheduled commercial aircraft. In one case, for example, a University of Havana history professor made reservations to come to Canada several weeks in advance of departure. He sent notices by mail of his arrival three weeks ahead. Upon landing in Toronto he announced having "escaped in danger of his life" and having "fled from persecution," and to that effect he was duly quoted in Canadian newspapers, radio, and television. He is now on the staff of the Voice of America broadcasting to Cuba.

[35] See Draper, p. 70.

[36] I am told by an informant I consider highly qualified and reliable that the event was not alarming at all either to Msgr. Díaz or to Catholic leaders because they knew of certain personal circumstances which discredited the two priests' claims despite their anti-Batista record. These circumstances would not have been, of course, known to many.

[37] See The Canadian Register, January 2, 1960; a shorter account had been given in NYT, December 15, 1959.

America, was that they had found it necessary to flee Cuba and take asylum in the United States. They charged that the Cuban regime was a communist dictatorship; that, therefore, the government persecuted the clergy and abridged the liberty of the Church; and finally that Castro had privately approached some Catholic priests with proposals about founding a national, schismatic Church. Of course, this did not at all tally with the sentiments expressed only a few days earlier by Msgr. Díaz who moreover, immediately "gave a formal denial to these statements."[38] He also revealed that Fathers Aguirre and O'Farrill had abandoned their posts without either authorization, permission, or consultation with himself.

It would be easy, but in my opinion quite mistaken, to say that Fathers Aguirre and O'Farrill had lied. Part of their accusation, that which concerns their alleged escape from persecution by a communist dictatorship can be explained by the fact that they wanted to leave in protest and perhaps in fear of the communism which, they suspected, was overtaking Cuba. This needed only to be stated in emotional and barely exaggerated terms for the equivocations of the story to begin. The answer to the question what did or did not constitute a communist dictatorship was, of course, very elastic. The judgment that it was such a dictatorship could have been as sincerely made in their case as it had already been made by many in Cuba and abroad. Hence, the two priests feared for the Church: Persecution could be said to have begun, because the possibility of a rift was clearly visible. Did not their own flight prove that it had in fact already begun?

[38] Julien, art. cit., p. 188; also reported in *NYT*, December 16, 1959.

The only bizarre aspect of their story concerns the alleged attempt to found a schismatic Church, a rumor which was henceforth to recur periodically and ever more insistently, principally in the North American Catholic press, during the next year and a half. To a person acquainted with the role of the Church in Cuban life the allegation must seem *prima facie* suspect. What could Castro have hoped to gain from it? The Church and any organized, institutional religious practice is to most Cubans, as has been mentioned, ridiculous and beneath contempt. Nevertheless, I can well believe Fathers Aguirre and O'Farrill sincerely expected such events to happen. I can believe it, because I have spoken with not a few Cuban Catholics, both lay and clerical, who have been of the same mind: Some of them still fear the likelihood of a national Church on the grounds that "the Communists always establish national churches, as they did in China, because they are afraid of the power of the Catholic faith."

As the revolution entered its second year it was evident that a large part of Catholic opinion, particularly among the regular clergy, was opposed to the government, and that it was hardening daily in direct proportion to the alienation of Havana from Washington. Early in the new year a document was circulated for signature among the Spanish clergy[39] in which they reaffirmed their loyalty to Franco. The meaning of this gesture could not escape anyone in Cuba, where the memory of the Spanish civil war is more alive than anywhere else in the world outside of Spain itself.

[39] See Julien, *La Rév. Cub.*, p. 191, who also says that several anti-Franco priests signed only under duress from their superiors, namely, under threat of being sent back to Spain. The document is also briefly alluded to in *Bohemia*, February 21, 1960.

The document amounted to a condemnation of Castro on the grounds that, as the Republican government had supposedly once done in Spain, Castro now was culpably betraying the revolution to communism. This explains in part why only a few months later Castro's favorite epithet for the clergy would be *cura falangista*—loosely, "Franco-following priest." The controversy among the Catholic intellectuals had meanwhile reached a most acrimonious peak,[40] and Msgr. Díaz found himself increasingly isolated in his support of the government.

Until early 1960, Castro had never expressed himself in public about the Church or about Catholics in any but the same terms that he had used on the day of victory. Whereas he had often spoken harshly about those whose opposition was avowedly based upon religious considerations, he had never alluded to their faith or indeed linked the Christian faith with their views. On January 20, however, he brought the religious question out into the open during a television program which did not lack some amusing sidelights. Many will remember the occasion when the Marquis de Lojendio, the Spanish Ambassador to Cuba, elbowed his way through a crowd during a live television program and demanded to be heard in reply to charges that Castro had made on the air only a few moments earlier.

What Castro had said was that unknown to the bishops, the heads of the religious congregations in Cuba had recently met secretly in the Spanish Embassy under the auspices of Lojendio to co-ordinate their opposition to the revolution. Castro's complaint was that it was unfortunate

[40] See, e.g., the controversy between Andrés Valdespino and Jose I. Rivero in *Bohemia*, February 14 and 21, 1960. Rivero, as the owner and editor of Cuba's oldest and largest newspaper, the *Diario de la Marina*, was one of the most influential anti-Castro Catholics.

enough for the Spanish priests to oppose the only popular government ever achieved by the country in which they were guests, but that to oppose it under the sponsorship of a foreign ambassador amounted to international conspiracy. Since Lojendio was not allowed to respond in front of the television cameras, we shall never know the full extent of the defense he intended to put up. It is impossible to doubt that the meeting at the Spanish Embassy took place,[41] but several constructions could be put upon the fact. One can well imagine that Lojendio merely served as host to a conference to discuss the trend of political events in Cuba; on the other hand, the views of the persons involved were no secret. In any event the incident was only a symptom of the progressive definition of categorical positions on both sides —as this other event was also a symptom of the geopolitics of American foreign policy in the cold war: At this same time, Eisenhower was visiting Franco in Spain.

More important were Castro's television remarks to the effect that among the clergy, as with every other segment of the population, there was a reactionary and counterrevolutionary element which was beginning to show itself. He stated that though he was not aware of all that went on within the Church, in his estimation the Church was divided both for and against the revolution. He then requested the bishops to put a stop to any possible subversive activities. A week later, on January 28, at a civic dinner commemorating the birthday of José Martí, Cuba's "Apostle of Independence," Msgr. Díaz appeared as a distinguished guest and went out of his way to appear cordial

[41] Fr. Guillermo Sardiñas has confirmed that the meeting took place and that all the religious superiors were in attendance, with the exception of the superior of the Christian Brothers, who was a Cuban; see *Bohemia*, May 21, 1961.

to his host: A photograph taken on that occasion shows him smiling and clasping Castro's right hand with both of his.[42]

But by this time Msgr. Díaz was almost alone. His futile gesture is significant only because it marks the end of a period in the history of Church–State relations in the Cuban revolution. For that gesture was the last he was to make.[43] Three weeks later Eduardo Boza Masvidal was appointed Auxiliary Bishop of Havana, and he immediately assumed the role of spokesman for the diocese and indeed, upon occasion, for the Cuban hierarchy. Msgr. Díaz was rarely heard thereafter.

Msgr. Boza's appointment was ominous. His stature as an uncompromising and militant anticommunist had been well documented: he used to publish a weekly bulletin expressing his views on the subject. He had proved himself in other ways. On February 5, 1960, within days of the civic dinner attended by Msgr. Díaz, Anastas Mikoyan had arrived in Havana. A public demonstration of disapproval ("*Cuba sí, Moscú no*"), had been organized by Catholic students, mostly from Villanova University, who jostled a

[42] Published on the cover of La Quincena, March 15, 1960. This is the only place I have seen this particular photograph, though other photographs of the event were published by the Cuban newspapers.

[43] It was the second to the last statement made by a Cuban bishop. When in mid-February Msgr. Rodríguez Rozas was appointed to the vacant diocese of Pinar del Rio, his first declaration to the press included a sentence in support of "the achievement of [Cuba's] total sovereignty": this was the sum of the Cuban hierarchy's vocal support of the government's foreign policy at any time. Msgr. Rodríguez also affirmed, in clear allusion to the term often used by Castro to describe his position, that "Cuba's humanism is equivalent to Christianism," *Bohemia*, February 21, 1960. Msgr. Rodríguez made no other public statement thereafter except in subscription of the collective pastoral and the open letter of the following autumn.

policeman and were put in jail overnight. Msgr. Boza, who was rector of Villanova, denied that he had actually called off lectures in order to encourage attendance: it is not reasonable to suppose he did, nor did he have to, of course. He did not, on the other hand, find it necessary to disapprove of the riot by his students. In any event, only a few days later his appointment to the episcopacy was announced.

We have seen how the establishment of Russo-Cuban commercial relations affected Cuban-American relations, especially when, on the following June the refineries refused to process Russian crude. The relations of the Church with the government followed a parallel course. On May 8, Raúl Roa, Minister of External affairs, announced the arrival of Ambassador Kudriatsev in Cuba and the restoration of Cuban–Russian diplomatic relations. On May 16, Msgr. Pérez Serantes issued a pastoral letter denouncing this development and adducing it as conclusive evidence, no longer "rumor or speculation," of an intolerable governmental policy regarding communism. In language strikingly reminiscent of that used by Rivero's editorial upon Mikoyan's departure from Cuba, Msgr. Pérez took Kudriatsev's arrival to mean that "the ranks are already marked between the Church and its enemies. This is neither rumor nor speculation. It cannot be said that the enemy is now at the doors, because actually it is within, speaking loudly, as though settled in its own domain."[44] Though the pastoral was not issued on behalf of the whole Cuban hierarchy, its influence was felt throughout the country, for it constituted

[44] From the translation reproduced in *Catholic Mind*, LXI, 1153 (January–February, 1961). The principal documents containing the official teaching of the Cuban hierarchy on the subject are analyzed in the Appendix, *The Theology of Counterrevolution*.

the first official and unequivocal justification of what Catholics and many others had so long felt. Castro's reply was not difficult to anticipate. On May 29 he said to a press conference: "we shall not fall into the error of anti-Communism,"[45] but he still refrained from direct reference to the Church. However, when in mid-June in full view of the impending clash with the oil refineries and the government's threat to seize them Msgr. Boza "chose to protest against the excess of state control in economic and social life,"[46] the government radio referred to him as "a reactionary in priestly vestments."[47] Then in July after the Cuban sugar quota had been cut and it was evident that thenceforth Cuba would have to sell her sugar to Russia, well advertized Masses began to be celebrated for such topical intentions as the victims of religious persecution in communist countries, and the anniversary of Franco's victory over international communism.[48] After-Mass clashes with government supporters resulted, and public disorder grew. At one point Msgr. Boza's church was bombed, and, in retaliation the church of Fr. Germán Lence, a government supporter, was also bombed.

On August 7, at the height of the economic battle with the United States (on the previous day Castro had national-

[45] J. Grignon-Dumoulin, *Fidel Castro Parle* (Paris, 1961), p. 161. Despite its title this book contains documentation on the Cuban revolution from a variety of sources, few of which are Castro's speeches. Though with reluctance, in view of the unavoidable inaccuracies that are introduced by translating into English from a French translation of the original Spanish, I shall use this source in a few instances in which the original documentation is not readily available.

[46] Julien, art. cit., p. 188.

[47] Julien, *La Rév. Cub.*, p. 191.

[48] Julien, *La Rév. Cub.*, p. 191; art. cit., p. 188.

ized the first American property), the Cuban hierarchy issued its first collective pastoral letter, condemning "the growing advance of Communism in our country." Religious riots multiplied in its wake. On August 9, Msgr. Díaz personally delivered an ultimatum to the Secretary of the Presidency: Unless the clergy and the churches and the faithful were protected from harm, the churches would be closed and the Church would officially declare itself to be persecuted and to have been silenced. On August 10 President Dorticós replied that "despite all the provocations," the government would "continue to respect all cults." He affirmed "certain persons wanted to convert the exercise of worship into a tribune against the revolution," and appealed for public order, and condemned as "a vile maneuver" every attempt "to enlist religion against the revolution."[49] On the same day Castro delivered a long speech in the course of which he said:

> Our revolution was not made against the priests, but against the landowners . . . Our countrymen know . . . that there is a clergy at the service of the poor which does not attain to high positions. They know that a part of the clergy sacrifice themselves without seeking honors, whereas the other part, higher in the hierarchy, serve the rich. I would like to see a pastoral that condemned the companies that exploited our people, and the imperialist aggression perpetrated against our country . . . whoever condemns a revolution like ours betrays Christ, and would be capable of crucifying Him all over again.[50]

This was, of course, partly false—though also partly true. For, intentionally or not, Castro misrepresented the motivation of the hierarchy, though it is possible he had in mind not motives, but net effect. What is beyond speculation is

[49] Julien, La Rév. Cub., p. 196.
[50] Ibid., p. 197.

that at no time before or since did the Cuban hierarchy, collectively or individually,[51] grant that there might have been some justice in Castro's claim against the United States. By this time, in any event, the break was all but complete. Very few Catholic intellectuals, even those who, as the colloquial expression went, "saw clearly," felt that they could continue to co-operate with the revolution since politically, if not ideologically, the government was distinctly abandoning neutralism.

On October 10 a new pastoral was issued by Msgr. Pérez Serantes vigorously rejecting the charge of unpatriotism and reasserting his position: "Cubans yes, slaves never." A few days later, Msgr. Boza in *La Quincena*, carefully and in greater detail than at any previous time, explained the position of the hierarchy. On November 21, Msgr. Pérez Serantes issued his third pastoral on the subject, this time against those Catholics who continued to support the revolution and who protested against the episcopal teaching on it. On December 4, the hierarchy issued their final joint document, this time an open letter to Castro challenging him for the last time to repudiate communism, and hoping "that the Lord may illumine you."[52] On December 16 Fidel Castro spoke on television and fired the last salvo in the war of words between the revolution and the Church:

In the first place we must say that the government does not have to render an account of its conduct to the bishops: the revolutionary government does not have to render an account of its political activities to the *falangista* clergy . . . One of the refrains that the bishops like to repeat is that government officials

[51] With the single exception that may have been implied in Msgr. Rodríguez' support of Cuba's sovereignty. See note 43.

[52] The full text in translation is reproduced by Warren Miller, *Ninety Miles from Home*, pp. 41 ff.

have said that to be anti-Communist is to be counterrevolutionary and that the government has not [denied it] . . . Do they
want us to clarify the matter? Do they want an answer? Well,
then, we do believe that to be anti-Communist is to be counterrevolutionary, just as it is counterrevolutionary to be anti-Catho-
lic, anti-Protestant or anti-anything that tends to divide Cubans.[53]

The same issue of Revolución which reported Castro's
speech also reported the following news. In pursuance of
February's trade agreement, bilateral contracts amounting
to $168 million had been signed with Russia along with a
three-year commercial treaty with Sweden. On the same day
that Eisenhower extended the sugar embargo into 1961, the
Bank of Nova Scotia had sold out all its Cuban assets to the
Cuban government for an unspecified amount of cash, and
a public subscription fund had been established towards the
reconstruction of the CMQ television studios which had
recently been bombed by terrorists—the MRR's "wave of
sabotage" had reached the city's heart.

On March 6, 1961, the conflict between the revolution
and the Church having been long since irrevocably confirmed, with terrorism about to culminate in invasion, Fidel
Castro made certain remarks on the situation which can be
appreciated only in the light of a historical anecdote concerning the early years of Cuba's colonization. The story was
familiar to every Cuban schoolchild. As the Spanish advanced into Cuba they enslaved, terrorized, and wantonly
killed the autochthonous race, the Siboney Indians who ultimately were exterminated within two generations. Early in
the conquest a small group of Siboneyes resisted the Spanish
under the leadership of their cacique, Hatuey. They were
soon vanquished, and Hatuey was captured and condemned

[53] Revolución, December 17, 1960.

to burn at the stake for the crime of "insurrection." As he was tied to the stake he was approached by a missionary who so entranced Hatuey with his description of Heaven that the latter showed some inclination to receive baptism. Torch was about to be put to faggot when a doubt arose: "Are there Spaniards in Heaven?" he asked. The priest, of course, said yes. "I don't want to go to Heaven, then," Hatuey replied, and refused to be baptized.

During his television speech of March 6, Castro said:

Did [the Cuban hierarchy] ever issue a pastoral against graft? Did any of you ever read a pastoral defending the sugar-plantation peasants? Or demanding schools for the children of peasants? Or condemning the murder of labor leaders and students? Or protesting the [exorbitant] prices [charged by the] electric and telephone companies? Did they ever protest against politicking? Against profiteering in food? Against high rents? Against smuggling?[54]

They say their differences with us are ideological. [The real difference] is the difference between those who were allied with those things and those who are the enemy of those things. Not a single sermon, not a single pastoral defending the people,[55] either recently or during the war of independence . . . [nor at any time] since they arrived in Cuba with those colonizers who burned the Indians alive. . . . So now I say: if the *latifundistas* go to heaven, we do not want to go; if the imperialists go to heaven, we do not want to go; if the criminals . . . [and] the exploiters go to heaven, we do not want to go.[56]

His feelings were, of course, as primitive as Hatuey's own, and are contestable. His facts are not.

[54] Public smuggling had been a very lucrative source of income for many highly placed *batistianos*.

[55] As we have seen, however, there had been sermons by the lower clergy.

[56] *Revolución*, March 7, 1961.

CHAPTER 10

FROM OPEN BREAK TO UNCONCEALED VIOLENCE

The immediate outcome of the rupture was that Castro took measures to make it impossible for the Church to speak publicly again. With the gradual disappearance of privately owned radio, television, and newspapers, communication media came under government control, and as the Church's opposition to the revolution solidified, her access to the public media became more and more difficult until it was ultimately altogether denied to her. By December, the Church had become restricted to her own press, the only uncontrolled medium remaining (with the exception of an American-owned, English-language daily newspaper). But it, too, was so harassed that before the year's end the last Catholic periodical, La Quincena, had ceased publication. The ensuing silence, broken only occasionally by such one-sided outbursts as that of March 6, was in a way a relief after the tension of the preceding summer and fall. On the other hand, the silence was deceptive. Catholics had passed from words to deeds.

We have already noted some facts concerning Catholic co-operation with the CIA's subversive activities. That co-operation culminated in Operation Pluto, the invasion of

April 17, 1961. Since the CIA distrusted, as a matter of principle, all those who, like Manuel Ray, had actively collaborated with the Cuban government after its victory, the better part of the invasion force was composed of two dissimilar factions: the *bastistianos* and the Catholics. The CIA's choice of Manuel Artime as commander was no more coincidental than was the choice of his lieutenant, José Pérez San Román, a former *bastistiano* Army captain. In great measure the operation was undertaken under the auspices of a specifically religious motivation symbolized by the shoulder patches worn by the invaders in the shape of a shield exhibiting in the center a Latin cross.[1]

Among the prisoners captured when the invasion was crushed were three Catholic priests, (all three Spanish nationals, regular clergy, but previous Cuban residents and members of Cuban religious houses), who had served as chaplains to the invaders both in the United States and Guatemala, and who had accompanied the men into battle. When they were interviewed on television and radio along with many other prisoners, they claimed that it was both their right and duty to minister to the religious needs of the invaders regardless of politics. Unfortunately among the documents captured with the prisoners was a proclamation composed by Fr. Ismael de Lugo, the head chaplain, apparently intended to be broadcast to the Cuban people,[2] which read as follows:

[1] Photographs of the insignia are reproduced in the MRR's *Dos Héroes* and in Lisandro Otero (ed.), *Playa Girón* (Havana, 1961), Vol. 1, appendix.

[2] The invasion force was equipped with a portable radio broadcasting station. It was never put into operation, having been destroyed when the *Houston* and the *Río Escondido*, two of the invasion ships, were sunk by Cuban aircraft.

The liberating forces have landed on the beaches of Cuba. We come in the name of God, Justice and Democracy to restore the rights that have been abridged, the freedom that has been trampled upon and the religion that has been subjugated and slandered. We do not come because of hatred, but because of love; we come to bring peace even if to earn it we must wage war. The Assault Brigade is constituted by thousands of Cubans who in their totality are Christian and Catholic. Our struggle is that of those who believe in God against the atheists, the struggle of spiritual values against materialism, the struggle of democracy against Communism. Ideologies can be vanquished only by a superior ideology, and the only ideology that can vanquish the Communist ideology is the Christian ideology. That is why we have come and that is why we fight.

Catholics of Cuba: our military might is crushing and invincible, and even greater is our moral strength and our faith in God and in His protection and His help. Cuban Catholics: I embrace you on behalf of the soldiers of the liberating army. Families, relatives, friends: soon you shall be reunited. Have faith, for victory is ours, because God is with us, and the Virgin of Charity cannot abandon her children. Catholics: long live Cuba, free, Democratic and Catholic. Long live Christ the King. Long live our glorious patroness.[3]

[3] The document was read by Castro during his May 1, 1961 speech (see Bohemia, May 7, 1961). I know of no independent confirmation of its accuracy; on the other hand, it has not been repudiated by Fr. de Lugo since his release from prison, though he has made public statements on other matters (see the Canadian Register, January 12, 1963). It was not true that the brigade was composed of Catholics in its totality, though their proportion was doubtlessly very high. It is known, however, that out of approximately 1,200 prisoners taken, 194 were former batistiano Armed Forces personnel (including José Franco Mira, the murderer of Sergio González, "the little priest,") and that about 100 were classifiable as belonging to the lower classes. About 500 were classifiable as wealthy or very wealthy, since collectively they either owned or were in direct line to inherit the following property: 27,556 caballerías of land (i.e., almost one million acres), 9,666 houses and apartment buildings, 70 industrial firms, 10 sugar mills, 3 banks, 5 mines, and 12 night clubs (see Aureliano Martínez, Historia de Una Agresión, [Havana, 1962], pp. 415–25).

Thus armed with concrete evidence that the opposition of the Church to the revolution had shifted from the ideological plane to that of concrete action, Castro struck back without delay. A good portion of his May 1, 1961, speech was devoted to announcing retaliatory measures. In this speech he blamed neither the Christian religion nor the Church as a whole. Rather, he placed the blame entirely upon Spanish fascism which, "through its priests [promotes] bloodshed and conspiracy in this country."[4] He announced that consequently the alien resident or visitor status of all foreign priests in Cuba would be individually reviewed, and only those would have their permits renewed who had abstained from counterrevolutionary activities. Moreover, he said, since the *curas falangistas* had been also active "openly, in every religious school, inculcating in the young people under their influence the poison of counterrevolution," which they had found particularly easy to do since "those schools were generally attended by the children of wealthy families," the Cuban government would immediately institute a system of exclusively free and public education, and to that effect all private schools would be immediately nationalized—without compensation, in the case of the Catholic ones. Castro specified that the Cuban government was not opposed to the teaching of religion, but that henceforth such teaching could take place only in churches: "the churches may continue open, and they can teach religion there."[5] And he continued: "Would it not be much better if, instead of this declared war . . . against the revolu-

[4] This and subsequent quotations from the May 1 speech are taken from *Bohemia*, May 7, 1961.

[5] Evidently, this restriction did not apply to seminaries and the like, which have continued to function normally. See Dorothy Day's report in the *Catholic Worker*, December, 1962.

tion . . . there were peace? Well, if they desire [peace] . . .
they may have it within the strict limits of the respect that
is owing to the Revolutionary Government and the people,
and under those conditions the Revolutionary Government
and the people will practice the same policy of respect and
consideration towards them. What they may not do is to
wage war on the people at the service of the exploiters [and]
. . . of imperialism, for that has nothing to do with religion."

Whether or not these words indicated a genuine desire to
improve mutual relations they certainly implied a warning
against further active opposition to the government. Evidently Castro's purpose was not to persecute the Church
militantly or to extirpate the Catholic religion. But insofar
as this policy may have been based upon the principle
that religion has nothing to do with politics or with social
and public life, Cuban Catholics found Castro's toleration
very difficult to accept—even when he added: "to our mind
it is true that [religion and the revolution] can coexist perfectly, and that the revolution is not in the least opposed to
religion, that it is they who have used religion as a pretext to
fight justice, to fight the workers and the peasants, to fight
the lowly: it is they who, forgetting Christ's saying that it is
easier for a camel to pass through the eye of a needle than
for the rich to enter the Kingdom of Heaven, landed here
with the *latifundistas*, with the sugar mill owners, with the
bankers, to murder lowly children of the people, to murder
workers and peasants, to murder Negroes and humble
Cubans."

The massive exodus of the Spanish clergy from Cuba was
soon completed. But since the expelled priests were Spanish nationals who strictly speaking had no legal right to
remain in the country, charges of religious persecution made

in their regard could not carry much weight with world opinion. However, many Cuban priests chagrined by the "persecution" chose this moment to leave the country in protest. Their departure provided a much better basis for reports in the North American Catholic press, which now began to relay the misrepresentation that even Cuban native clergy were being expelled.[6]

Otherwise the new situation concerning Church–State relations remained unaltered in any fundamental respect. Of course, just as the invasion crisis had brought renewed support for the government from many citizens who otherwise had been inclined to be disaffected, a number of Catholics also rallied, if only briefly, to the cause of the revolution. Fr. Guillermo Sardiñas, for example, spoke on television at this time in terms more frankly dissident than even Fr. Lence had ever used; yet unlike him, managed to escape all ecclesiastical censure. On Mothers' Day, Fr. Sardiñas celebrated an open-air Mass in the Plaza Cívica in ostentatious support of the revolution. In his television appearance he attributed the clergy's attitude essentially to their Spanish outlook. More interestingly, he revealed that "even bishops, when they tried to curtail some of [the Spanish clergy's] privileges, were impeded access to [Catholic schools], and a veto was forthcoming from Rome, where the 'leverage' of the religious communities is great."[7] Fr. Sardiñas concluded:

[6] See, e.g., the NCWC report in *The Canadian Register*, July 8, 1961.

[7] *Bohemia*, May 21, 1961; (the quotation following in the text refers to the same source). It seems certain that when Msgr. Boza, though only an auxiliary bishop, displaced the coadjutor in all but name, he did not act without authoritative support. For reasons that shall appear below it is difficult to believe that this support originated either with the Nuncio or with the Pope.

"More than sixty years ago Pope Leo XIII issued the encyclical *Rerum Novarum* . . . What is the Church waiting
for? Until there happens in every country what happened in
Cuba?"

Fr. Biaín, the editor of *La Quincena* who had been deposed by Msgr. Boza in 1960 for his views on the revolution, also broke at this time his long silence in a letter to a
newly founded Catholic publication, the *Avanzada Radical
Cristiana*, edited by a Catholic journalist, Nicolas Ríos. In
the letter he congratulated Ríos for his constructive posture
regarding the revolution, an attitude, he thought, that was
"Most logical, keynoted by serenity, dictated by high aims
and procedures without entering into wrathful and intolerant polemics."[8] Although the letter did not express any
new views on the question of the Cuban revolution it merits
fuller reproduction, because it reaffirmed his position even
at this late date[9]:

To take an aggressive stand against the present system when
it is well known how assiduously was coexistence cultivated with
that of other times . . . seems to me a grave mistake for anyone,
but graver still for a Christian . . . I think it is the duty of Christians to help towards the rapid and happy culmination of this
[revolutionary] process, since from the national and social point
of view it exhibits the achievement of advantages the true dimension of which history shall judge in due course, but whose
reality is tangible already. The Christians of tomorrow—those
who do not have a broken backbone[10]—shall judge us very

[8] *Ibid.* The following quotation refers to the same source.

[9] In recent times Fr. Biaín has been granted regular space in the
government-controlled newspaper *El Mundo*, where he writes a
column on religious matters.

[10] *Siquitrillado*, i.e., one who has a broken backbone. This colloquial expression emerged into general use in 1959 from the argot
of cock-fighting to designate a person, specifically a non-*batistiano*,
whose interests had been damaged by the social measures adopted
by revolution.

severely if this process culminates without our co-operation or, which would be worse, with our aversion . . . This would be a repetition of the mistake of 1896, when the problem of Cuban independence . . . was [put in terms] of civilization against barbarism. We all now know that this problem was badly posed and badly solved, with no excuse afforded by [the fact that there were] certain confusing elements [in the independence movement] . . . My conscience, my mentality, my appreciation of the American problem, forbid my taking an aggressive posture . . . against the revolution, whatever may be the episodes, the incidents and even the disagreeable details that stain its development, about all of which there could be much to talk and argue.

Fr. Biaín and the Catholics of the opposite persuasion at all levels were talking at cross-purposes. For Fr. Biaín there was much to talk about, much to argue with and, certainly, much to change within, the revolution. But all this was to be done within a basic commitment, if not to the revolution, at least to revolution. For the others, however, not only was such a commitment lacking, but "the disagreeable details" were the only things worth deciding about.

Probably the most improbable clerical supporter of the revolution to have expressed himself as such at this point was Fr. Rodolfo. Czechoslovakian by ancestry and birth, Fr. Rodolfo as a young man during the thirties had emigrated to Cuba where he was ordained a priest and later acquired Cuban citizenship. During the Sierra days he had first co-operated underground with the revolution and finally become a chaplain to the guerrillas. Since the end of the armed struggle he had spent some time in Czechoslovakia visiting his family, and later had become Principal of the Salesian School of Guanabacoa, an across-the-bay suburb of Havana. Coincidentally, this school had been one of Marta Fernández de Batista's Catholic charities, and its director had been her confessor. Fr. Rodolfo had not previously figured publicly in the debate concerning the revolution and the Church, but he now chose to make known his feelings by joining the militia and by insisting in taking his turn at guard duty. At other times his white soutane was worn along with the olive-green beret of a militiaman. He was elected president of the neighborhood branch of the Committees for the Defense of the Revolution. Asked what he thought of those among the clergy who were leaving the country though they were not required by the government to do so, he replied: "Either they are influenced by bad propaganda or by an absurd fear or because some of them are implicated in things they should not be implicated in . . . They do not fulfill their mission . . . when they [quit Cuba]. I can assure you of this, and it would be a good thing if you make it known: the Apostolic Delegate, [Msgr. Luis Centoz], blesses all those who remain in the field of the apostolate. Whoever does not do so fails to comply with the wishes of the personal and spiritual representative of His Holiness."[11]

Fr. Rodolfo did not explain why he did not quote diocesan sources. But asked whether he based his support of the revolution upon his understanding that priests ought not to interfere in politics "he realized the trap hidden in the question and parried . . . 'What they may not do is to engage in counterrevolution if the revolution, such as Cuba's, is a crusade for the people . . . The clergy should not be against the people anywhere in the world."

Fathers Biaín, Sardiñas, and Rodolfo were presumably simply following their consciences, for as was entirely predictable none of their activities changed anything. It was too late for that, since the statement that "the ranks were

[11] *Bohemia,* May 28, 1961. The following quotation refers to the same source.

already marked" between the Church and her enemies was no longer a clarion call but a plain fact. Theirs were the last Catholic voices to be raised in Cuba in defense of any aspect of the revolution. Indeed, henceforth, in virtue of the logic of total and absolute condemnation of Castro, Cuban Catholics began openly and without qualification to long for the Cuba "that not long ago used to be prosperous and happy."[12] It had finally come to that.

[12] *Información Católica Cubana* (a Bulletin published by the Committee of Cuban Catholics in Exile in Miami), No. 7 (November 15, 1961).

CHAPTER 11

FROM NUNCIO'S DOORSTEP
TO VATICAN HALLS

An uneasy and short-lived truce followed upon the em-
barkation of the last Spanish priests, but early in the fall an
incident took place which led to new and harsh reprisals by
the government. On Sunday, September 10, "several thou-
sand [Catholics] turned a [religious] procession into a vocif-
erous anti-Communist demonstration,"[1] which clashed with
government sympathizers. The government blamed Msgr.
Boza since the riot had begun in his church.

A comparative analysis of the government's White Paper[2]
and Msgr. Boza's version[3] leaves no doubt on the following
points. First, the riot was premeditated. Msgr. Boza's statement that it was spontaneous is inconsistent not only with
some known facts, but even with his own line of defence.
There is, however, no evidence that Msgr. Boza participated
in or actively encouraged the plan—it is certain that he
had notice of it in advance. Second, Ramiro Valdés, the
Minister of the Interior, and his Undersecretary repeatedly
asked, indeed demanded, that Msgr. Boza take action to
prevent public disorder. Third, though several opportunities

[1] *G&M*, September 11, 1961.
[2] Reproduced in the Havana newspapers on September 12, and in
Bohemia, September 17, 1961.
[3] *The Canadian Register*, October 28, 1961 (NCWC report).

to act presented themselves, Msgr. Boza persistently refused to intervene—not even after it had become evident that the congregation that had gathered in his church, at his call, and in his name, was about to rampage. The riot's toll was one killed and "a score" wounded among the participants on both sides.

The official government account of the incident was prepared on September 11, but was not published in the newspapers until the morning of September 12. On September 12, Msgr. Boza was "summoned by the nuncio,"[4] Msgr. Centoz. If the Nuncio's purpose was to hear Msgr. Boza's side of the story, he was disappointed. As Msgr. Boza prepared to keep his rendezvous he was arrested on the very doorstep of Msgr. Centoz' palace and held incommunicado. On September 17, together with 135 other priests, including about 45 Cuban nationals and comprising nearly half of Cuba's remaining clergy, Ramiro Valdés put Msgr. Boza bodily aboard the Spanish liner *Covadonga* bound for La Coruña, Spain.[5]

Two days later Castro spoke at length on the religious question and announced that "since the permits granted to hold processions have been used by the counterrevolutionaries in order to provoke incidents, that's the end of permits for processions! The permits have simply come to an end. Let them practice their cult within the churches; let them hold functions within the church; and that's the end of it!"[6] He also explained that:

In living proof that the revolution knows how to make distinctions, and that the struggle is not against religion, Cuban and foreign priests have remained in this country against whom

[4] *Ibid.*
[5] *G&M*, September 18, 1961.
[6] *Revolución*, September 20, 1961.

no accusation has been made and no measure taken . . . [But] we shall [henceforth] deprive of his citizenship any priest who, being a Cuban national, conspires against the country in the service of foreign powers . . . That shall be our attitude: those priests who act correctly and devote themselves to the acts of worship and who exercise their true mission shall be respected. Those who adulterate it will have to leave the country. And if unfortunately the number of priests became so reduced as to hinder the conduct of services we shall try to resolve it in some way . . . and we even offer the use of television [for pro-revolutionary priests to say Mass on Sundays] so that . . . the believers among the people are not deprived of services.

On the next day, September 20, Pope John XXIII made a public statement: "We ardently desire the welfare of this beloved people [of Cuba], their social progress, their internal harmony and the exercise of their religious liberties. And we still trust that good will, calmness in decisions and a sincere search to safeguard the values of a Christian civilization . . . may prevail over hasty deliberations."[7] The Pope's words were not without effect. For with Msgr. Boza's absence from Cuba, Msgr. Luis Centoz' suggestions for a diplomatic approach began to be heeded. Just as Msgr. Pérez Serantes and Msgr. Boza had once projected the image that they were the voice of the Cuban hierarchy and the personification of the Church's view, it now seemed as if Msgr. Centoz had assumed that role. Since the events of September, 1961, no Cuban bishop has been seen in public, but Msgr. Centoz has been in evidence (and photographed by newspapers) in attendance at public events in the company of public officials—his capacity as dean of the foreign diplomatic corps having provided the occasion for such appearances.[8] It can be safely presumed that the subsequent course of State–Church relations in Cuba insofar as they depended upon

[7] The Catholic Messenger, September 28, 1961.
[8] Msgr. Centoz was replaced early in 1963 by Msgr. Cesare Zacchi.

the Church, and more specifically in what concerned official relations with the Vatican, was due to his having prevailed over the Cuban hierarchy. And it may be pertinent to remark at this point, as an indication of how dangerous simplified generalizations can be, that Msgr. Luis Centoz is a Spaniard.

The ascendancy of Msgr. Centoz after the September riot was noticeable, in the first instance, in a negative way. Though Fidel Castro and Ramiro Valdés had unmistakably violated Canon Law by preventing Msgr. Boza's exercise of his episcopal functions, no excommunication decree was issued by the Vatican against them or against any Cuban official. This was an extraordinary omission. In 1955 Argentina's President Juan Perón had come under explicit censure for the same offence. More striking still, almost simultaneously with Castro's impunity, the government of Haiti came under similar censure even though the bishop in that case was not like Msgr. Boza, a national, but a foreigner.[9] The intentional character of the omission was discreetly made explicit by the Vatican three months later.

On January 2, 1962, the Vatican had made a routine announcement listing diplomatic representatives to the Holy See. Among other less newsworthy items the brief notice mentioned that the Cuban Government had appointed an ambassador to the Papal Court. Once before, Castro had appointed a representative to the Vatican who had presented his credentials in March, 1960, and had been recalled the following December during the closing days of the government's feud with the Cuban hierarchy.[10] On January 3, the

[9] A first excommunication decree was issued on January 12, 1961, on account of the expulsion of two bishops. A second decree was issued on November 22, 1962, on account of the expulsion of a third. See *NYT*, November 23, 1962.

[10] *G&M*, January 3, 1962.

Rome correspondent of the Associated Press evidently try-ing to follow up the story of the new appointment raised the question of Cuba's relations with the Holy See and asked a Vatican spokesman, Archbishop Dino Staffa, to comment on the excommunication of Fidel Castro. Msgr. Staffa replied that "excommunication had been incurred without formal announcement by the Vatican."[11] This was quite correct, but hardly novel: what was unusual was pre-cisely that no formal decree had been issued. Hence further explanation was sought by the correspondent: it came from anonymous "Vatican sources" which "speculated that the pope had made no announcement in an effort to avoid further strain in relations between the Vatican and Cuba."[12]

The announcement concerning the appointment of a Vatican ambassador had been heralded a few days earlier by an exchange of season's greetings between the Pope and Cuba's President Osvaldo Dorticós. Though the Associated Press carefully explained that "the pope's reply [to Dorticós' message] was a courtesy required by diplomatic protocol, like the pope's to the birthday greetings . . . Khrushchev sent the pontiff,"[13] there is some reason to think that the com-parison was less than apt in view of the fact that the pope sent more than a mere greeting: he had also sent as a "per-sonal present" to Dorticós a collection of religious medals which were delivered to their intended recipient by Msgr. Centoz at a private audience.[14] The new ambassador pre-

---

[11] The Toronto Star, January 3, 1962 (Associated Press report).
[12] Ibid.
[13] G&M, January 4, 1962.
[14] News from Cuba, No. 4 (February, 1962). This is a monthly publication issued by the Cuban Embassy to Canada. Early in 1963 the Pope sent another medal to Dorticós commemorating the Sec-ond Vatican Council.

sented his credentials to the Vatican on February 29, during a special audience granted him by the Holy Father.

Later that year, when the Vatican Council was due to open on October 12, many countries sent special diplomatic missions to the opening ceremonies. Despite the fact that Cuba was laboring under considerable difficulties at the time—it will be remembered that this was ten days before the Cuban crisis broke, and that an American invasion was generally considered imminent—Cuba was among those nations that found it possible to send special missions. The missions from all countries were received at a special audience on opening day. Now, the United States government does not maintain diplomatic relations with the Holy See, which sometimes spares the Vatican's Chief of Protocol certain embarrassing complications. The absence of special protocol difficulties was particularly fortunate on that day. For when in the course of the audience John XXIII spoke to the Cuban ambassador, Luis Amado Blanco, the Pope asked him to convey a message to the Cuban people. The message was to "have hope, faith and courage."[15]

The Church–State problem in Cuba may not have come to an end, but it seems to have reached a plateau. Msgr. Boza continues to reaffirm his stand from Venezuela, where he now resides. It is more difficult to know how the remaining Cuban bishops feel, or what lessons they have derived from their reflections on the recent past. One hopes their plans do not hinge upon the day when things in Cuba shall be once again as before. Positive and ambitious goals for the Church in Cuba are not unreasonable, if they are grounded on reality and not on dreams.

[15] G&M, October 13, 1962 (Associated Press report).

CHAPTER 12

FROM CUBAN PROBLEM
TO UNIVERSAL DILEMMA

For the Universal Church the problem posed by the history
of the Cuban revolution is not, I believe, whether the
Cuban hierarchy was prudent or not in allowing its voice to
become discredited. It is more important to consider
whether the Cuban Church was ready to meet social and
political change of any radical sort. But recent Cuban history raises for Catholics everywhere an even more basic
problem: How did the Cuban Church come to so conceive
itself and its relations to the secular world that the question
whether the revolution was or was not communist became
the only matter worth judging? The problem, in other
words, is to understand how the Church arrived at the position that Christianity and anticommunism are convertible,
and that the only way to meet the risk—or the suspicion—
of communism is head on, with the assurance that what is
not anticommunism is abominable and whatever is otherwise is at least negotiable. The problem thus is essentially
an ecclesiological one. What we need to ask ourselves is
what was the nature of the Cuban Church's implicit ecclesiology, particularly in what concerns the sanctity of the
Church; whether that ecclesiology is the only possible one

within orthodoxy; whether it is adequate; and, finally, whether we wish to share it or not.

The situation of the Cuban Church in relation to the revolution is closely parallel in several respects to that of the sixteenth-century Church in relation to Protestantism. The basic facts concerning the well-known evils that plagued the Church are not important in themselves except insofar as they may have contributed to the creation of certain conditions in which the Protestant Reformation could flourish. Of greater importance, for instance, might be the fact that medieval Christendom was so enamored of its own handiwork, of the civilization it had created, that it thought that era would endure forever, unchanged in all essential respects as a monument to testify to the Church's faith and to its love of Christ. The integration of the Christian order and the secular order was, though far from perfect, adequate enough to make it difficult to distinguish between them. It became easy, therefore, to think that to be a Christian was the same as to preserve the existing state of affairs. This gave the Church a tactical inflexibility which ultimately led to the notorious events that precipitated the greatest tragedy in its history.

Moreover, sixteenth-century Christianity appears to have thought that the Church, being holy, being the Body and the Bride of Christ, needed no humility—as if Christ himself, because he was God, had not chosen to be humble. This idea of the Church's sanctity always tends to go hand in hand with that curious conception of the Church which is reluctant to admit the consequences of the parallel between the dual nature of the Christ whose Body is the Church, and the Church which incarnates Christ, but in our human nature, not in His. The humanity of Christ's

Mystical Body is our humanity, a humanity that is subject to passion, disposed to blindness, and prone to sin. Therefore, the Church as such is subject to passion, blindness and sin— insofar as humanity truly and essentially belongs to the Body of Christ. In other words, to take away our sinfulness from the nature of the Church would be a sort of importation of Monophysitism into the mystery of the incarnation of Christ in the Church.

To the same degree that the Church mistook itself, it also misunderstood Protestantism. It failed to see that Protestantism was not just another heresy, but the result of a long historical process of irresistible change which orthodoxy itself had originally generated. The process was so inevitable that when it aborted in the sixteenth century its force was, though repressed, still unspent: Four centuries later Catholics have found it necessary to become considerably "Protestant" themselves. Thus, to have met Protestantism head on was the only strategy doomed to fail. Orthodoxy was saved, of course, but little else, and that only at a great spiritual cost, with deep wounds in the flesh. The idea that tolerance does not mean surrender had not yet been born.

The Cuban Church's pride was nurtured not by luxury, but by poverty, and not by great popular success, but by great popular indifference. It felt so harassed, so imperiled, that it thought it could do nothing except trust in Christ's promises. It thought of itself as a monument whose function was to stand still—patient, holy, and untouched by time and space—a testimony to the power of God. The dissociation of the Christian and the secular order, though far from complete, was severe enough to make it difficult for the hierarchy and clergy to understand how any society but a medieval, sacral one could be Christian. It became easy, therefore, to think that to be a Christian was the same as to withdraw from the world's sullying contact. This gave the Church a tactical inflexibility which ultimately led to its eclipse.

The Cuban Church seems to have thought that, having been rejected by its world, it needed no longer to live in it, as if the Word Himself, because He was God, had not chosen to become man and sanctify the world by sharing the world, by sharing bread, wine, water, with mankind. To the same degree that it mistook itself, it also misunderstood the nature of the sociopolitical events around it: It failed to see that the problem was not simply one of communism but of the beginning of Cuba's emergence from medieval life, with all the painful dislocations due to the process of rapid, violent, overdue, historical change. Not even success would have justified attacking this process head on. Orthodoxy was saved, but little else; fortunately without any deep wounds in the flesh. There remains a faint hope that within the Cuban Church the idea that tolerance does not mean surrender might yet one day be born.

The problem that the Universal Church is ever increasingly pressed to meet is not essentially different from that which was faced in Cuba. The problem, which one cannot adequately begin to pose, least of all solve, without an ecclesiology rather different from that of Msgrs. Pérez Serantes and Boza, may be formulated as follows: How shall the Body of Christ as it ages and matures, and as it finally comes to its childhood's end, adapt to an emerging world-wide civilization (a civilization which being catholic may be presumed to be naturally Catholic by disposition and unconscious desire), adapt to a civilization which liquidates not only the medieval, but also the "modern," post-medieval world along with its own foundations in the cultural forms inherited from the classical Greco-Roman world.

The Church is faced with an unprecedented, extremely rapid, and radical change on a multitude of planes and on a world scale. It must cope with socio-politico-economic problems of the emerging post-Western contemporary world. To reduce it to the dimensions of how to cope with Russian imperialism and the appeal of Marxism-Leninism reveals a failure of imagination to comprehend the range and magnitude of the problem.

There are, of course, important differences between the problems of the Cuban Church and our own. The Cuban Church has already passed the critical point: It has survived, but it cannot be said to have succeeded. Other churches have also had their brushes with the twentieth century, with the concrete problems of the new world. But the Universal Church has not as a whole yet reached the peak of its crisis: though it appears to be steadily drawing towards it. Perhaps the Church in North America above all should take stock and consider whether it too in its own way is not beginning to encounter the challenge. Does not the problem of world war, for instance, constitute for it a moral trial analogous to that suffered by the Cuban Church? Perhaps it shall be the last to undergo the great temptation. It would be inadvisable to believe that it shall be altogether spared.

It is worth underlining once more the fact that the Church risks above all a spiritual failure. What must be feared is not so much the danger of persecution as the possibility that the emerging catholic universe might remain outside the World Church. What must be feared is not so much that it shall suffer as that it might fail; not so much that the world might crush it as that the world might pass it by; not so much that the Church's mission might be opposed by others as that it might be left unfulfilled by us. What must be feared is not so much that the gentiles shall reject the Church bodily as that the Church may not spiritually conquer the gentiles.

III. THE CHRISTIAN CRISIS AND THE CHALLENGE OF HISTORY

The principal foundation on which the present state of relative calm rests is fear. Each of the groups, into which the human family is divided, tolerates the existence of the other, because it does not wish itself to perish. By thus avoiding a fatal risk, the two groups do not live together: they co-exist. . . . The most obvious absurdity of the situation resultant from such a wretched state of affairs is this: current political practice, while dreading war as the greatest of catastrophes, at the same time puts all its trust in war, as if it were the only expedient for subsistence and the only means of regulating international relations. . . . Although it is a sad thing to note that the present rupture of the human race took place, in the beginning, between men who knew and adored the same Saviour, Jesus Christ, still there appears to Us to be a well founded hope that, in His name too, a bridge of peace may yet be built between opposing shores, and that the common bond, so sadly broken, be re-established.

—Pope Pius XII. (*Christmas Message*, 1954.)

The study of the Church–State problem in Cuba confirms that the present moment, for Christianity, is a critical one. If so many Christians find it difficult to view the crisis with serious concern, part of the reason may be a cynical feeling that pessimism is the prophet's stock in trade. However, to suggest the danger of the crisis is not to gratify a fear of failure but to bring to consciousness the existence of opportunity and occasion—however true it may be that with these temptation comes also. Moreover, the outlook is bright. To understand the nature of the crisis is also to understand the reasons why, for the Christian, this is precisely the time for looking forward to the future with trust.

Others who scoff at the prophecy of crisis do not so much misunderstand as disbelieve. The reason is that they find it difficult to suppose that there might be anything unique or even very different about our times—a crisis is, by definition, an extraordinary time.

No doubt, we are chronocentric. No interpretation of history which does not constantly seek to correct its contemporary bias, its tendency to understand all times in terms of its own, can escape distortion. But the paradox is that a dismissal of the present crisis of Christianity on the grounds that the present could not differ much from the past is only an expression of that same contemporary bias. If one wishes to assert that the present is not a truly critical time, one should do so not a priori, but only after a historical appreciation of the nature of today.

An impartial and fair consideration of history will in fact show that the Christian crisis at this time is of unprecedented magnitude and kind. For, surely no Christian crisis could be less momentous than the crisis of the world in which Christianity lives at any given time—and it would be difficult to deny that the qualitative and quantitative proportions of the world crisis today are less real than are newspaper headlines.

It is, therefore, not simply a matter of personal disposition if the Christian becomes apprehensive about our age. It may be a matter of fact and not of feeling for which intelligent concern is required. Above all the crisis requires understanding by him who professes the Christian faith.

CHAPTER 13

THE NATURE OF THE CHRISTIAN CRISIS

It is possible to determine the nature and causes of the crisis of Christianity in the twentieth century. But first it is important to explain what they are not. The crisis is not essentially moral, and its causes are not man's infidelity to God's law. It is true that we experience grave moral problems. In fact, the crisis is lent a greater urgency because of the magnitude and consequence of the moral issues at stake. But we should not confuse urgency and crisis. The moment is critical because it brings us to a point of no return, to a juncture at which decisions of great moment, for good or for evil, can no longer be put off. The crisis brings moral urgency only to those who care vitally whether these decisions are morally right or wrong.

Nor have we good reason to affirm the alleged moral corruption of the modern world. We have done great wrongs, as has every other age, but we have some virtues as well. It may, indeed, be argued—though the point is irrelevant—that the modern world shows on the whole a better moral complexion than any previous age. Though standards by which to measure it are notoriously difficult to come by, the moral tone of Christian cultures, whatever our individual and collective sins, appears to show a steady trend toward

ever greater elevation. This is signified, for instance, by the
ever higher level of refinement in comportment to which
civilization naturally leads: The measure of this moral elevation is the measure of civilization itself. Of course, our
civilization can scandalize us. But we should not be deceived by the fact that the depths to which we may sink are
correspondingly greater as our soul is nobler. If our sins
seem more shocking today and more grave than ever before,
the reason may be that our moral life has reached a higher
plane.

But even if it were otherwise and the world more evil today than in the past, what we need for our own guidance
and government is to understand, not to blame. For this
reason we should observe that the crisis as such is due to
causes which in themselves are neither morally good nor
evil and which, as to other values, are in themselves nothing
but good. The Christian crisis, which is at one with that of
the modern world, has been brought about by the fact that
man, Christian or not, resides in history. Its cause is that all
of man's experience accumulates and leads him on. We
Christians, the Church as much as other men, carry with us
the weight of years: to do so is normal to any living reality
as it develops, grows, and becomes. Our crisis is that we are
reaching the end of a spiritual stage.

The contemporary world, which Christianity has helped
to shape in so many fundamental respects, is a growing
world not simply because it has more years behind it, but
because being older it has more experience and knowledge
to heighten its consciousness—if not always to make it more
wise. Man not only knows; man hoards knowledge. Thus his
racial, collective knowledge reaches well beyond the boundaries of any one man's life span.

However, this knowledge brings problems in its wake. First, we cannot know without becoming different. Knowledge is transforming and therefore requires readjustment. Whenever one knows one finds it necessary to do something with one's knowledge and also to do something with oneself. Naturally, we are not always able or willing to adjust: Obviously, then, knowledge can cause maladjustment to the world. Now this has always been the case; it is not a unique problem we face today. But man does not simply store knowledge; he also invests it. We use knowledge to multiply our knowledge, and that is one reason why the more we know the more we can know. Therefore, the more we readjust the more readjustment is required of us. But deficiencies in human readjustment to the world, do not slow down the rate at which knowledge grows. Under these conditions the growth of knowledge becames unbearable. Thus there arise not only maladjustments to the world on account of knowledge, but maladjustments to knowledge itself. Eventually, a point in development is reached when man produces knowledge at a faster rate, as it were, than he can digest it—faster than he can incorporate it into the organization of human life. This is the sort of problem that knowledge brings us today; this is the reason why the growth of knowledge means the disturbing headlong rush of modern change.

But the meaning of this can be easily missed. If modern change creates a difficult problem, the reason is not that there is too much of it but, rather, that the rate of required change has outstripped the rate of organization. The problem is not caused by the quantity of knowledge as such but, more precisely, by the ratio, or the quality of the relationship, between knowledge and change. In other words: Our human institutions make allowances on the basis of past experience for adjustment to change—but at obsolete rates. Therefore, the institutions themselves have become obsolescent. This is the second type of problem posed by knowledge, the sort we had never experienced before. To put it succinctly: the trouble is not as many think that we are changing too rapidly but, quite the contrary, that we are not changing fast enough.

For these reasons the crisis of today must be adjudged by the most impartial observer to be unprecedented and unique, since the problems created by our fund of knowledge and power and by the rate of contemporary change are beyond doubt unprecedented and unique.

It might be objected that this simply means that it is not the accumulation and possession of knowledge, but our inability to handle, administer, and generally, use it well that actually constitutes our problem. But this is not exactly true. If what one searches for is the seat of the blame one cannot quarrel with the allegation that it is we human beings who are at fault rather than knowledge itself. That we should blame ourselves because we cannot cope with our knowledge is as true as it is irrelevant, because to exhort ourselves to do the right thing is, by itself, less than useless: it is a nagging distraction and a bore at a time when our trouble begins with utter perplexity and dismay. We do suffer from an inability to manage our knowledge. But our trouble is not simply that we will not manage it correctly—our affliction is that, in the first place, we do not know how to do so.

Anyone who thinks it is easy to know what the trouble is with the world is also likely to give cheap advice to us all. He will probably enjoin us *a priori* that we should do what is right, we should abide by God's will, we should make the correct choices. The voice of such a Christian witness is not likely to be heard. Or if heard, not heeded, because for a priori guidance we need seek no one's advice. To know whom to blame, namely ourselves, is useful only insofar as it means that we wholesomely face our own guilt rather than blaspheme God or make a scapegoat out of Satan. It is useful, that is, if it compels us to think. Although our problems are caused by knowledge, our hope remains in the mind, for the mind is all we have, either to cause problems or to solve them—it is all we have of ourselves to do God's bidding, and what we need to use, even with grace.

Moreover, although we have doubtlessly long misused the power of our knowledge our problem is not just how to correct the past, but how to plan for the future. The present moment is critical not only because we have troubles, but also because we have not yet committed ourselves irrevocably to use our contemporary knowledge in one or another decisive way. We have only too recently (recently, that is, as these things are measured in the scale, for instance, of human palaeontology, not to consider scales of broader scope), acquired enough knowledge to enable us radically to refashion our world and to conceive radically new ways of human life and thought. No final or even long-range commitment in this respect has yet been made by man. We have not done much good with our knowledge— nor much bad. We have not yet used it to do as much for evil or good as its potential allows for both.

The symbol of this crisis is, of course, thermonuclear power, which is undeniably good in itself. We have not begun to use it unequivocally well. We have to choose the kind of thermonuclear world we want. But the fission-fusion-fission process is only a symbol, standing for the power of *all* we know. It portends, for the moment, death. More important, it is a sign that our collective decisions must now be taken with a longer and broader sweep of mind than heretofore. We are now deciding, as it were, on an adult scale of historical change. We must now commit ourselves for longer, with ever fewer opportunities of later changing our minds. It is an entire historical age that is being fashioned today. We are not simply the actors on a historical stage already set: We are the creators of a whole world to come.

This is not the occasion to relate the history of how we arrived at the crisis of modern knowledge. It is more relevant to note that there is a twofold historical process by which the crisis was brought about. Pope John XXIII, with a keen historical sense, has clearly abstracted this and brought it to the attention of Christians everywhere. "One of the typical factors which characterize our age," he writes in *Mater et Magistra*, "is socialization, understood as the progressive multiplication of relations in society, with different forms of life and activity, and juridical institutionalization. This is one of many historical factors, among which must be numbered technical and scientific progress, a greater productive efficiency and a higher standard of living among citizens."[1] But, as the pope also points out, the intensification of social relations implies the intensification of every human process and therefore also of all the problems that man and society must face: "socialization multiplies the form of organization and makes the periodical control of relations between men of every walk of life ever more detailed."

[1] This and subsequent quotations from *Mater et Magistra* are taken from the official English translation reprinted as a supplement to *Our Sunday Visitor*, August 6, 1961.

Since some misunderstanding has been evidenced by Catholics on this point, it may be well to underline that John XXIII's doctrine of socialization is in the first instance not normative, but descriptive of a human process which, in point of fact, is taking place with increasing rapidity in the modern world. Moreover, it is primarily not political, but sociological. Once noted that it is a current phenomenon, the question may then be asked whether this process is of itself harmful to man, either from the natural or from the Christian point of view. Pope John's teaching is that, of itself, the process of socialization is natural to man and in accordance with both reason and freedom, for it is "a creation of men, of beings conscious, free and intended by nature to work in a responsible way." Of course, like every other human creation it can return disadvantages and it can open up new dangers: "Hence we consider that socialization can and ought to be realized in such a way as to draw from it the advantages contained therein and to remove or restrain the negative aspects."

So far we have examined the nature of the world crisis, assuming that it was relevant to Christianity only because Christianity happens to exist in that world. In reality this relevance is substantial: The world crisis is the crisis of the Christian Church.

The reason is that although the Church is not of the world, the world is of the Church. We do not happen to exist in the world—as if we might have existed elsewhere, but the lot fell to the world. To us the world may be distant, but it can never be an alien domain. It is not a foreign land—it is our home. The reason is simple: The world in which the Church exists is the only real, human, earthly world that exists—there is no other. It is this world, therefore, the real one, that is our inheritance to be gained, our prize to be earned or, better, our charge to tend and care for. It matters little if the world does not always know this —or knows it and does not admit it.

Our crisis, then, is that we are charged with a Messianic task toward a world in crisis. Thus, it is for the very fulfillment of the mission of the Church as such that we have a call to care about this world. "Today," writes John XXIII, "the Church is confronted with the immense task of giving a human and Christian note to modern civilization, a note that is required and is almost asked for by that civilization itself for its further development and even for its continued existence."

But this could be understood in a narrowly proselytic way, as if it meant that the world should be given moral and ideological help in the same way it might be given a handful of rice that would dispose it to humor our missionary whim and accept baptism. This would be spiritual pride at its superb height—a height that is not strategic in our campaign of spiritual conquest. We do not give our love to the world so that it may come into the Church; the Church was placed on earth so that we might give our love to the world. We do not want the world to embrace the Church; we want the Church to embrace the world.

For this reason, to see to it that the hungry of the world are fed, the sick healed and the ignorant taught, and that order, law, and peace prevail among men is not simply an accidental, optional task for the Christian Church, nor a merely instrumental one to serve an other-worldly end— nor least of all, a means to alleviate the conditions that foment Communist infiltration. It is essential, it is commanded and, moreover, it is to be undertaken for its own sake—however true it may also be that the transcendence of charity transforms its own sake into Another's, and that it transposes its finality to an End beyond its end.

The difficulties of "the immense task" are many, but one should be mentioned, because it is especially trying. The world is inadequate to the task required of it. But we, too, have our own inadequacies, our own unlovable habits, our past dispositions, our thorns in the flesh. We are prey to our peculiar temptations. Worst of all, we have the weight of our own history to hold us back. In brief, insofar as its solution may depend upon us "the immense task" is made especially difficult by the condition of the Church today.

No doubt we are changing very rapidly, and the second Vatican Council, even at this early date may be thought to mark a watershed in the history of the Church. But while the hope that we shall quickly become adequately prepared to the task is sustained daily by new developments, we must understand, precisely in order to facilitate the renewal already underway, that our self-satisfaction, our ecclesiastical, that is, our collective pride constitutes the most basic inadequacy for the fulfillment of this immense task. The promise of Christ that the gates of Hell shall not prevail against us is neither an assurance that the success of the Church shall be at any time (but least of all at its end), measurable by the standards of worldly success—nor does it mean that we cannot sinfully fail to discharge our mission, to our own peril and risk. The infidelities of the scribes and pharisees are not less likely in the new Israel than in the old: Our pride may well begin at the moment when we imagine otherwise. And though the terms of the new Covenant do not simply repeat, but fulfill and perfect those of the old (thereby granting additional privileges to the

Church, pre-eminently that of an unfailing faith), the Church is not impeccable in each and every respect. For the Church is responsible and free. We shall stand not only individually but collectively in front of God on the last day.

This does not mean that the moral life of the Church today is inferior to that of any other time. On the contrary, every sign is reassuring. What our pride has fed is our fear, and our fear our self-pity. Our self-pity has fed our contempt for God's earthly world, and that contempt has fed our ignorance. That ignorance is our divorce from reality, and that divorce the stagnation of our progress. Perhaps the best measure of our dissociation from the world, as it really is, is our feeling that we already exist in eternity, the feeling that though all human things exist in time, we, the Church, singularly blessed, do not. If we still sometimes remember that we must redeem the time, we tend to feel we can, and should do so, without immersing ourselves in it, as if Christ himself had not deigned to live within it and as if, indeed, Jahweh before Him, had not chosen to enter human history and human time. In a word, we lack historical perspective, and we can hardly expect ourselves to lend to the times a human and Christian note if we are blind to the *historical* realities of the times.[2]

Just as it is possible to trace in detail the history of the

[2] The renewal of the Church in every sphere is bound up with the renewal of the collective historical self-concept of the Church. The revolutionary character of Pope John XXIII's opening address to the Second Vatican Council on October 11, 1962, seems to me to be given, above all, by the adoption of a *historical* perspective, by its conviction that "history . . . is . . . the teacher of life." It would not be an exaggeration to say that the substance of the pope's exhortation to the Council Fathers was to adopt the historical perspective of time.

process whereby the contemporary world has arrived at its critical present, it is also perfectly possible to trace in detail the history, both the chronology and the dialectic, of the process whereby the Church has arrived at hers. Now, like charity, history begins at home. The most urgent and immediate task for the Christian is to become aware of the present age of the Church; thus, the immediate task for us is intelligent self-examination and self-criticism.

To criticize is, of course, to discriminate. We need to discriminate between what we ought to be, but are not, and what we are, and ought not to be. We need to criticize ourselves, favorably where truth and humility so indicate, unfavorably where the evidence may require it. We are self-critical in order to gain self-awareness. We need self-criticism because we need increased consciousness: Heightened self-awareness and wholesome self-consciousness are the conditions of spiritual and temporal human growth.

CHAPTER 14

THE FOUNDATION OF CHRISTIAN
ANTICOMMUNISM

It would be logical at this point to examine the condition of some of our public means of self-awareness, namely, our communication media (from the most concrete, like type and electron, to the most abstract, like epistemology and gnoseology—for nothing so reveals, or so binds, a culture as the theory of knowledge it assumes). Here, too, the Cuban revolution is a sign; it is a faithful mirror of the processes of collective perception in our times. But the indications already given should suffice and therefore I shall proceed to the first question of substance that emerges from the study of the Cuban revolution as seen against the background of the Christian crisis.

We have observed the decisive, almost exclusive role played in the Church's conduct towards the Cuban revolution by the question of the Christian's view of communism, and enough has been said to cast doubt upon the correctness of the Cuban Catholic position. How, then, should we rule ourselves in confrontation with communism?

First, we should analyze what the rather commonly assumed answer implies, that is the view that the obliteration of communism is good in itself, and that if any hesitation or scruple is reasonable in this matter it could refer only to the moral quality of the means to that end. This is the position of anticommunism, formally and properly so called.

There are ascertainable psychological, economic, social, and cultural factors that contribute to the creation of formal anticommunism—and there is also a specifically religious component: this component depends, at least in part, upon the assumption that from the truth of the Christian faith prudential judgments such as those of the social and political orders can be deduced by a simple process of inference and, moreover, that this process can be made to yield unique conclusions. This helps explain the recurring appeal to the manifest contradiction between Christian theism and communist atheism to justify indiscriminate opposition to whatever and in any way is communist. It also helps explain why otherwise well-formed Christian consciences do not feel uncomfortable when close to the thin ice of suspicion, rash judgment, defamation, and the spread of contempt, dissension, and hatred. Only our best instincts and our best dispositions have saved us, so far, from drawing all the conclusions logically implied in formal anticommunism.

Prudential judgments, however, seem to be related to faith, to hope, and to charity rather differently. We make prudential judgments in virtue of the total configuration of our person and, as it were, by consulting our inclinations of heart and mind toward the object judged. Since the theological virtues qualify our heart and mind, then those virtues may be said truly to inspire our decisions. But we cannot deduce the one and only right decision from the truths of faith. We can only trust that faith, hope, and charity have so perfected us that our judgments will be correct—or as close to correct as they can be, given the actual moral condition in which each one of us may find himself.

Consequently, it is difficult for the Christian conscience to know the right thing to do. Indeed, we can never strictly know, we can only believe what we ought to do—which need not take away from the firmness of our moral convictions; for, in moral questions, we can never have other than "moral certainty," but moral certainty can be hardier than human life. Nor can we know the solution to a moral problem simply because we have known the solution to another or, least of all, because we have known the solution to a typical case. Nor can we, finally, delegate our moral responsibility to anyone—as would be possible in principle if moral reason had the objectivity of logical thought. In short, what this means is that we ought to avoid that torpor of conscience which is facilitated by mental inertia, moral ovinity, and spiritual hedonism.

In the order of political ethics the latter dispositions may account for the ease of our assumptions that the world is, in metaphysical fact, and in moral right ought to be, polarized into contradictory opposites, in which the existence of one depends upon the non-existence of the other; or that all of us ought to submerge our differences in order to present a united anticommunist front. For that reason, in turn, we are asked to uphold Western civilization, though imperfect and earthly, as the defender of the faith —without regard to the consequent inevitable compromise of the faith. Of course, co-operation, even close and intimate, is desirable and possible between State and Church. But the existence of the faith cannot be conditioned upon natural institutions—not so much because by being beholden we might be captured, but because by being espoused we might be captivated.

None of the foregoing denies the incompatibility of Christianity and Marxism-Leninism. The question is whether Christianity is convertible with anticommunism. The suggestion made here is that it is not, and that, formally speaking, to be a Christian is not to be anticommunist. To think otherwise may materially imply a sort of sociopolitical Manichaeanism that some Christians appear ready to accept as a simple corollary to the Apostles' Creed.

But these conclusions are merely negative, the purpose of this analysis having been to bring to light some implications of formal anticommunism. The questions remain: What is a Christian alternative to anticommunism? How far should one, as a Christian, pursue the consequences of the argument here suggested? How open a mind should one keep in order to judge the political world of today?

For it might be thought, for instance, that even if it were agreed that to be a Christian is not formally speaking to be anticommunist, we could nevertheless uphold every practical decision we have taken and every policy we have followed if we merely distinguished between communism and communists. We must love communists, Christians would generally grant—but we must hate communism. Is this the conclusion to draw in a Christian political philosophy from the opposition of Christianity and Marxism-Leninism? This is the problem to which we must now turn.

CHAPTER 15

THE HISTORICAL CHALLENGE
OF COMMUNISM

To say that Christianity and communism are mutually contradictory is to say that the two are related by an opposition which mutually excludes their simultaneous falsity and truth. But a relation of contradictory opposition is, of course, a logical relation. To establish such a logical relation is not to determine what the actual, existential relation between them has been in the past, is at present, and will or ought to be in the future. Prone as we are to confuse the logical order with that of existence, we tend to think that once contradiction between ideas is discovered every ideological question is settled. In fact this solves nothing, because the relations among ideas do not reflect or correspond to the relations among realities.

Christianity is neither an abstraction nor an idea: It is not even an ideology. The substance of our belief is an existential, historical reality, concrete in a nation, Israel, the Church. Moreover, it is a historical reality not only in the psychological, social, natural order, as even non-believers could affirm, but also, as we are required to *believe*, in the spiritual, supernatural realm. This needs emphasis: To believe in the Judaeo-Christian revelation is to believe that we exist in a certain historical condition definable by certain events—all of which might have been otherwise. For instance, the creation of man in a certain existential condition is one such event. And our whole religion, our duty to worship God, is required by a contingent event, namely, God's free decision to enter into and be present to human history (or, rather, to bring man into existence in His presence) and, thus, to create the only human history which in reality exists.

The point is that the confrontation between Christianity and communism is a confrontation in history, an encounter between two realities both of which actually exist. Although we may fail to realize this consciously we unwittingly confess it in the same breath with which we propose Christianity's adoption of political forces and cultural energies as a novel, twentieth-century form of the inquisitional secular arm that shall serve our Christian ends. For the conflict is between Rome and Moscow. Msgr. Pérez Serantes was in this respect perfectly correct.

But Rome is not God, nor Moscow subsistent evil itself. If the confrontation takes place in history, the confrontation takes place among men who, be they godly or evil, are men. For some of us may be incorporated in Christ, whereas some of us may have been grouped under the sign of withdrawal from Him: this does not diminish the humanity of either body nor the confrontation as a historical event.

The theology exemplified by Msgr. Pérez was twice wrong and, thirdly, inconsistent. In order to identify the Rome–Moscow conflict with the antithesis of subsistent evil and God, he had to grant Moscow less than human reality, and that is why he converted communism into a pure idea.

But in order to maintain that identity he also had to take away from Christianity all its humanity—and that is why he converted the Church into pure God. The inconsistency lies in his having sought a human ally to champion God in His struggle with an Idea—it would have been more to the point to lend Him Occam's razor or a sharp syllogism.

If this is correct, the problem of our relation to communism is not adequately met at the level of homiletics and, instead, should be posed at the level of political ethics: it is a special part of the more general Church-State question. Let us consider, therefore, certain relevant aspects of the relation of Church to State.

State in the twentieth century means national state. A national state is, by definition, a limited and partial society. Since no agent can be expected to act except within the limitations of its own natural finality, no national state can be expected to seek any ends that may conflict with its own good. National sovereignty, national safety, national survival, and national dignity are thus perfectly legitimate national ends. But for that reason also national states cannot be expected to pursue the common good of mankind as a whole. This does not mean, of course, that national states never seek, even with great inconvenience and sacrifice to themselves, the good of other states: for example, the official bounty of the United States toward many nations and the personal generosity of the American people toward countless international charities are renowned. It remains true, nevertheless, that the strictest requirement that can be self-imposed by the most tender official conscience of a national state is a negative one: that it should not adopt ends that conflict with international justice.

We should understand, therefore, why national states

(especially at this time when the unprecedented levels of socialization and internationalization intensify the political rivalries among countries) offer particularly unstable and morally risky political structures on which to rest Catholic hopes. For it has always been easier to be fair to oneself at the expense of others than to be fair to oneself only within the limits of the strictest fairness to all. But moreover, when socialization reaches today's heights, the problems of mutual justice reach such a level of intensity and complexity that it often becomes impossible even for those with the best of intentions to determine what the rights and wrongs of international disputes may be. Not unintelligibly, national states tend to err (or tend to be perceived by others as if they erred) on their side of the doubt. Border disputes of modern times are a case in point: They are invariably clouded by the length of their history. It all depends on how far back in time one goes—or how far back one refuses to go.

Thus, world relations among national states can be ruled, at best, by the principle of commutative justice. But international, universal distributive justice cannot be reasonable expected from them. We need not be long detained by three considerations pertaining to the increasingly problematic and unworkable character of international justice. First, international commutative justice, that is, the equitable intercourse among national states, is itself impaired by the emergent unity of the human race. It is gradually becoming impossible to be just to another nation or even to one's own without being just to the whole human race. Therefore, international distributive justice, that is, the equitable ordering of the common good of the whole world is not optional in today's world, nor is it an ideal: It is indispensably required by the nature of the contemporary world as it already exists, and it is demanded for the very sake of justice to each and every nation and, ultimately, to each and every man.

Second, the political socialization of the world cannot continue much longer to lag behind socialization in other respects and, therefore, new political structures on a world scale (and proportionate political institutions as well) must and shall emerge in due course. Finally, and more pertinent to Christian political philosophy, the suggestion can also be made that the concept of justice itself, at least in the context of politics, needs recasting in order to take into account the requirements of such a politically socialized world.

Consequently, what in the past has been legitimate, normal, and even indispensable, e.g., association into national states, can be under contemporary conditions a grave temptation and an occasion of sin. What once was legitimate, and even what may still remain so in other respects, may not be adequate for the needs of the Church today.

But the point is not only that national states are decreasingly able to administer international justice: Even if it were otherwise, they cannot be expected to be either Catholic or charitable. The concern of Christianity, however, must be both. When we presume to use national states for our own purposes we run the risk that, knowingly or not, these states may drag us down to their own moral level or, in any event, to their uncatholicity.

This is not to condone international injustice, nor to canonize the parochialism of national states. It is only to recognize the reality of both. It is only to affirm that Christians cannot guide themselves in such a way or restrict in the slightest the catholicity of the humanist concern from which they derive their own name. If we are Catholic, then, the welfare of the whole world, communists included, is our concern. Precisely for that reason the logical relation of opposition between our faith and communism poses a genuine, serious, and pressing dilemma.

But though the dilemma is as problematical as it is real, its alternatives may be badly posed. We make it seem as if we had to choose between faith and charity. Obviously, this cannot be true. We have, in fact, tended to choose between them: the lesson to be learned above all from Cuba is that we cannot continue to prefer the certitude of wounded charity over the possibility of broken faith. How, then, are we to do justice to both the claims of charity and the requirements of faith? Three suggestions may be made.

First, Christians have a special interest in the maintenance of peace with the communist world. Christians cannot remain indifferent to the peaceful outcome of any political struggle, but there is a special reason in the case at hand, namely, the very ideological opposition between communism and Christianity. That opposition, precisely ideological, would remain unresolved if the political struggle were to result in war.

There is ample historical precedent to warn us of the damage that accrues to our own faith when ideological conflicts of great depth are left unresolved because the intellectual confrontation aborts in war. The wars of religion, quite apart from the physical and cultural evils they inflicted on both sides, reached a mutually unsatisfactory spiritual conclusion which has benefited neither Catholic nor Protestant Christianity. The ideological cleavage of the sixteenth century has been perpetuated through four centuries largely because the peace was not kept. The stagnation of the Catholic Church is only part of the price we have had to pay for whatever may have been our share of the guilt.

War, as a solution to any conflict, but least of all an ideological one, is simply not efficient: It is more precipitate than it is final. It is more cathartic of passion than of thought. For the sake of our belief, then, and of the responsibilities faith puts on us, it may be in our interest to see to it that a nuclear war does not in the near future remove the possibility—perhaps forever—of solving the spiritual impasse between the Christian and the communist worlds. It is not, therefore, only for humanitarian reasons having to do with charity, but also for ideological reasons having to do with faith, that we bear a heavy responsibility in this respect.

This means that although the faith does need defending, active peacemaking may defend our belief more efficiently than waging or even threatening war. To work for peace, however, may be more arduous than the weakness of our belief can bear—to live for peace in the world may need rather more courage, imagination, daring, ingenuity, and heroism than to die for Ideas on the sands of pagan shores.

Second, it may be suggested that we are apt to use the distinction between communism and communists as a blind behind which we can indulge our hostility toward both. Communism can be found in reality only in communists, and communists are such only by reason of their communism. It is as tempting to nullify the distinction by treating it as a separation, as to blur it by invoking it only at convenient times. For example, it is easy to recognize that communism and communists, though distinct, are found only together in existential reality when (legitimately so, of course) we warn ourselves that we cannot deal with communists as if they did not really believe in communism —in a word, as if they were not firm believers in an ethic that contradicts our own.

This only means that communists cannot be trusted: It is merely a circular reaffirmation of the originally granted premise, that there is a genuine mutual exclusion of truth and falsity between Christianity and communism. If we could trust communists we would not have the immense problem that challenges us: We would have a common ethical foundation upon which to build higher. However, the trustworthiness of communists is not a necessary prerequisite: If the foundation does not exist the foundation must be laid. The problem, therefore, must be solved at a basic level; that is, our first aim must be eventually to make communists trustworthy. Now, for precisely the same reasons it goes without saying that we cannot ask them to trust us, and that therefore our first aim may be reciprocally defined as our eventually becoming trustworthy to them. The required basis for negotiations, thus, is not necessarily mutual trust: Evidence of mutual interest is quite enough.

There is another consequence from the truth that we must beware of communists precisely because of their communism: We cannot in actual existence deal with communism as if it did not involve communists. Therefore, if we are committed to dealing fairly with communists, we must also be disposed toward dealing fairly with communism—our charity toward them would be essentially impaired by anything short of the strictest justice toward their belief. For example, if communism, by reason of its falsity is not accorded the right to be heard, the rights of communists could be jeopardized. Or if the suspicion of communism cannot be granted the same benefits of doubt as those granted to other political accusations, communists are unfairly deprived of their social and political rights. And all this we can do while sincerely affirming that we wish no harm to communists, but only to communism.

We invented this sort of sincere but insidious self-deception long ago. The year was 1229 when, at the end of the Albigensian Crusade, the synod of Toulouse, frankly recognizing the mutual excesses of the war, addressed itself to the task of preventing a recurrence of such calamities. The result, which may well have been the best that could be envisaged by a Christian imagination conditioned by its times, was predicated upon the idea that it was more economical, as it were, and in everybody's best interests, including in the first place the heretic's own, to inflict on him pain even unto death to purge him from his false belief and to bar its socially disruptive propagation. It was thus that the first Inquisition was born. Thermonuclear inquisition is surely not the best that our imagination can conceive today.

Perhaps the most consequential and common way in which we tend to be unjust to communism precisely as an ideology is by judging it not upon what it is, but upon what we ascribe to it, both with and without a foundation in fact. Here, again, we must beware of thinking that the contradiction between communism and Christianity is sufficient grounds to judge anything except the concept that if we adhere to one we cannot adhere to the other, or that if we affirm the truth of our faith we deny the truth of communism. What it does not entitle us to judge is what in actual fact communism is or what it proposes. It is true, no doubt, that this contradiction is not the only ground on which we judge communism. The ordinary information publicly available concerning the historical events of the last forty years wherever communism has ruled is enough, even if allowances are made for undoubtedly biased reporting, to enable us all correctly to judge that communism has unleashed much physical, psychological, and moral evil upon the world. Communists have no one to blame but themselves and their ideology if deep prejudices, both correct and incorrect, are widespread over most of the world. For all that, if we are to judge communism fairly, we have to judge it as it is and not as we imagine it or as we would like it to be if certain prior propositions are to remain safe —or if certain indulged passions are to remain justified in the sight of both man and God.

In this respect, too, the parallel between Protestant and communist relations to the Catholic faith is valid. The opposition between Protestant and Catholic belief is genuine enough in important and essential respects: For all their agreement in many basic views, one cannot affirm the truth of both at the same time. But the mutual imputation of absurdities is not justified by that opposition or profitable for anyone. Only recently both sides have begun to realize that it may be mutually advantageous to ascertain exactly how we differ from each other and exactly how we do not. Or, to take an example from a different sphere of Catholic experience: Nothing can be easier for the Christian philosopher than to judge Descartes or Spinoza, Bergson or Kant, Heidegger or Sartre in the typical fashion of some neo-scholastics. The fact that they judge chimaeras and that they know beforehand that the dragon must be slain works to no one's greater disadvantage than their own.

This brings us to the third and final remark. Bearing in mind that communism is an ideology, what sort of general objective is it possible for us to have?

Now, the nature of our own absolute objectives is determined by the nature of our ideology—and nothing else. But our objectives relative to communism are essentially affected by the nature of communism—and, in the first place, by the fact that communism is an ideology. The distinction between communism and communists is particularly important at this point: If we ignore it we are apt to treat whatever may be false in the other as we might whatever may be evil in the one. Communists are persons, free agents, subject to passions and capable of action—free agents, moreover, with a record which does not recommend them to anyone's trust. But that is not the point. The point is that we can easily confuse, on the one hand, the justified defensive reaction we have against the specifically communist threat posed by communism, and, on the other, an unnecessary, self-defeating, aggressive reaction toward the ideology behind that threat—even when the threat stems from the ideology itself.

Consequently, for the Christian the result of the distinction between communism and the communist is highly paradoxical. It is the communist, not communism, who is subject to hate and who, indeed, may well have provoked it, whether with unilateral guilt or not. But it is those whom we can hate that we should love; it is those who really threaten us that we are enjoined to forgive; it is those who are dangerous whom we are asked to negotiate with. Communism, the ideology, on the other hand, is merely an abstraction from the human reality of communists. Within that human reality, its reality is that of a product of thought. It is not, therefore, except metaphorically, subject to being hated or loved; it can be neither fought nor embraced.[1] It exists, rather, to be faced, to be considered, to

[1] This does not take away from the reality of an ideology's affective and aesthetic component. Perhaps the most distasteful feature of communist ideological life is the spectacle of its peculiar inconsistency: the typical dogmatism, the blind faith, the uncriticalness,

be exposed to public examination as an object to judge and to understand. For the Christian believer communism is an object of *thought*.

Consider again the parallel with Protestantism. Only recently we have begun to realize that the unfortunate division of the Western Christian mind in the sixteenth century, though in itself an unmixed evil, can be made to yield good fruit. For we have fought and hated Protestantism even after we made our peace with Protestants. Now we begin to perceive that we can profit, within our own order (and quite apart from any thought of an eventual reunion), if we no more that encounter Protestant thought and if we enter into a "dialogue" with the ideology of Protestant minds. We now recognize, all the while disagreeing with Protestantism, that it may be to our advantage to turn its original inspiration into our own, that is, to rediscover, reinvent, and refashion it. We now propose, in effect, to catholicize Protestantism—within ourselves, that is, and with our own purposes in mind. We no longer strive to "convert" it—except insofar as it may be converted by our own conversion of ourselves.

Much the same may be true of communism. We have not generally discerned that we might, on the one hand, take advantage of it for our own purposes and, on the other, that we should strive to redeem it, that is, make it truly, not spuriously, serve its own best motives and achieve its own self-realization not in error but in truth. In brief, the

---

the thoughtlessness, all in relation to an avowedly unmysterious, rationalist, materiality-based doctrine. Our own repulsiveness to them may not be far from the diametrically opposite inconsistency: the pseudo-rationalization, the intellectual duplicity, the placidity, the ineffectualness, all in relation to an avowedly mysterious, disturbing, existential, transcendent faith.

suggestion here made is that though communists may well constitute for Christians a menace, communism is to the Church a challenge and not a threat.

For these reasons, it would not be quite accurate to say that, regarding communism, our objective should be that of conversion. That might be more properly said of communists, in regards to whom a totally free and self-determined conversion, solicited by the appeal of our example, must be the Christian aim. Regarding communism precisely as an ideological challenge, however, there is a twofold result we might hope to obtain. We might hope that our consideration and reworking of it might have a transforming effect upon it analogous to the conversion of the communist. We might call this the *redemption* of communism, that is, the realization and actualization of communism's aspiration to truth by its transformation in the Christian intellect. No doubt, this is more easily said than done, but there is ample precedent in our history for striving to do so. If we once did it with such an essentially pagan and alien civilization as the Roman empire; and if we once did it, as in the thirteenth century, with such an essentially pagan and alien religion as Aristotelianism, there cannot be much doubt that something can be done with an ideology that, culturally, is less of a monument than the Roman empire and, philosophically, has less sophistication than much pre-Socratic thought.

Hence we can also hope for a second result, this time in relation to ourselves. For we have now begun to grasp, as Pope John XXIII has repeatedly taught, that the Messianic task of the Catholic Church toward "all nations" is best and most faithfully initiated through the inner purification and the universal sanctification of the Assembly of the Faithful, the Church. A Christian dialogue with communism[2] might be redemptive of communism not simply and, perhaps, not primarily, by our adaptation and adoption of whatever good and truth communism might have to offer but, above all, by such inner purification and ever stricter sanctification of our faith and of our Church as would attend upon that dialogue. That has always been, since the beginning, the traditional means that we have used in order to help redeem the world.

It would be impossible to forecast either failure or success for such a dialogue. What is certain, as the experience of centuries shows, is that ideas cannot be destroyed by fire and sword. Gamma-radiation swords and thermonuclear fire are probably not much more efficient in this respect than the other kind. The suggestion here made, consequently, is that total victory over communism must be, indeed, the only policy the Christian conscience should entertain. But we must understand it as total spiritual victory. A merely political, not to speak of a merely physical, victory over communism would be, at an unlikely best, only partial and bitter, and hardly enough to satisfy the unbounded ambition of Christian charity. If communism is wrong, then precisely because it is such, what we should do to it is not destroy it, but do what it cannot do for itself, namely, make it find its proper perfection and its proper truth.

[2] Many European Catholics have already entered into a Catholic-Marxist dialogue, most notably Fr. Marcel Reding, of the Free University of Berlin. *Nuova Presenza*, a quarterly journal edited by Italian Catholics, devoted a special issue to the question in the spring, 1961. In France the dialogue is well advanced. As this goes to press the publication in *Blackfriars* of a paper by Prof. J. D. Bernal may hopefully herald a similar development in Great Britain.

IV. THE POLITICAL AND RELIGIOUS CONTEXT OF THE WORLD CRISIS

One result of leaving everything to the politician or the herd leader is that the individual conscience, left dormant, becomes atrophied. . . . No religion allows the evasion of unilateral responsibility in the soul's final judgment. And this is what I mean by unilateral responsibility: . . . if I had anything to do with participation in the war, I could not get away with quoting Pope Pius XII in any sense at all. God would hold me responsible to my own conscience.

—Archbishop Thomas D. Roberts, S.J., formerly of Bombay. (Address to the Anglican Pacifist Fellowship, London, July, 1962.)

Msgr. Pérez Serantes with eloquence and force, and Msgr. Boza together with every other Cuban bishop by direct implication of word and deed, argued in favor of the championship of Christianity by the United States: Their argument may be and has been extended without serious strain to the whole of the West. The question may be raised whether such championship is practically, that is, ethically, justified.

Practical justification should be distinguished from pragmatic. The latter is usually narrower than the former, because pragmatism restricts the order of the practical to the instrumental. Pragmatism takes means as pure means, without ethical value precisely as means. Pragmatism, however, need not be gross: It can be subtle and spiritual. The Chris-

tian who reduced all things to the condition of instruments
in the service of God would be a spiritual pragmatist. Practical justification, thus, must depend upon the moral nature
of the means. But because means are not simple instruments, the moral quality of means can be ascertained only
empirically: In order to act, the Christian has to find out
what the world is really like.

When we ask, therefore, whether it is practically justified
for the Church to bestow championship upon the United
States, or upon democracy, or upon the West, the answer
depends in great part upon the nature of political and cultural realities in the United States, in democracy, and in the
West.

The question, thus, really means: What sort of world, as
seen from the viewpoint of Christian political ethics, do we
really exist in? Is that world really as the Cuban hierarchy
thought? What is the actual political and religious world
context in which the struggle took place between the
Cuban revolution and the Church?

The issue at stake, obviously, goes well beyond whether
the Cuban bishops can be proved wrong. The substance of
the matter is the definition of the moral foundations of
Church–State relations in our time and, consequently, the
role that Christianity should undertake in the political life
of the thermonuclear world.

CHAPTER 16

THE AMERICAN POLITICAL CHARACTER
AND THE WORLD SITUATION TODAY

What is the nature of American culture as a political force
in the world of today? How could it be defined and described? What is its meaning? As with individuals, we shall
search for clues to the dynamics of the deeper psychic forces
of the collective American political personality among the
experiential manifestations found in immediate consciousness. There can be no doubt, therefore, as to which American experience we must consider first.

"If one probes beneath the chrome-plated surface, he
comes inescapably to the conclusion that the American
people by and large are not happy," remarks an American
politician of great perceptiveness and historical sense. "It
would be helpful, I think, if the developing science of psy-
chiatry could make a study of national egos and motives and
personalities; for it seems that nations have quite as hard a
time understanding themselves as do individuals. I believe
that such a study would conclude that America's trouble is
basically one of aimlessness at home and frustration
abroad."[1]

[1] Sen. James W. Fulbright, quoted by John Cogley, "Natural Law
and Modern Society," Commonweal, LXXVII, 16 (January 11,
1963), pp. 405–406.

The predominant feeling in American political life today, as it has been during recent years, is a chronic, intense, generalized, inexplicable, and frustrating disappointment with the international situation. Americans are unhappy with Russia. They are unhappy or at least impatient with neutrals and with allies. The thirst for unconditional friends and friendship is unquenchable, in the sense that anything less than agreement with American policies is often regarded as hostile (in the case of an opponent), as outrageous (in the case of a neutral) or, at best, as impertinent (in the case of an ally). This tendency, insofar as it is reflected by American foreign policy, has measurably increased to the same degree as the involuntary involvement of the United States in world affairs since the end of World War II. This impatience has been avowed most clearly and outspokenly of all by President Kennedy, who has made it a principle of his foreign policy. The American people, thus, are least happy of all with themselves, since they experience the frustration and despair of witnessing that "all the good will in the world" seems inadequate—and perhaps irrelevant—to the task of ensuring and preserving international peace.

Unfortunately, this disappointment, this feeling of discomfort is conceptualized falsely and is explained away too quickly and superficially. "We act in good will," Americans tell themselves, "we sincerely want peace, yet we get nowhere with the Russians. The impasse, therefore, is in no way of our own making. The polarization of the world is wholly the product of Russian international politics." However, this merely defines the perceived situation. The question remains: Why is it experienced as frustrating? Why is the reaction to an apparently wholly undeserved threat not essentially one of dismay, terror, and aggressiveness, however much the frustration may contain these components? "Since the situation"—so continues the myth—"is basically simple, i.e., the guilt is wholly or at least predominantly on one side, there must be in principle a simple solution to it, whether military or diplomatic, whether capitulation or war. Thus, if we cannot solve it once for all we must be in some way deficient and, therefore, to blame. Either we lack the resolve to do what needs to be done, or the ability to determine what needs to be done or, most fundamentally, the will to determine and to do what needs to be done." Hence follow the interminable "great debates" on national purpose, the wrangles on foreign policy, and, ultimately, the ascription of frustration and discomfort to a "reluctance to take up our role as leaders of the Western world."

The desire to find a solution once and for all expresses, of course, the perfectly normal wish to find a stable solution to any problem: In this case, to live not simply in a state of peace, but in a state of stable peace. Could any national aspiration be more reasonable? This may be why the solution to the cold war adopted by American foreign policy since 1950, namely, permanently postponing war is both frustrating and essentially unstable. It is no accident that the same Kennedy who has repeatedly made it clear that he seeks "no final solutions, because there are none,"[2] has also decided "to follow up his Cuban [crisis] success by exerting stronger leadership over the West's cold war policies—even at the risk of offending sensitive allies."[3] The "patience" required to live with an insoluble Russian problem and a perma-

[2] Stewart Alsop, "Kennedy's Grand Strategy," *Sat. Eve. Post*, March 31, 1962.
[3] *G&M*, January 2, 1963.

nently unsatisfactory state of world affairs must be mined elsewhere. Now it can be extracted out of relations with allies and neutrals. Will this source last forever? If and when it becomes exhausted the United States will be driven to seek a final solution but, by the terms of the process, at such a point the final solution may well be only the sort recommended by the Catos among us, that Russia must be destroyed. In the meantime, Kennedy's new determination to lead whether or not others wish to follow may be taken as a reflection of diplomatic inadequacy. This is not to be understood in a personal sense: Though the obvious strength of his success drive and that of his closest advisors accelerates the process of development of American foreign policy (thus making the inadequacy more apparent) this inadequacy is not peculiar to him or to them. It is an element of American diplomatic history.

It is significant that the United States does not actually engage in aggression against the perceived "conspiracy"— though the danger is ever present that the truculence of verbalized aggressive feelings may be translated into action[4] —and it is a disquieting thought that one cannot recall any case in Western history where national frustration of a comparable extremity has been endured without eventual war. Yet, so far, and for whatever cause—reasonable fear of the awful consequences of nuclear war is part of it, of course

[4] "I have no doubt that the balance of terror is now more stable *against sane actions of rational governments* than it was a few years ago . . . I have not the slightest doubt that the main danger today is not from the rational act of responsibile statesmen, but is due to essentially irrational acts of irresponsible, frightened, humiliated, revengeful or just mad people—or perhaps, more likely still, from the confused actions of well-meaning people overwhelmed by complex circumstances beyond their mental or moral ceiling," P.M.S. Blackett, *Studies of War* (New York, 1962), pp. 139, 143.

—hostility feelings are largely introjected, only to reappear on the surface of national consciousness in the amply described syndrome of national malaise.

However unpleasant the introjection of hostility may be, few would think that nuclear aggression would be preferable. But while prudence and reasonableness may account for the United States not lightly entering into thermonuclear conflict, the question remains why a decision that is thought to be and in fact is reasonable and prudent is nevertheless experienced as highly dissatisfying and frustrating. Could it be true, after all, that the United States is motivated by some aggressive drive (whose true name is either "capitalism," or "imperialism," or the like) which is only superficially overlaid by peacefulness and rationality? Now, I would not want to dissimulate the rapacity of the United States, e.g., in Latin America, during the last hundred years. But that does not quite explain away the basic American dispositions toward peace and democracy to which Americans often pay much more than lip service and to which the very endurance of frustration testifies: If the United States has not already gone to war there cannot be any doubt that the fundamental disposition is definitely on the side of peace. Therefore, this is an oversimplified hypothesis. The answer is rather more elaborate.

The difficulty with the popular diagnosis of the American mind is that there is enough truth in it to constitute a potent source of resistance to analysis and insight. Let us, then, first apply ourselves to this proferred diagnosis, to this apparent "reluctance" to discharge the duties of Western leadership. It yields a colorable image because after World War II the United States long hesitated to commit itself to the complex system of international relations which was required for the survival of European civilization. The Marshall Plan, for example, was presented to, and perceived by, the American people as a gesture of friendship and charity, or else as a business-like operation of pragmatic altruism, rather than as the stroke of political wisdom it really was.

The immediate reasons for this hesitation are not far to seek: The United States thought that even in the second half of the twentieth century some form of isolationism might be viable, if no longer behind the moats of the two oceans which technology had shrunk, at least behind the curtain of secrecy afforded by the atomic monopoly. Why did the United States, despite expert scientific assurance that the atomic monopoly could not be long maintained, nevertheless seize upon it as the last basis of isolationism? One notes a similar inability today to face the fact that it is only a matter of time before membership in the nuclear club is attainable by at least half the nations in the world, including China. Clearly, only a strong prior attachment to isolationism could make such a train of thought appear reasonable. But when the hope of atomic isolationism, as vain as it was short-lived, was shattered first by Russia's matching of nuclear fission, then by her thermonuclear lead, and finally by her prowess in rocketry, the United States lost no time, during Dulles' long tenure, erecting a diplomatic maze of international alliances, commitments, and roles.

Therefore, if the United States nevertheless fails to experience comfort and satisfaction it is not because it can truthfully accuse itself of having shrunk from taking the initiative, nor because it has lacked the intellectual, diplomatic, economic, and physical capacity to do whatever its safety required. (Is it not curious that the most powerful nation in the world should feel physically insecure?) The ambiguity of the diagnosis of "reluctance to assume the role of Western leadership" is made especially clear when we note the relish and zeal with which the American people and the American government discharge their international role. Americans enjoy being the leaders of the West and the mightiest world power, as well they might, since they do so on the whole (the Caribbean is an aberration), within the boundaries of international justice, democracy, and respect for human values. The idea that the United States should return to a secondary position among Western nations is simply inconceivable, and no one has seriously proposed it. Even the contemporary advocates of conscious isolationism base their arguments upon the weakness of the allies and the ability of the United States to fight alone if need be.

Therefore, we must make this distinction. The United States was reluctant to abandon isolationism in favor of collective security. It did so because it was militarily safer, not because isolationism seemed politically undesirable. The root of the inner conflict, therefore, according to this analysis, is that the United States can find security today only collectively rather than in isolation. But collective security is an ambivalent object. It is desired insofar as it is rationally viewed as the best possible goal at present; it is hated insofar as it produces an unaccountable feeling of acute discomfort.

The feeling is unaccountable only if it is not confronted and broken down by enquiry. It is not frivolous to suggest that if collective security is distasteful to Americans it is because it is collective and not because it is security. It is distasteful because it requires them to enter into close international human relations and consequently to suffer a proportionate loss of independence. The American people dimly and instinctively perceive that collective security requires them to give up a relatively large measure of self-sufficiency if their world leadership is to be exercised democratically and not despotically. International democracy, thus, requires them to give up a relatively large measure of their highly valued ideals of self-determination and independence. Therefore, the apparent reluctance to face up to the task and the consequent experience of discomfort are more than the remnant of nineteenth-century isolationism. They are manifestations of a new, updated isolationism which in uneasy compromise permits outward international participation (because it is indispensable for security) while preserving inner isolation (because it is necessary for the continuity and integration of the national personality).

If the United States cannot confidently occupy the central position among Western countries the reason has to do with its original marginal relation to European culture. The early American society adapted to cultural severance by accepting it à outrance, that is by investing it with social value. Note the symbolization in the quotation inscribed on the base of the Statue of Liberty the ambivalent feelings toward European "refuse" and the evident satisfaction with the ability of the United States to revalue what Europe has rejected (for in so doing, the United States is revaluing itself). The cultural idealization of self-sufficiency and self-reliance was only part of a trend toward national encapsulation. A culture developed in which the absence of relations with the outside, and its temporal analogue, absence of relation to the past, were counted among the highest values. Hence, for instance, the attraction of the new and of the home-grown.

This is not the place to enquire how this national character emerged during the first century and a half of the early settlements, nor how it reached maturity during the second quarter of the nineteenth century. The relevant point here is that the very national character that accounts for the motive force behind the development of American greatness and power is fast becoming a liability. For it is becoming the cause of pain. Pain is, of course, physiologically and psychologically a danger sign: Perhaps it is dangerous culturally as well.

It is generally recognized that isolationism is a present impossibility: The American sense of reality is strong enough to see this. But it would be unrealistic to think that isolationism in the military order is all that must be transcended; in that consisted Secretary Dulles' myopia. National security is no longer a simple military matter. There was a time when isolated survival being possible, military defence from outer aggression sufficed for security, and economic, social, and political matters could be considered "purely internal affairs." Today, however, it is not so. Since science, population growth, and political consciousness have reduced the world to a fraction of its former size, we are now, all together embarked upon a common cosmic mission. More accurately, if national security has become essentially dependent upon international relationships, then all human affairs and, specifically, all economic, social, and political matters have become essentially collective affairs.

Now, why should the United States have been sufficiently realistic and reasonable to give up isolationism in one form and yet have remained sufficiently blind and inflexible not to give it up completely? The answer is not simply that the one form was physically impossible to maintain, but not the other; nor simply that cultural habits and social institutions change slowly and die hard. It is more important to observe that the compromise formation I have described permits outward change to mask inner immobility. If so, we can now begin to define the basic etiology created by the disparity between environmental needs merely outwardly met and the inner dispositions of the American psyche; and this may account for the symptoms of discomfort and frustration which we took as our original clues. Evidently, the cause of frustration is a character inadequacy that inhibits relations to others and, more specifically, creates a difficulty in perceiving others empathically and thus facilitating the other's empathic perception of the United States. Translated into less psychological terms, the defence mechanism I am trying to describe is the transmutation of isolationism into ethnocentricity.

What is the difference? The isolationist group lives alone and likes it, and survives partly because this is intrinsically possible and partly because it understands others and is able to avoid trouble with them, thus enhancing the viability of its solitude. The ethnocentric group, if it is a society that can no longer maintain its previous isolation, lives with others and hates it; and because it cannot understand others it gets into trouble with them and thus prejudices the very society it needs. In other words, the American problem can be defined as disbelief in the total impossibility of isolationism. Americans think they have overcome isolationism. In fact they do not realize how impossible isolationism really is—nor how isolationist the United States has remained and is tempted to remain by the very dynamics of its domestic political life as well as by the weight of the tradition of its foreign policy.

If it is true, as I suggest, that the fundamental American

inadequacy is an inability to understand the world as other, I need hardly elaborate upon the danger presented by American national and international policies if they are guided by ethnocentric cultural forms. If the United States lacks empathic ability it will find it difficult to realize how transparent its feelings and intentions can become to others.

Lack of empathic ability means, moreover, that the United States will judge and evaluate others only upon the assumption that others are like themselves. Consequently, the American projection of foreign behavior, both as to allies and as to enemies, is often disastrously mistaken.

For instance, when popular opinion feels that "we have all the good will in the world and yet get nowhere, therefore the impasse is in no way our own making," the mistake in perception due to numbed empathy is twofold. First, there is an ambiguity in having "all the good will in the world." It is easy to pass from "we have all the good will that is required of us" to "we have all the good will that is available." (It is difficult for either of these conditions to be satisfied, anyway, and even more difficult for either to be ascertained.) To assume even the first, if not the second, is to run the risk thereafter of reasoning circularly—perhaps paranoidally. Second, and more important, the impasse in no event can be unilaterally determined. Even with all the good will in the world—in fact, the more easily with all the good will in the world—one's perception of hostile behavior can be distorted precisely because it seems unwarrantedly hostile. To filter our perceptions of another through the coloring experience of disappointment at the ineffectualness of our good will is one of the most powerful biases we can permit ourselves: It is exactly what is commonly called self-righteous bitterness and cyncism.

It is scarcely necessary to remark that no nation is capable of perfect empathy or wholly devoid of ethnocentricity: that is why international misunderstandings even when unilaterally begun quickly become bilaterally compounded. But there is a difference between American ethnocentricity and that of others. The ethnocentricity of other countries tends to be shaped by ignorance, provincialism, or even backwardness: Primitive peoples, of course, are typically ethnocentric. On occasion it may be due to a deliberately introduced communication bias. But this ethnocentricity is not usually built into the national character and is therefore, at least in principle, easy to overcome, since it is not consciously sanctioned by the basic social values. That is why even the Russians, for all their ignorance and prejudice about the United States, can understand and, therefore, can predict American behavior with, on the whole, rather remarkable accuracy, even when the categories in which they couch their understanding are inadequate and contrived.

For example, the American inability to understand Canada is proverbial in that country. But, curiously, Canadians reveal their own bias when they misconceptualize their insight into American behavior in terms such as: "Americans don't know enough about Canada." Canadians seem faintly to imply that there is something unfair and unrequiting in American empathetic deficiency. What is required in any case is not knowledge, but understanding, and it is amusing when professional truth-mongers in Canada open-mindedly set out to prove that the Canadian complaint is unfounded because Canadians know just as little about the United States. Scientific surveys may well prove something about Canadian education, prejudices, biases, and attitudes. But for all that, Canadians do understand the United States remarkably well. Indeed, under the circumstances they do so disturbingly well, for it may be that the development of the Canadian national character is hampered by a too vivid background of the American way against which the Canadians must fashion their own values, habits, and culture.

This distinction between knowledge and understanding is important. It explains, for instance, why lack of empathy is found not only in the masses, but also among American intellectuals. It is surely symptomatic that a quite justly respected American sociologist, Nathan Glazer, could recently write: "I cannot conceive of myself acting as Castro acted and acts . . . I understand politics through myself— what I would do, what I would feel, that I might conceivably do, what I might conceivably feel. What Lenin did, I could not do, nor what Castro."[5] A country where such a statement, particularly by a sociologist, echoes the national feeling, could not possibly have begun to understand the world revolution of the twentieth century even though, living within it, it experiences its effects too closely and too well.

Granted the basic accuracy of the foregoing analysis, should one write off American culture as a radically hopeless means for the realization of Christian finalities or Western purposes? This would be an unwarranted conclusion. Christianity, like the non-American West, can serve its ends more adequately than otherwise by continuing and, indeed, strengthening its close association with American culture—but only on condition that that association can be made to produce a reorientation of the American politi-

[5] See the symposium on "Revolution and Liberal Conscience," *Council for Correspondence Newsletter*, No. 13 (January, 1962).

cal character. This reorientation, in turn, depends on whether Americans take advantage of certain character reserves. Naturally, it also depends on whether Christians, American and non-American, will facilitate that reorientation.

Consider that paradigm of the American view of World War II in Europe, William Shirer's *The Rise and Fall of the Third Reich* as a current illustration; any other instance of the average, collectively formed American perception of almost any international political event would do just as well. Shirer's appreciation of the question is, of course, vastly more elaborate and factually competent than that of the ordinary American, but for all its wealth of knowledge and all its documentation it yields a pedestrian view of Nazi Germany (i.e., a view we all had beforehand which Shirer merely enlarges) which is fundamentally untruthful and without insight. I need not add that I do not myself diverge significantly from Shirer's own moral conclusion about the evil of Nazism or Hitler's guilt. Indeed, my judgment is probably harsher than his in what concerns the German nation's unfortunately aberrant participation in Nazism and its complicity with Hitler. But I would maintain that Nazism is historically, culturally, and anthropologically intelligible: Shirer's recurrent expression is one of disbelief, horror, amazement, and wonder. He is unable to empathize with Nazi Germany. For Nazi Germany was evil; and evil he finds impossible to empathize with.

One should empathize with evil if one is genuinely to understand it and one must understand evil if one is to understand realistically the affairs of men. He who understands evil, he who is truly aware of the evil of evil, of its human reality not less than of its enormity, is he not in the best position to evaluate it reasonably and to judge it; that is, to conquer it by reason in so much as reason can? Like Shirer's, the average American's understanding of the Nazi evil is untruthful because evil scandalizes him. It may be, on the contrary, that if one wishes to understand what truly happened in Nazi Germany one's moral judgment of it, however correct, is not the relevant category in which to cast one's thought. For the moral conclusions we may reach, though indispensable for our own self-government, our own self-understanding, and our own self-respect, are irrelevant to our empathetic relations to the other. Though it is true that human behavior, individual or social, does not lie beyond good and evil, it is also true that human behavior is not made to be what it is because it is good or evil. On the contrary, because it is what it is, it can be evaluated as evil or good.

Why should Americans be scandalized by evil? Why should they find it so difficult to empathize with it? The ethnocentricity previously described does not of itself account for this. In fact, let us recall that if any nation has ever been consciously and purposively ethnocentric none was ever more so than Nazi Germany, where ethnocentricity became a political philosophy. Yet, Germany's ethnocentricity did not appreciably blunt her empathic capacity: Hitler's political craft and diplomatic skill cannot be gainsaid. Nor did it produce great inner conflict. American ethnocentricity by itself would neither produce national frustration nor be pragmatically inadequate. Trouble arises because of an inopportune coincidence of ethnocentricity and moral sense. For Americans are much too committed to a humanist morality to allow their ethnocentricity to generate the master-race complex which ethnocentricity,

boosted by power, would naturally evoke. Americans sometimes talk, especially in the face of hostility, as if they
thought otherwise. But when it comes to doing, their better
nature prevails. American diplomacy is sometimes immoral
—it is rarely Machiavellian. In other words, just as there can
be a non-ethnocentric Machiavellism, such as the traditional one of the early modern world, and an ethnocentric
Machiavellism, such as Nazi Germany's, there is also a non-
Machiavellian ethnocentricity: And, this is what afflicts the
United States today. The fact that this ethnocentricity is
non-Machiavellian does not make it without hazard. It may,
on the other hand, make it superable.

One need not go far to seek the reason why American
ethnocentricity should be non-Machiavellian. For the
American alienation from the Old World had more than
one edge. By cutting themselves off from European culture
in order to develop independently, Americans also cut
themselves off from the accelerating decay in European
political morality. The United States does not have a non-
conformist origin for nothing. Particularly in what pertains
to fidelity to the sense of right and wrong in statecraft the
United States has preserved—so far—all that is best in the
faith of the Puritans and the Quakers. It is undeniable that
the ideals of freedom for all, religious toleration, political
pluralism, and, indeed, all the social and political values of
an ever traduced Christian humanism are deeply imbedded
in the fabric of American culture.

It is highly cynical of some Americans, however, to interpret the conflict in question—a sort of a struggle between
ego needs and super-ego imperatives—in such terms as those
preferred by Kennedy's advisors: "the trouble with us is
that we aren't tough-minded enough," as if callousness were

the proper corrective for a bad conscience. It is to be feared
that the ascendancy of this moralizing cynicism is one of
the most notable contributions to American diplomatic history made to date by Kennedy's regime. Nor should one
wryly conclude that it is the American people's bad luck that
their chance to sin came only when sin could no longer be
committed in comfort. Yet, there is truth in both these
reactions. If Great Britain, Germany, and France were successfully Machiavellian, the reason is that their Machiavellism flourished at the right time, namely, when it could exist
in the vacuum left by the disintegration of medieval Christianity. But as a crypto-Christian, secular humanist morality came into being at the end of the nineteenth century,
Machiavellism gradually became impossible, and Europe
has been sufficiently realistic to behave accordingly. Thus,
Great Britain has given it up, on the whole, rather gra-
ciously; Italy, quite unconsciously; France, however, only
painfully; and Germany only indecisively and inchoatively.
(In this view Hitler's Machiavellism was essentially anach-
ronistic. He wanted Europe to revert to the eighteenth-
century pattern of peace, diplomacy, war, and politics. He
was, therefore, quite out of touch with the realities of the
times: in that consisted his "madness.") There is, therefore,
a time when one can get away with international murder
and a time when one cannot. The United States would do
well even on pragmatic grounds alone not to entertain the
thought of trying to turn history backwards. Nor can it
enter into relations with a Europe and a world which no
longer exist.

There is also truth in the notion that strength of character must be trained for and developed by the United
States. But strength of character is not the same as the

"Spartan quality," the "lean and mean" self-conceit which President Kennedy's inner circle seems dangerously to prescribe. Americans should not presume to improve the inadequacies of ethnocentricity by pursuing a Machiavellism that they are basically too spiritually wise and too morally innocent to make succeed. The failure of Machiavellian policies in Laos, in Cuba, and in the U-2 incident indicates that the Americans are too moral a people to adopt successfully the dispositions of political amorality as an acknowledged way of life.

It is, rather, in that weakness, in that inability to fight fire with fire, in their instinctive lawfulness, as Professor Roger Fisher has argued,[6] that lies the great strength of the United States. There is enough good will—even if it is not all the good will in the world—and enough moral habituation in the American people, to inspire a reasonable confidence in the Western world and in the Christian mind that if Americans give themselves enough time, and if they can avoid being tripped up by their own logic, they will eventually do the right thing, even when the task is as Herculean as transcending the horizons of ethnocentricity.

Some may dismiss these opinions as being "anti-American." But, the distinction between being critical and being against must be made. I believe these observations express a greater faith in the American character than do the "pro-American" statements which unconditionally agree with every venture of American diplomacy. Such uncritical "friends" of the United States perform in its regard the same toadying role that communists monotonously undertake toward the Soviet Union, that of the apologist and the

[6] "Fighting Fire with Fire," *Council for Correspondence News-letter,* No. 6 (June, 1961).

sycophant. It is an expression of faith to conclude that the
United States, after all, does have the spiritual resources required to reorient the entropic course of its political history.
This faith is not entirely a matter of feeling. It seems to me,
for the reasons I have advanced, that the tension set up by
the opposition between ethnocentricity and ethical humanism may well provide the motive for the United States to
understand itself and the world. Heightened self-awareness
is the ordinary means to human progress as such.

Other than possible lack of time, the great obstacle in the
way of achieving this is the temptation to cut the Gordian
knot of tangled international affairs. For instance, the tension might become so unbearable that the United States
might in despair convince itself not only of the feasibility
but also of the morality of preventive war. The role that
American Catholics will choose to play in this regard is,
perhaps, decisive. There are reasons to hope in them. For
instance a nucleus of American Catholics has been formed
whose novel idea is that peacemaking is an essential Christian activity, and their number grows. The name of Thomas
Merton requires special mention in this respect. The foundation of an American chapter of PAX in 1962 was a milestone in the path of the American Catholic peace movement, and Dorothy Day's activities had been an earlier one.

But complacency would be ridiculous. Despite official reassurances that the United States will not seek "total victory" by war, the official government policy, though
couched in ambiguities, seems to retain the goal of "total
victory" while avoiding war. It is certain, at any rate that
this goal has not been officially rejected. The danger, therefore, is not so much that the United States will set out to
conquer communism by war, but that the attempt to con-

quer communism otherwise—say, by subversion, as in
Cuba—will set off a war. Nor is the danger so much
that the American people will consciously generate the
desire to impose their will by force upon the world, but
that they may be seduced unwittingly through the dynamics
of two agencies, government and fourth estate. These two,
while simply, even innocently and in good will serving the
people, often bring out the worst in them, even as the people often bring out the worst in the politician and journalist. It is no one's isolated madness that we need fear: It is
the *folie à deux*, and that *à trois, à quatre, à cent mille.*

The critical time when these matters shall be decided,
particularly the ultimate orientation of American foreign
policy either toward total victory or co-existence with Russia
and communism, is probably not too far off. One hopes and
believes that the United States and the West will choose
not merely to co-exist with the East, but also, resorting to
Pius XII's distinction, to live together and to co-operate
with it in the creation of one human world.

I should stress that this is a faith and a hope—not in any
American administration or in any one nation of the West,
but in the evolutionary, creative cultural forces that have
produced the United States as well as every other Western
democracy. It is, if you will, a faith in certain cultural values, a faith in democracy itself, and in the self-transcending
possibilities of Western culture under the guidance of
Christianity and in the service of mankind. If events prove
this faith and this hope to have been misplaced, then we
shall all know—if we survive the literally shattering blow—
that democracy cannot work, and that the suicide of Western culture was, after all, an emergency therapeutic operation, a sort of spiritual surgical excision, as it were, per-
formed upon itself by the genus Man.

CHAPTER 17

THE CUBAN QUESTION AS AN INTERNATIONAL PROBLEM

Having examined some of the cultural, social, historical, and ideological processes which, as they relate to the United States, make up the fundamental context of the world crisis of which the Cuban question became a focal point, we may now review some of the processes which make up its contemporary political context.

From the point of view of contemporary political history the Cuban question obviously should be defined in terms of that semi-military, semi-diplomatic struggle between Russia and the United States which we call the cold war. If so, Cuban events should be viewed from exactly the same perspective as we view the emancipation movements of the various colonial areas since the end of World War II: To a very great extent the diplomatic and military battlefields of the cold war have been provided by the nations emerging from colonial or neo-colonial conditions. Thus, the interaction of the colonial policies of the United States and Russia is an essential part of the problem.

As we all know, the Russian policy since the end of World War II has been consistently to lend her support, to a greater or lesser degree, and whether politically only or also economically and militarily, to the so-called "movements of national liberation" which raged predominantly in Asia during the first half of the fifties and in Africa during the second. This policy was not originally a cause of tension with the United States. In fact, the natural sympathies of the United States made it lean toward passive if not active sympathy with the colonies. But we must remember that at this time, at the end of the war, and even after the beginning of the cold war in Europe, the people of the United States were not yet convinced that the goal of Russian policy was to conquer the world, a conviction they did not begin to acquire (not, at least, with consciousness and feeling) until the early years of the last decade. Moreover, that conviction did not become the nearly universal American belief it is today until the second half of the fifties, partly because the United States had been so confident of its invincibility that it could not seriously believe that any nation would have the temerity to challenge its supremacy. What seems above all to have lent force to the common persuasion that Russia intended to conquer the world was the rather sudden realization that Russia possessed the power to succeed in such an ambition. This view gained currency suddenly and spectacularly only after October 5, 1957, when the first Russian sputnik was successfully launched, and was followed by an unbroken string of ever more spectacular feats of space exploration. "I don't think most Americans realize the way the situation has changed," Kennedy said: "as late as 1954 the balance in air power, in the nuclear weapons, was all on our side. The change began about 1958 or 1959, with the missiles. Now we have got to realize that both sides have these annihilating weapons, and that changes the problem."[1]

[1] Quoted by Stewart Alsop, art. cit.

Human beings are, on the whole, so chronocentric, so ready to assume that these things have always been and probably shall continue to be the way they are at present, that it is necessary to make an effort of memory to recall the vastly different quality of popular American and, more generally, Western feeling toward Russia before these events. Though we all knew that war was a possibility we did not live in fear of its imminence. This does not mean that American hostility to Russia is the exclusive result of fear. But it is important that we remain open to the possibility that fear may have exaggerated the response to real danger from Russia. If we understand this, moreover, we might also begin to understand the reciprocal, fearful exaggeration in the Soviet response to whatever real danger might similarly accrue to them from the more powerful American military establishment. And that may be worth understanding. For we cannot reasonably expect anyone to bear imperturbably the threat posed by the mere existence of nuclear arms regardless of their possessors' apparent good intentions. We cannot, moreover, expect greater trust in one's opponent to be displayed by the weaker party.[2] In any case, the result of the development of these two convictions by the United States was a marked and rapid shift in its attitude toward the nations emerging from colonial stature.

The process leading from American apprehensiveness to actual dread and alarm began shortly after the end of the war as Russia began to realize its expansionist aims in Eastern Europe through the creation, typically by the use of internal subversion, of a satellite system out of the terri-

[2] And yet, as P. M. S. Blackett put it, some strategists propose the truly psychopathic doctrine which in essence means that "the West must plan on the enemy's capability, but the U.S.S.R. should plan on the West's intentions," Blackett, p. 138.

tories she had occupied at the end of the war. Moreover, her unsuccessful efforts extended beyond these territories, as in Greece. And Italy and France, too, seemed for a while to be close to the adoption of communism. We should also remember Russia's insistence on the partition of Germany and the shifting of Poland's Eastern and Western frontiers.[2a]

However, though the creation of satellites by internal subversion is neither a democratic nor a justifiable mode of international behavior (indeed, from the point of view of political ethics certain of its aspects are rather more immoral than aggressive war itself), there is a clearly perceptible difference between willingness to subvert a country for one's national gain, and the ideological need to conquer it by war if necessary. The United States has tended to let its thinking pass over insensibly from the former to the latter. A student of Russian diplomacy whose opinion cannot be ignored has explained:

Although the injury which the Soviet leaders wished to work upon the Western countries was as serious as many of the injuries nations have sought in the past to work on other nations by the normal devices of war ... it was not by these normal devices of war that Moscow itself set about to operate. The Marxist-Leninist ideology did not suggest that it was by a single grand military conflict between the world of Communism and the world of capitalism that these aims were to be achieved. I cannot

[2a] Whatever the justice of Russia's claims in these two crucial respects may be, this is another case in which much depends on how far back one goes, or refuses to go, in history. Russia could claim that in her relations with the West since the early Middle Ages she has been more frequently the invaded than the invader. It is true, at any rate, as Pius XII wrote, that the Russian-Western rupture "took place, in the beginning, between men who knew and adored the same Savior, Jesus Christ," for it harks back to the struggle between Latin Christianity and Holy Russia, with Moscow as the third Rome.

think of a time when the Soviet Government desired that there should be such a conflict, planned to launch it, or staked its hopes and expectations for the victory of world socialism on the effects of such an encounter . . . I have labored many hours to explain . . . the nature of the Soviet threat as I saw it; in no respect have I found it so difficult to obtain understanding as in the presentation of this one simple fact.[3]

It may be as unwise to overestimate as to underestimate the extent and nature of the threat posed by Russia. If the United States had been able to view events in Eastern Europe with sufficient objectivity and historical perspective it would have been able to see Russia's policy for the *Realpolitik* that it was and, therefore, might have dealt with what was a real danger in a realistic way. Instead, it chose to view the Russian policy not simply as ideologically moti-

[3] George F. Kennan, *Russia and the West* (Boston, 1961), p. 389. This does not mean that the policy goals recommended by Kennan (see "The Sources of Soviet Conduct," *Foreign Affairs,* V, 25; July, 1947), are vastly different from what they would have been had he perceived Russia as his audiences did. Indeed, if it is true, as is contended by W. A. Williams in his *American–Russian Relations, 1781–1947* (New York, 1952), pp. 258 ff., that Kennan's role in the formation of postwar American policy toward Russia was decisive, it may be that the root of what I shall describe below as the American theory of the permanent postponability of war with Russia is to be found at such points as Kennan's premise that "the theory of the inevitability of the eventual fall of capitalism has the fortunate connotation that there is no hurry about it," and that, therefore, "the Kremlin is under no ideological compulsion to accomplish its purposes in a hurry" (art. cit.). This is the point at which a Marxoid historical determinism introduced itself into or, rather, was uncritically absorbed by, postwar American policy makers. The implication of Kennan's words seems to be that although American policy need not count on an early, wartype showdown, the hostile antinomy is permanent of its own nature and shall remain so until the disappearance of one party or another—that is, an acceptance of the concept of dialectical, historical determinism on which is superimposed a rejection of its projected outcome in favor of socialism.

vated, which it certainly was (for Russia's expansionism was compounded of national ambition and the communist brand of cosmopolitan humanism), but also as ideologically necessitated, which it was not—and, hence, projectible to an absolute degree.

When Americans say today that Russia is bent upon world conquest they do not mean merely that Russia's ambitions are so great that if she could she would conquer the world in order to appropriate to herself the resources of other nations; nor even that Russia, either by reason of intolerance or misapprehension concerning foreign threats wishes to protect the viability of her ideology by forcibly voiding real or imagined threats to it. If that were all, the problem would not be half as serious as it is. What Americans seem to mean is that there is something in the very nature and existence of Russian Communism that, first, requires her to work for the forcible subjection of the world, by war if necessary, and for no other essential end than the imposition of her ideology; and that, second, once such an ideology is adopted by a country its violent conflict with nations disposed otherwise is ultimately unavoidable. This is what is meant by the view that communism is "irrevocably committed to the overthrow of the Free World."[4]

If war, though in itself unavoidable in virtue of that commitment, is nevertheless not actualized, the reason is that the United States does not have a corresponding will to war. Consequently, war, while remaining essentially unavoidable, can be permanently postponed—as long, that is, as superior power deters the communist will. Since that will is conceived as committed permanently and irrevocably, the

[4] David Wills and Peg Eck, *Total Victory Without Atomic War* (Washington, 1962), p. 3.

postponement-through-deterrence must be projected as a permanent requirement of peace—and by this Orwellian dialectic we find ourselves in an arms race for the sake of peace. For the only alternative is "unthinkable": to allow weakness to elicit an enemy attack. For this reason the United States sees itself as reluctantly, sorrowfully, and resignedly committed, first, to the view that the cold war is essentially insoluble unless Russia abandons communism, and second, to a permanent arms race in order to maintain deterrent superiority.

But the American solution is neither as flawless nor as permanent as it may seem at first. Nuclear deterrence may have prevented war, but it has produced perils of its own, like war by accident or by miscalculation.[5] It is said, somewhat circularly, that it must work, because it has prevented war. Perhaps—but what is beyond argument is that it has not prevented the danger of war, and this may be the costliest contradiction in the reliance upon nuclear deterrence: The fact that the very raising of war potential to astronomical figures produces no more than that sham security known as the "balance of terror." In any event, it has not prevented war without a number of economic, social,

[5] Part of Kennedy's military strategy, based upon the idea that exclusively nuclear deterrence is inadequate to Russia's "peripheral probings" in virtue of the all-or-none character of such weapons, is to balance the American armory with non-nuclear deterrents. This is advantageous to the United States in that it may help prevent further military gains by Russian-armed "movements of national liberation." But it is now too late for this to make much political difference to the long-range world situation: Non-nuclear forces are not likely to find new battlefields in the cold war. On the fallacies of nuclear deterrence strategy see Arthur I. Waskow, *The Limits of Defense* (Garden City, 1962), and Michael J. Brower, "President Kennedy's choice of nuclear strategy," *Council for Correspondence Newsletter*, No. 17 (June, 1962).

political, cultural and psychological consequences which are
already undesirable and which threaten to become intolerable. This last point should touch the Christian conscience
with some asperity: Under the constant pressure of a culture bound to a war economy, to a war-threatened way of
life, the temptation to become subservient to needs other
than those of the Christian mission becomes particularly
trying: "never was opposition to war more urgent and more
necessary than now. Never was religious protest so badly
needed. Silence, passivity, or outright belligerence seem to
be characteristic official and unofficial Christian reactions to
the H-bomb."[6] Finally, from the point of view of third parties, whether neutral or allied with either side, the American solution threatens ever more to diminish the autonomy
and development of all those nations caught in the struggle:
they are increasingly required to make choices in terms of
what may satisfy one side or the other or both. Even if a
Pax Americana were perfectly satisfactory to the United
States it can hardly satisfy all other nations, not even the
American allies.

Now, the American conceptualization of the danger of
communism which we have just examined is a curious
phenomenon. It means that the United States adopted a
theory of historical determinism which is itself largely
Marxist in origin and nature. That is why I have placed
emphasis on the difference between these two: On the one
hand, the opinion that Russia is a threat, either because she
is ambitious, or because she would like to further the cause
of communism and is not scrupulous as to the means, or
because she feels that communism's security is best
achieved by the destruction of her enemies; on the other

[6] Thomas Merton, *Breakthrough to Peace* (New York, 1962), p.
88.

hand, the opinion that she is a threat because the destruction of democracy, militarily or *otherwise*, is required by communism in virtue of its nature and existence as a historical force.

As is well known, Marxism does affirm that the course of history is determined by economic forces, which guarantees that capitalism will disappear, annihilated by its own inner contradictions. There is a difference however, between the historical determinism of Marxism and that of American diplomacy. The course of history, according to Marxists, is determined by the dialectical development of reality which, for them, is matter—and matter alone. American foreign policy appears to assume, all the more dogmatically because it does so tacitly, that the course of history is similarly and strictly determined by the dialectic of ideas—and ideas alone. It is not necessary at this point to defend the view that human history is not determined, but that it is open to possibilities which cannot be defined beforehand. The issue is that though both the American and the communist views of history share a common belief in determinism, the Marxist view permits Russia a diplomatic flexibility which is denied to the United States. That flexibility may be healthier for the world, in the long run, than the "idealism" of American diplomacy. For the Marxist view of history maintains touch with reality, however mistaken its notion of reality may be—whereas the American version of determinism, however correct in its opposition to materialism, is inclined to pattern reality after the rules of thought. The first falsifies reality: The second substitutes logical fictions for reality. The practical consequences of these two errors are quite different. The second is, in the long run, more dangerous to peace than the first.

Because the United States conceives political realities in

absolute and ideal terms it did not merely recognize that Russia posed a genuine threat to world peace; it also believed that the opposition between Russia and the West was a struggle to the death fated by history, sanctioned by ethics, and hallowed by sincerely good intentions: a struggle between the forces of evil and the forces of good. And, just as Americans would recognize that neither their country nor their democracy is perfect, they are also willing to admit, and immediately to dismiss as irrelevant, the possibility that there may be some accidental good in both Russia and communism. If the frank recognition of all this changes nothing the reason is that the foregoing requires them to adhere to the view that the contest is not essentially one between human concretions but between superhuman forces. Both Russia and the United States are but pawns of history: In reality and quite literally the conflict is between God and the Devil. In this consists the American historical, determinist idealism.

It was out of this American absolutization and idealization of the cold war that arose the doctrine that neutrality ought to be forbidden, not simply on the grounds that it is disadvantageous to American policy (which would have made it negotiable), but on the grounds that every non-communist nation had the moral duty to support the United States against the common enemy of man and "the free world" (which made it a matter of principle). In this connection one may remember Dulles' own formula, "neutralism is immoral."

The difficulty with American opposition to neutralism was that the emerging nations, with exceptions, of course, were on the one hand, more or less indebted to Russia for political support while, on the other hand, the United

States had been more or less neutral in their struggle for independence from countries, principally Great Britain and France, which were the staunchest American allies. Not surprisingly therefore the new nations did not relish alignment: while non-alignment became a policy increasingly distasteful to the United States. The ambiguities of this distaste were symbolized by the paradox of American support of a communist Government in Yugoslavia in order to reinforce its neutralism away from Russia simultaneously with an ill-concealed impatience with the neutralism of a democratic country such as India. Gradually the original American sympathy with colonial emancipation began to be subordinated to the abhorrence of neutralism.

If the foregoing is correct, then it is rather superficial and unduly cynical to think—as many do in Canada, Great Britain, and France—that the United States did not object to colonial emancipation when it was the empires of Britain, France, the Netherlands and Belgium that were affected, but that it awoke when its own Nasser, in the person of Castro, injured its colonial interests. Actually the role played by economic self-interest in the American policy towards Cuba was rather more indirect. We have already briefly studied the economic side of the dispute. We have seen, however, that the opposition of the United States to Castro was not simply economic, but that its economics was bound to its logic of politics. American hostility toward Russia had become greatly exacerbated between 1956 and 1959 and verged on the hysterical. Let us remember once more how alarming and galling had been the Russian successes in space. When Castro tried to achieve, not only more ineptly and quixotically but also much later and faster the same national aims that had been elsewhere fought for with universal success, he met an unprecedented obstacle: the determination of the United States to deny to Russia the supposed advantage of Cuban neutralism. In other words, American political fear and political suspicion of communism made the economic dispute with Cuba initially acute and ultimately insoluble. The failure of American diplomacy consisted in not having foreseen that an unresolved economic problem radiates political consequences. American diplomacy, thus, fulfilled its own worst predictions.

By the same token, it is imprecise to say that Cuba turned to Russia because the United States tried to throttle Cuba when the latter freed herself from American economic colonialism. In the first place it was part of Cuba's policy—as it had been that of other colonies in their own way—to draw closer to Russia precisely in order to enhance Cuba's independence from the United States. We have seen for instance, that some diversification of markets and production was indispensable to Cuba. It is quite true, on the other hand, that the United States tried to throttle Cuba economically in retaliation for her emancipation— which, in turn, necessitated the turn of Cuba's policy toward greater economic reliance upon Russia. In brief, it was Cuba that struck the first blow—the blow of her emancipation.

This has been somewhat obscured because sequence of causes is not the same as priority of reasons. The sequence of events in the American policy of aggression against Cuba was: first, subversive violence; second, economic warfare; third (after the culmination of subversion into the open violence of the invasion), diplomatic, political hostilities. But the order of American motivation was the opposite.

First of all there was a political end—to forbid Cuba's neutralism. But, as Professor W. A. Williams has observed, the traditional political philosophy underlying American diplomacy includes a very strict definition of good and evil economics. Therefore, a second motive came into play: to retain economic ascendancy over Cuba, not merely for the sake of lucrative economic advantages, but primarily perhaps for the sake of advancing certain economic ideas, namely, international capitalism and free enterprise. Violence was only a means to these ends.

If this analysis is correct, Kennedy's and Eisenhower's gravest offense to political morality in this matter was quite the opposite of what many relatively liberal Americans think—that the invasion was an ethically indefensible means to an otherwise justified end.[7] It seems to me that Kennedy's and Eisenhower's culpability lay in having adopted ends that were much more immoral than the means themselves. For the overarching purpose of the

[7] The more commonly debated question is, rather, whether the invasion was pragmatically adequate and, particularly, whether it was Kennedy's fault that it failed when "he left the men stranded on the beach." It seems to me that from the point of view of tactics Kennedy did not make any glaring mistakes. This does not mean that the invasion brigade alone could ever have overthrown Castro—or that the CIA failed to estimate correctly the strength of Cuban support of Castro. It means that the failure was not caused by Kennedy's withholding additional emergency forces to what would have been originally sufficient strength. My hypothesis is that it was not Kennedy's understanding that a second stage of massive participation by American forces had been an indispensable part of the operation from the beginning; and that if there was any blunder on anyone's part it was the CIA's overestimation of its ability to manipulate Kennedy under pressure into doing its will, namely, to take Cuba by the open use of American forces in supposed aid of a hastily recognized Cuban government-in-arms. Kennedy's mistake, if so, was strategic: not seeing until April 19 what he could have suspected long before.

Cuban policies of two American Administrations has been, in effect, to prevent at all costs Cuba's autonomy. American diplomacy has preferred Cuba's Communism over Cuba's full emancipation. I say full emancipation, because there was never any question of allowing none at all. Castro once remarked, speaking of Cuba's bourgeoisie, that it wanted "revolution, yes, but not too much revolution." The same might have been said of the United States.

Exactly how much revolution was the United States ready to allow? The question is such that one can only speculate. American diplomacy, largely in virtue of the ponderous dynamics of domestic politics, develops slowly, changes painfully, and adapts only in reaction and under duress. In time, the United States might have grudgingly allowed more freedom than was acceptable to it in 1959. What Matyas Rakosi once called "salami tactics" do work well with the United States, because American public life is itself its best exponent. For these reasons one may estimate premising a faith in the fundamental humanism of the United States—that the United States would have eventually reconciled itself to mere economic loss in Cuba, especially in an amount which, after all, was not unbearable. But the unconditional opposition to neutralism demanded an immediate opposition to Castro. It was, therefore, not only Castro who moved too fast. The United States, too, did not allow itself sufficient time to adapt, nor did it give Cuba an opportunity to learn.

The United States government did not oppose (any more than did the Cuban Church) the social revolution because it was a social revolution. But, like Boza and Pérez, Kennedy and Eisenhower opposed it despite its having been basically just and humanly required. The United States might have supported it at least passively, and within the framework of that support striven to avoid whatever political consequences it thought undesirable. But, like the Church, the United States conditioned its support of the social revolution's actualities upon the annihilation of certain political possibilities. It preferred the wrong likelihood over the right risk. Ironically, the likelihood was not a certainty—the Cuban policy of the United States has succeeded only in making out of its Cuban dispute an international question and, indeed, a particularly grave threat to world peace.

Only three basic alternatives remain open to the United States regarding Cuba. First, it could persevere in its stated determination to overthrow the Cuban government by one means or another, and, at the appropriate moment, follow through that decision to its logical end. In view of the Cuban people's and Castro's equally firm determination to remain independent, the internationalization of the Cuban question has made this course the equivalent of war with Russia. Ironically, this was ratified by Kennedy's own diplomacy. He failed to perceive that under "balance of terror" conditions the diplomatic efficiency of greater power is almost none: Overkill does not overpersuade. Thus, Kennedy's choice to inflate the presence of Russian missile bases in Cuba into the Cuban crisis of November, 1962, was exploited by Russia with such diplomatic skill that the paradoxical net result of the crisis included a virtual American guarantee of Cuba's sovereignty: To break that guarantee now would signal nuclear war.[8]

[8] It is fairly certain that Kennedy exaggerated the capabilities of the Cuban missiles and the nature of their threat for the purpose of rallying the support of American opinion (see, e.g., Richard H. Rovere, "Letter from Washington," the New Yorker, March 2,

Second, the United States could do nothing—or nothing significant. It could persist in its desultory, pointless, cruel game of sabotage, subversion, and harassment—or, for that matter, it could stop. It could go on, for instance, hoping for an unlikely internal collapse in Cuba; it could toy with temptation while it expected reality to disappear. The worst part of this alternative is that although it is the most enticing—for it works by inertia and requires no initiative—it is also essentially unstable. It is the local application of the general doctrine that world war can be permanently postponed. But since the international situation cannot be stabilized without the resolution of the Cuban question, this policy would also advocate, in effect, the permanent postponement of world peace. Unfortunately for this doctrine, if it is true that war is not permanently postponable, neither is peace.

The third alternative is the one that American diplomacy has tried so hard to avoid: the decision, if not to sponsor the revolution, to at least leave it alone; to cease diplomatic and economic hostilities; to negotiate with the Cuban revolution on a footing of equality in dignity and from a

---

1963); but that is not nearly as important as his having resorted to the illegal "brinkmanship" of a blockade. However, from the point of view of diplomacy there can be little doubt that Kennedy's response played into Russian hands in almost every respect. His diplomacy succeeded in isolating the United States from NATO, in guaranteeing the defensive build-up of Cuban military forces and in guaranteeing Cuba from direct American attack. I have developed some of these points at greater length in my paper "Russia's Cuban policy: an interpretation," first published in the Council for Correspondence Newsletter, No. 21 (October, 1962), pp. 17–24, and republished under the title "The prospects for peace," in Liberation, VII, 10 (December, 1962), pp. 5–10. A briefer version, revised in the light of later perspective, appeared as "Cuba: catalyst of peace," in the Nation, CXCVI, 6 (February 9, 1963), pp. 113–5. See also my paper on Cuba and the cold war, an expanded version of parts of this chapter, in Liberation, VII, 1 (March, 1963), pp. 16–22.

position of mutual respect; finally, to open up trade with Cuba on the basis of bilateral agreements pursued to mutual advantage and interest, so that Cuba's independence from both Russia and the United States might be allowed to increase. In brief, this alternative would mean a return to November 13, 1959, and the acceptance of Raúl Roa's proposals from first to last. This would mean taking a loss—but perhaps it would be the cheapest option in the long run. The price would be not so much economic, since Cuba is ready to make some compensation. Its cost in pride would be more difficult to pay; but perhaps the most serious loss would be political. A return to November 13 would mean that the price of not having tolerated Cuba's neutralism then would be having to tolerate Cuba's Marxism now. This is a loss that the United States can afford—and would do well to take.

It is impossible to tell which of these courses shall be followed by the United States. All are unlikely; none is impossible. However, although the second alternative, doing nothing, is the most enticing, it is also in the long run the least likely: It is too late now for that. For the shape of world events over the remaining decades of the century, is likely to be sketched out in broad but essential outline over the next few years—say, over the remaining years of the Kennedy administration, if we suppose a second term. This is merely to reaffirm the reality of the world crisis of today. A more decisive Cuban policy would be required before the end of this period if the world is to avoid war.[9]

[9] But a more decisive Cuban policy means a more decisive world-wide policy. Where does decisiveness begin?

Both Russia and the United States believe each other morally capable of aggression but themselves incapable of it. Both sides are correct in the first respect. Therefore, both sides deceive themselves in the second. If so, both sides are also correct in denouncing the

However, if by the end of this decade or so we have not reached an international economic depression homologous to that of 1929, if the rate of progress toward the political integration of the world has not slackened, if war has been averted, and if the ideological polarization is not replaced by a racial one, we shall also have achieved a great deal more than negatively to have avoided these evils. We shall have established the foundations of the first stable world peace, the first unified world, the first world economy on the basis of universal equity and the first universal civilization of Man. The reason is that the situation of the world is so straitened that it has become impossible for the world to avoid any of those evils except by making considerable progress toward the achievement of those goods. The converse, therefore, is also true. Unless we adopt those goals and consciously and assiduously work toward their achievement, to suffer the corresponding evils shall be our inevitable lot.

---

naïvete of those who propose that it is all a question of mutual misunderstanding, of lacking mutual trust, of misreading each other's peaceful intentions. For the "peaceful intentions" of both sides are highly ambivalent. Both sides intend peace—but both sides are ready to risk war. The fountainhead of trouble, thus, is that although both sides are hypothetically committed to peace, both sides are unconditionally committed to war as a last resort. Both sides, therefore, are at least psychologically if not morally ready to deliver a devastating, forestalling, first thermonuclear blow. The mutual fears and distrust are, in this sense, *mutually justified.*

That is the explosive situation that requires defusing: the reality, not the appearance, of a mutually hostile and aggressive political morality. But since this problem is of human creation it is in principle soluble by human consciousness. If so, it is fairly evident what the foundations of a decisive policy of peace may be. The first reality of which each side must become conscious is not so much the potential peacefulness of the other side as the latent aggressiveness in its own. The unilateralism required for peace is not essentially military, but political.

CHAPTER 18

THE CHRISTIAN UN-CONSCIENCE
AND THE PROBLEM OF WAR

We have considered some aspects of the political context
of the Cuban revolution in order to discern the political
foundations for alternative proposals which a Christian
political ethics might suggest. However, the larger context
of the Cuban revolution as a focal point of the crisis of the
world and of the Christian Church, is a religious one. It is
a context definable as a Christian world—and a world
Church in which it is possible for their members with a
perfectly clear conscience to wage modern war upon each
other.

This is not to say that we always wage war joyously, or
that we never try to avoid war, or that world statesmen are
totally irresponsible—though the institutional glorification
of war, the large cultural and economic component in the
causes of all modern wars, and the frequent culpability of
statesmen in these respects, show that even the judgments
of a lax conscience are not always abided by. The point to
be discussed here, in other words, is not whether we are
guilty, but whether our conscience is well-formed—indeed,
whether we have consciously formed our conscience on this
matter or whether we have not, on the contrary, developed
an un-conscience of war.

The Catholic conscience seems, on the whole, to have remained not deeply troubled about modern war.[1] It is not so much that Catholics have not made up their minds about it, but that they have not generally considered it in its existential reality. For instance, most Catholics do have an opinion, usually affirmative, on the question whether it is lawful, in principle, to use nuclear weapons for licit ends— as if that question mattered much. To have arrived at that answer through a coherent train of syllogistic thought is not to have solved a problem in ethics, but to have engaged in an exercise in logic.

The confusion between ethical and logical thought, which explains why Catholic moral theology has become permeated with rationalism and apriorism, also explains why Catholics have tended, at least asymptotically, to religious pragmatism—to the view that all's fair in God's love and God's war. For if we are religious pragmatists, then we have no problems of conscience: Our moral perplexity is spent in trying to determine under which category our particular case falls. To rationalize, on this scheme, is to define our particular case with a certain principle already in mind— and the principle invariably turns out to justify whatever we want. With a little habituation to this method an invincible un-conscience is developed. And once one develops an un-conscience one is free to devote all one's time to the pursuit of the salvation of one's immortal soul.

When I say Catholics have not been deeply concerned by the reality of war I mean that although they have thought about it, their thought has been for the most part

[1] All the more surprisingly because the two pontiffs of the nuclear age have both been very much troubled by it. Pius XII's main writings on the question have been collected by Harry W. Flannery in *Pattern for Peace* (Westminster, Md., 1962).

a fairly transparent rationalization of war. Efforts have been spent largely in disquisitions about the *justification of war* —it is a historical fact that Catholics have not put nearly as much effort, either intellectual or practical, into the promotion of peace.

In contrast, there are some non-Catholic groups that have expressed moral concern with war and, particularly, with the prospect of thermonuclear strife. Their position is usually not wholly satisfactory to the Catholic mind—with some reason, perhaps. Though the quantity of destruction through war has become so vast that vital urgency and gravity are lent to the problem, we should not let urgency and gravity disperse our attention. Our moral problem should not be formally stated in terms of an unusually high explosive. Our problem is nuclear war, not nuclear power. More precisely, our problem is the kind of war in which, if nuclear power were not available we would invent something else to take its place. Nor is our problem formally posed by the perfection of our science and technology, which would make it quite feasible to devise more lethal weapons than nuclear warheads. Our problem is more nearly defined in terms of escalation, which did not begin with nuclear power nor during the twentieth century, but which is the emergent product of the history of civilized man. To ban the bomb, even bilaterally, would be a palliative: Alone, it would solve nothing. In the long run we can solve the problem of nuclear war power only by solving the problem of nuclear war.

To see why the relevant consideration is the quality of war and not the *amount* of war potential, we should remind ourselves that the concept of war has undergone a complete revolution beginning most remotely with the introduction of gunpowder but more particularly since the introduction of warheads. Because warheads themselves were introduced into the technology of war through the use of explosives it was especially difficult for man to realize the radical change that imperceptibly took place in the very substance of armed conflict. The bullet naturally seemed only an elaboration of the hand-thrown projectile; the warhead an elaboration of the bullet. In the human reality of war, however, the concomitant change is from the traditional condition of personal involvement, individual risk, personal and individual combat, to the condition of impersonal and general conflict, mechanized destruction, mass slaughter, total hatred, and strife. There was a time, from the stone age until rather recently, when war, however reprehensible, could be regarded as an art. That was radically changed when war acquired the impersonal and mechanical configuration that has been brought to perfection in the second half of our century.

The complexity of our problem today is compounded by the ancient (though by no means either apostolic or patristic) tradition since St. Augustine against the unconditional rejection of war—though in reality St. Augustine's theory of the "just war" is not exactly the one on which we base our more recent rejection of pacifism,[2] understood as the doctrine of "peace at all costs." In any event, this rejection rests upon two principles, both of which are as authoritative as they are reasonable. The first is that under certain conditions war can be justified. Christians have long thought that physical violence is neither good nor evil in itself and that, therefore, its use is either good or evil

[2] This point has been textually documented by Thomas Merton in unpublished studies.

depending upon the moral quality of the effect it essentially achieves.[3] The surgeon, for instance, inflicts pain, wounds the flesh, and sheds blood, but he is perfectly justified in doing so. Similarly, though every war has some evil effects which, if sought for themselves or for an evil end, would render war unjust, some wars are rendered just if they are the only possible means to achieve a necessary, lawful end. On this foundation Christians have distinguished between aggressive war, which is never just, and defensive war, which may be justified and even a duty at times.

Consequently, the present trend of Catholic thought on the question is shaped by two distinct strains. On the one hand, the developing tradition just mentioned and the foregoing conception of moral theology have tended to make us assume that there is no need to consider all over again a question which seems definitively settled. On the other hand, this reassuring tradition could resist several centuries of geometric growth in war potential because the changes took place so gradually that we became conditioned to them.

Let us first recall the quality of primitive war. There surely must have been within its texture an element of humanness that suggested a legitimate distinction, for example, between honorable and dishonorable combat. There can be, after all, a heroic element to some war, and it is possible to admire the qualities of selflessness and courage that could

[3] Though it is not my purpose to criticize this argument on its own *a priori* grounds, but to shift the problem to an existential level, I should remark that the argument is useless: There is no such moral reality as physical violence in itself. Moral realities are always in situation. What this argument tells us is that physical violence may or may not be justified. Whether war is or is not justified is not affected. Put otherwise: it is invalid to argue on the basis of a supposed proportionality between, say, a surgical operation and war.

come out of it. Sometimes war could exhibit even a certain sporting quality. One can well understand and share the feelings that were enshrined in classical epic poetry and in the early medieval geste. It is significant, however, that by the end of the sixteenth century Cervantes could sketch a profoundly ironic portrait of knighthood. The knight had already ceased to be a hero, and the signs of his derangement were plain for all to see and for Cervantes to satirize. As gradual changes were introduced into the weaponry of war, parallel changes took place in its political under-structure—I do not speak of them as cause and effect, but as part of that mutual involution of causes which enables history to free-wheel down a certain incline. The socio-logical meaning of war was similarly altered. Before the end of the eighteenth century a prototype of the world war had made its appearance in Europe, and though actual mass de-struction and killing (that is, collective destruction and kill-ing rather than mere destruction and killing on a very large scale) still remained to come, mass suffering and mass involvement in war were becoming so acute that our culture became immunized to deeper changes yet to come.

Frederick the Great in that century is well remembered for his contribution to the evolution of war in the creation of the modern army: And von Clausewitz, early in the nine-teenth century, transmuted war from a fine art into an exact science. The important point, however, is not that war began to acquire efficiency, nor that it began to involve an ever increasing number and proportion of people but, rather, that it began to acquire the impersonal and inhuman configuration that reaches its proper form in the aseptic and detached competence of modern, twentieth century, mech-anized war:

Just as mathematics, business and technology needed the discovery of zero in order to develop, so too political and economic power needed the faceless abstractions of state and corporation, with their unlimited irresponsibility, to attain to unlimited sovereignty. Hence the paradox that in the past ages usually regarded as times of slavery the individual actually counted for much more than he does in the alienation of modern economic, military and political totalism. At the same time it is the modern, irresponsible, faceless, alienated man, the man whose thinking and decisions are the work of an anonymous organization, who becomes the perfect instrument of the power process. Under such conditions, the process itself becomes totally self-sufficient and all absorbing. As a result the life and death not only of individual persons, families and cities, but of entire nations and civilizations must submit to the blind force of amoral and inhuman forces. The "freedom" and "autonomy" of a certain minority may still seem to exist: it consists in little more than understanding the direction of the historically predetermined current and rowing with the stream instead of against it. There should be no need to point out the demonic potentialities of such a situation.[4]

Unlimited war requires unlimited irresponsibility. It is when war is no one's fault and when it takes place against everyone's wishes that war is most irrational and immoral. The gravest indictment of thermonuclear war is that it can take place by accident. Surely there is something wrong with the international political structure of a world which not only permits this situation to obtain but, indeed, encourages it and finds itself prepared to contemplate its projection even into the end of the world. By the same token, the unlimited irresponsibility of modern war requires the complete irresponsibility of each man: The argument that war has become too complex a political issue for any one man's conscience to judge amounts to the suggestion that each person should abdicate his moral responsibility in

[4] Thomas Merton, unpublished study.

favor of Leviathan, and that Leviathan should entrust its
soul to Beelzebub.

It is pertinent to observe that the dehumanization of
war is intimately connected with its totalization. It was not
until the second half of World War I that the last vestige
of humanness appears to have been shed by war when
Ludendorff introduced the concept of total war into the
political life of our times, a concept which, elaborated into
a full-fledged theory in his *Der Totale Krieg* served as the
foundation of the military apparatus of Nazi Germany and
of the theory of war accepted by both sides in World War
II. In this conception war was no longer to involve simply
large numbers, but collectivities and, indeed, totalities in
every respect. For example, the normal, peacetime economy
of a country adopting the idea of total war becomes a
Wehrwirtschaft, a war economy, as it did in Germany
before World War II and as it has more recently among
all the participants in the cold war. The nation preparing to
wage total war must be geared to war even during peace;
peace thus becomes an abnormal economic condition bearable only because the totality of the citizens is engaged in
the peacetime "war effort."

World War I began as a war between armies, but it
ended as Europe's civil war. It began as an intensified form
of traditional modern war, but it ended as the new, modern
war, that is, genomachy, no longer simply deadly, but gen-
ocidal war. The armory of war in parallel now became
qualitatively altered and not merely quantitatively increased. More, and more lethal, weapons were devised; the whole range of machinery available to man
was thrown into the fray. Eventually the distinction between military supplies and consumer goods became one of

degree alone. The Boer war was fought with cavalry, saber, and gun. The equipment essentially was a highly elaborate form of that used by Hannibal with the possible exception of artillery, if we consider it as more than a quantitative improvement over the catapult. But World War I saw the introduction of the automatic machine gun, the tank, the airship, the airplane, poison gas, the mine, the flame thrower and the submarine. The peace of Versailles was only a reflection of the sort of war that had been waged with such an arsenal. Total defeat, naturally, became the price thenceforth to be paid for losing a total war.

But there were some refinements to be added to the concept of total war. During World War I, the distinction between civilian and combatant with isolated exceptions, though considerably strained still received general social sanction. Though total involvement was a matter of fact, a certain prejudice still reigned that inconsistently strove to maintain a distinction between total slaughter and indiscriminate carnage.

We know to the minute the time when this inconsistency was finally dissolved. April 26, 1937, was a Monday. Monday was market day in the town of Guernica, in the province of Vizcaya near the north coast of Spain.[5] On that day Guernica was crowded with farmers bringing their produce to the weekly fair. At half past four in the afternoon an air raid warning was given but, of course, it was useless: there was nowhere to go except indoors. Ten minutes later the Luftwaffe's first wave of bombers arrived and began to drop bombs on the town. As people tried to run away from the town, fighter aircraft strafed the roads, thus herding them

[5] This account summarizes that of Hugh Thomas, *The Spanish Civil War* (London, 1961), p. 419.

back. Half-ton incendiaries and high-explosive bombs were dropped on Guernica by wave after wave of German aircraft for over three hours until a quarter to eight in the evening. More than 1500 people including women and children were killed, and the total number of casualties reached 2500—the town had a population of about 7000. The concept of open city, of Christian origin, ceased to exist on that day.

Every citizen and every piece of property having now become fair targets for killing and destruction by every available or devisable effective means, total war had achieved its proper perfection. Nothing else was lacking. Nothing else needed to be taken away. When the atomic bomb was dropped over Hiroshima, the magnitude of the explosive power or the extent of personal and property damage per kiloton did not appreciably change the nature of modern war. Naturally, one cannot argue that it makes no difference whether to the arsenals of World War II we add the refinements of fission-fusion-fission warheads delivered by rocket-launched ballistic missiles. The point is that nuclear war is not evil because it is nuclear but, on the contrary, that nuclear war is nuclear because it is evil in the first place.

There is some reason to think, therefore, that total war, as the concept has developed in political theory and in historical fact does not simply mean a war pursued relentlessly. It means a war pursued relentlessly because victory has been adopted as the *raison d'être* of the society at war. This comes about when a society mistakes the inalienable right to self-defense for the absolute right to exist which, in the Judaeo-Christian tradition, no creature can ever possess.

This may be the turning point. A society waging total war

must seek total victory, that is, it must be disposed to seek the final and permanent destruction of the enemy. To wage total war is to identify the existence and end of man with the existence and end of one society to the exclusion of another. It is a matter of historical fact that, as it became total, modern war did begin to claim for determinate countries, races, and nations the totality of the right to exist. This was the logical conclusion of claiming for them the totality of the right to survive.

If we claim for one society to the exclusion of another the right to survive—and, thus, the exclusive right to exist —is it possible for that society to justify a war as defensive on the grounds that it ensures its survival? Survival and defense are not necessarily the same. Defensive war is justified despite its being war, not because of it. But when war seeks to kill and destroy as a matter of right, which is exactly what we do when we claim the right to promote our nation's or our society's survival to the exclusion of another's, war is no longer defensive except accidentally. It is defensive only insofar as it produces our survival, but it remains substantially aggressive, and the accidentally produced defense is not enough to justify the adoption of a means, aggressive war, that is intrinsically wrong. In short, war can remain defensive as long as it does not of its very nature deny to the enemy the right to exist. If it does so of itself (and it matters little whether scattered survivors will manage in fact to escape), then war has become essentially aggressive, even when it is waged in reaction to prior, unjust aggression itself.[6]

[6] In this discussion I have been concerned with the morals of war, thermonuclear or otherwise. I may submit, with specific reference to nuclear war, that no nuclear weapons yet devised or presently imaginable, not even "tactical" warheads or such apparently defensive

Total war is essentially antisocial and antihuman: Its totality denies the concept of the unity of mankind. Defensive war may well be—indeed, surely is—perfectly justified[7]:

---

weapons as anti-aircraft nuclear missiles, are morally justified. The reason has not to do with their destructiveness, but with the fact that they, like almost every non-nuclear weapon deployed today by either Russia or the United States, exist and function only in virtue of a certain strategy which morally defines them. Their essential and direct role is not that of defending property or human lives, but of preserving and protecting the "nuclear deterrent." What they defend directly is not the society from harm, but our other weapons of directly aggressive design—in the jargon of modern strategy this is known as the "shield and sword concept." The shield does not shield man; it shields the sword.

As for the latter, the missile- and aircraft-delivered "nuclear swords," their immorality is fairly evident. They deter not as an impregnable fortification would, namely, by making credible to the potential enemy the efficiency of one's defense, nor even as would a steel sword, which can be used to parry—or which, even if to thrust, can be used to meet the enemy's attack. Nuclear deterrents deter only by threatening either retaliation (i.e., a revenge of unacceptable consequences to the enemy), or a first strike (i.e., a nakedly aggressive attack). Of course, aggression, and the threat of aggression or of revenge do deter. Therefore, they have an indirect, accidentally defensive value. But directly aggressive war, whether wanton, retaliatory, or preventive, has never been condoned by Christian morality. I do not see in the contemporary nuclear strategy any condition that would substantially affect the traditional view. Moreover, no other nuclear strategy has been devised, and it is difficult to see how any other could be devised. In sum, every nuclear war imaginable at present seems radically incompatible with Christian morality not only in virtue of its totality but specifically in view of its essentially aggressive nature precisely as thermonuclear.

[7] In April, 1961, Cuba engaged, in my opinion, in a perfectly legitimate, justified, defensive war. If the United States attacked Cuba today it would be perpetrating aggression upon Cuba, and in this eventuality, again, Cuba's self-defensive war against the United States would be morally justified: there would be no question of Cuba's denying to the United States the right to exist. On the other hand, Cuba would be wrong to adopt the strategy of nuclear deterrence through the threat of retaliation or first strike. In this sense, but only in this sense, I would oppose on moral grounds Cuba's

But modern war does not qualify. It may be, in other words, that the Judaeo-Christian tradition excludes not only the doctrine of peace at all costs, but also that which total war in effect proposes in its place, namely survival at all costs. Obviously, there is only one means remaining, now that defensive war has become impossible, whereby we can defend ourselves from unjust aggression. That means is to make war itself impossible. It is, then, for the sake of surviving with a clear conscience, surviving with sufficient innocence to make survival worthwhile, that we must condemn war. We may not wish to call this pacifism; what matters is not what we call it. The adoption of the goal and the directing of one's intellectual and physical effort toward it is what solicits the Christian conscience today.

Now the theory of just war rests not only on the right to self-defense. It depends, even more fundamentally, upon the principle that mere biological survival is not the supreme value of human existence. Christians have always held that there are many values to which life, limb, and possessions may have to be sacrificed. It is paradoxical that this very principle which justifies defensive war engenders the gravest and most radical condemnation of modern, total war. For if it is true that we must be ready to inflict death upon others in virtue of the principle that certain values are more precious than human life, we must also be ready to lay down our own, even at the hands of the

---

acquisition of missiles or nuclear warheads. My reason would not be that Cuba has less of a right than the United States to do so, but that neither nation has the moral right to pose that sort of threat to the other—or to anyone. I am quite unable to follow the reasoning of those who object to nuclear missiles in Cuba, but not in the United States.

unjust, rather than to let injustice take possession of us. What may be most questionable about our international policies today is the assumption that survival is the highest value to which every other value must be subordinated. We seem to think for instance that our social, political, and religious ideologies entitle us to ensure our survival and our victory irrespective of consequences—even the spiritual consequences to ourselves. It may be that the truth and nobility of our ideologies create obligations that are rather less comfortable than the doctrine of survival at all costs. It may well be that the truth of our religious faith and our political creeds requires us heroically to choose to run the risk of either enslavement or ultimate destruction rather than to commit nuclear genocide.

Catholics commonly believe that many advocates of "nuclear sanity" and of "survival," whether intentionally so or because they argue poorly, appear to subordinate higher values to mere life, that "survival" really means "survival at all costs"—instead, say the Catholics, we must stand on principle. What we do not so often realize is that the advocates of "total victory" repeat exactly the same mistake by subordinating higher values to "national security" and to "the safety of the free world." There is little difference between standing on principle, if the principle on which one stands is survival, and advocating survival, if one advocates it as a matter of principle. Perhaps we should adopt the principle that all things, including personal safety, national security, and physical freedom must be subordinated to our right action and to our human conduct. Like both the survivalists and the chauvinists one may believe that nuclear destruction must be risked, if necessary: not for the paradoxical sake of safety, but for the sake of integrity. For a much greater tragedy could befall us than to suffer nuclear destruction, whether because we were unprepared for war or because we unleashed it: It might be much worse to win a nuclear war than to lose one.

Of course, if the promotion of our security, whether individual or collective, is our supreme political principle it would be folly to envisage anything but victory. Yet, the rare irony of this wisdom is that, for all its immorality, it does not in the end ensure survival and, indeed, may well impair it somewhat. For the Russians, no less pragmatic than ourselves, reason just as we do: Many on our side even among the proponents of nuclear deterrence will grant that the greatest immediate threat to peace arises from the political symmetry between East and West. Pope Pius XII seems to have foreseen so too when shortly after the onset of the cold war he wrote: "Both parties want peace while both endanger it: on the one side by arousing distrust, on the other by promoting a security which can prepare the way for aggression. Thus both, without wishing it, compromise the cause of peace at the very time when the human race . . . shudders at the thought of a future catastrophe."[8] What is not symmetrical is the spiritual responsibility we bear if we promote such security or if we prefer physical survival, of any sort, above all.

This does not mean that the only alternative open to us is either innocently to suffer death or sinfully to inflict it. The real alternative is whether we shall drift and do nothing and keep on going exactly the way we are, and let it come to that, or whether we shall make sure that it does not come to that. The genuine alternative is not whether we shall

[8] *Christmas Message*, 1948.

neither inflict nor suffer death but, instead, whether we shall or not guiltlessly survive. The physically and morally vital issue, then, is the abolition of war. It may be that the only type of defensive war the Christian can wage today is on war itself.

THE POLITICAL VOCATION
OF CHRISTIANITY TODAY

Two questions underlie every problem raised in this study: One is philosophical, the other theological. From the point of view of Christian philosophy the question is that of the nature of human freedom. From the point of view of Christian theology it is that of the nature of the Church.

Concerning the second I will remark only this, not by way of solution, but only in order to give some precision to the question itself. The problem is whether the Church is a reality anterior to human beings: Whether the Church, for all its divinity, is integrated prior to human membership or only out of that membership. For it may well be that the Church is integrated by Christ, in virtue of His principal and gratuitous agency, but that it is integrated by Him only out of human beings—and nothing else. It is true that every society is, as it were, more than the sum of its parts. This is most especially true of the Catholic Church. But if the Church is not a reality prior to its parts, then its members make up the Church. If we are engrafted onto the vine, we are the vine: We do not make up the Church as ornaments make up a Christmas tree.

The idea that the reality of the Church is separated from

the reality of men leads to the conception of the Church as a totalitarian polity. The impersonal, inhuman Church becomes then a Leviathan to serve, a Juggernaut who requires human sacrifice. Yet, like the Sabbath, man was not made for the Church, but the Church for man, and the Universal Church for all men.

What I would comment upon rather less summarily is the other question, namely, that which concerns the Christian condition and the rational nature of human freedom. The inordinate influence of Greek philosophy on the Christian conception of man, particularly since early in the twelfth century, has been canonized in a concept of human freedom which may be more or less deficient regarding the individual human person, but which is totally so regarding society and history. We believe in human freedom, but, like the Greeks, we assume the determinism of society and of history. This is why we have not really solved the antinomies of the individual and society and of personal responsibility and historical conditioning. We know that some integration of their opposite claims must be made—our Christian instinct suffices for that—and we hobble along in practice, trying our best to do so. We have not yet managed to devise a theory to explain the nature of that integration. The suggestion made here is that both society and history, being human, are as free as the human person is, and that all three realities are free in essentially the same way. Whatever we predicate of individual freedom should be essentially predicable of both society and history.

If, despite the instinctive inclination of the Christian intellect to the contrary, we have persisted in assuming some sort of social and historical determinism, the reason, in part, is that Christian political thought has been unduly dominated by the basic form of enquiry of the *Republic* and the *Politics*. Only the content of these two sources of our political philosophies has been controverted or adopted, modified, or developed, baptized or traduced. The idea has remained generally unquestioned that the political philosopher seeks, like Plato, to define the nature of justice in order to know how the second-order reality of human actions should conform to it. Or, as in Aristotle's elaboration of this doctrine, the idea that "our purpose [in politics] is to consider what form of political community is best of all for those who are most able to realize their ideal of life."[1] However empirical it may be in execution, this procedure is essentially a priori in nature: Once one adopts it, the Kantian ethics and the Hegelian politics are only a matter of time.

Do we really seek to apply ethical principles to prospective human social and political behavior? This question can be answered in the affirmative only if we assume that there is an ideal social or political condition, determined beforehand by an agency either demiurgic or divine, to which our behavior must conform as to a plan drawn ahead of time. But unlike the Greeks we Christians need not assume the supreme regulative reality of fate. We believe that we are free—there is the source of our responsibility and the condition of our genuinely moral status: "our misfortune," when we betray our responsibility and our freedom, "is precisely that there is no scenario written by God in advance (it would be less sinister): and that the ill-omened element of the drama comes from created existents, ourselves: and from the fact that God plays fair."[2] The point is that this is as true of the individual as it is of society and of history.

If the speculative enquiry of the philosopher into practi-

---

[1] Aristotle, *Politics*, II, I (1260 b 28).
[2] Jacques Maritain, *Existence and the Existent* (New York, 1948), p. 120.

cal, human affairs has any meaning and any Christian value
the reason is that what the Christian philosopher is trying
to do is not to puzzle out as Plato and Aristotle did, the
riddle of a perversely enigmatic god's preconceived order
(whether social, political, economic, or personal) but,
rather, to work out with his intellect, creatively, arduously,
and faithfully, a plan or an order by which he can discharge,
individually, collectively, and historically, the responsibilities of the freedom in which he has been created and of the
supernatural vocation to which he has been called by God.
The Greeks needed to presuppose "ideals" because they
never doubted the bondage of fate. We believe, instead, in
human freedom, individual, collective, and historical, and
in the invitational challenge of man by God. To live by
ideals is the best that pagans can do: It is not even the least
that Christians are required to achieve.

An utopian element is apt to insinuate itself into political
philosophy even if one asks no more than what is the ideal
for this particular situation here and now. The proposition
I question is that there is an ideal, even for here and now.
When we enquire about what we should do if we are to do
the right thing, we enquire about what we have to do to
bring into existence what does not yet exist. For what is
brought into existence is a thing only after it is brought into
existence. What makes it the right one, thus, is not its
nature prior to existence, but its being brought into existence in the right way, that is, according to the requirements
of the actual situation (pre-eminently, of course, if we are
believers, the actual situation in which we find ourselves in
relation to God). The moral law is, in this concept, not a
pattern according to which we cut the pre-existing, pre-
alloted bolt of the fabric of life, but the loom and the scis-

sors, the needle and the thread, which we use to weave, design, and put together our existence. We do not put on a moral quality. We are a moral life. All this, too, should be applicable to society and history. For our actual situation—most especially so for the Christian—is a social and historical one.

If we return now to the problem of war, a great deal of conscious and unconscious determinism seems to underlie many of our attitudes. Some even assume that it is impossible to abolish war, "human nature being what it is." More commonly we argue, for instance, that the problem of war and peace in the nuclear age is not entirely of our own making and that, therefore, we are not free to choose how to pose it. The dilemma, it might be thought, is created by Russia or, at least, by communism: The arguments above even if valid, provide only self-righteous consolation in the afternoon of deathtime—all they give us is a reason to die self-satisfied, and the advocate of either holy war or nuclear quietism can do that more successfully than they can.

But problems of behavior, even on a world scale, and whether on a political, physical, metaphysical, or supernatural plane, are not the result of confronting a stimulus which is the cause of our response, nor are they posed by an other which lies beyond oneself. We should question the conventional view that our problems, international or otherwise, are formally defined by "circumstances beyond our control." When I say this I do not primarily have in mind that the contemporary world, communism, atheism and all, is entirely of our own making, for it is a world that has issued wholly out of Christendom. Nor do I wish to suggest that a problem of conduct arises out of the interaction between subject and circumstance, as if the dialectics of history were God's cruel sport with man. A problem of conduct is always an inner problem, a problem of conscience, a problem essentially circumscribed by the fact that we are trying to determine how we must behave and how we must bring into being our human existence. This is, indeed, the dignity, the practicality, the realism, and the existentialism of Christian morality: that it is grounded on the exercise and not merely the ornamental possession of human freedom. Freedom, in brief, is not a faculty: It is a way to be.

Of course, we exist in a world, we exist against circumstance, we exist with one another. The sort of being that behaves and therefore experiences the perplexities of moral alternatives, is not simply a being but an existent, a subject. Only if subjectivity were to depend upon a prior alienation from one another would problems of conduct be posed for us by another, or arise out of the interaction of each self with others. Above all, in what pertains to the spiritual plane we must follow through upon our persuasion that God does play fair, not only with each one of us individually, but with man collectively, and with the generations from father to son—for if He were not fair to society and to history He would not be fair to any man, and on judgment day we could accuse Him of having set the trap of fate for mankind to fall into at the end of the pointless, stupid tragedy of life. For man is essentially both social and historical: It was God who disposed it that way.

It is good that we remember the fallen nature of man—fallen and redeemed. But have we become so insensibly won over to the idea of the "state of nature" that we make man essentially asocial, and society a convenient if exasperating, unfair, indispensable device? For the moral quandaries of society—the problem of war, for instance, or of the political organization of the world as a whole—would be either insoluble, or soluble by means of a restriction of human freedom, only if man were essentially asocial, and the common good of man only a mirage.

If a morally good social life and a peaceful world are possible to free agents the reason is that their problems of conduct arise out of their consciousness and subjectivity rather than out of their struggle with society and with their kind. There lies the radical freedom of man. We are truly responsible for our conduct, and no one else, no other man, no other group, no other time, can as such do away with our moral freedom. Only we ourselves can. The political order, thus, must be grounded on the social and historical freedom of man.

To illustrate the role of autonomy in international politics I will recast very schematically David Riesman's typology to fit the history of international relations. It might be said that the foreign policy making of the classical world was tradition-directed. It was largely unreflective, non-calculating, primitive, non-Machiavellian and ordered toward the preservation of traditional values and the avoidance of disruptive change. The idea of progress had yet to make its weight felt. This was the heroic and epic moment of war, which continued beyond the dissolution of Greece and Rome into the earlier stages of the Christian world. In Western civilization, however, national—or rather, tribal—relations gradually became inner-directed, that is, oriented toward the achievement of national needs. We had progressed to nation from city and tribe. Machiavellism was the climax of this process, and it resulted in the emergence of a fragmented Europe in which, paradoxically, as principalities coalesced into nations, the feudal bonds expanded into wider loyalties to an impersonal fatherland while nations, more radically than ever before, became mutually alienated by the concept of national sovereignty. We had gone from nation to national state. This was the strategic, dramatic moment of war. With increasing rapidity this stage had to give way to an other-directed type of international relations, that is, directed toward the achievement of a *modus vivendi* with the complex interests and many parties that Machiavellism itself, no less than the accumulation of knowledge, had brought about.

It was then that the world began to become too small for a race with such an ill-bred history as ours, and the problem of having to reorient the course of history began to emerge. Instead we produced high diplomacy. War, in the well-known maxim of von Clausewitz, was simply the extention of diplomacy by extraordinary means—conversely, the modern standards of conduct of international diplomacy are but the less violent form of modern war. Thus arrived the tragic, baroque moment of war. We would be wrong to think it had not passed away long ago, or that from a world of national states we had not begun to become a world of one race. For "balance of power" is no longer possible in a world in which "capability" is enough and "superiority" is superfluous. If one nation alone can, in principle, strike at any alliance, no effective *modus vivendi* can be achieved by any realignment of powers. Thus, the accelerated political polarization of the world is not the cause of but, rather, a symptom of the obsolescence of balance-of-power techniques and of other-direction in the formulation of international policies. Perhaps we need to guide ourselves in the solution of international problems by *autonomy*, otherwise we shall bring about the irrational, suicidal moment of war.

Since David Riesman's categories are sociological, they would fit equally well the historical development of the Christian Church, but it would be unwarranted to continue the simile beyond this point. Spiritually as well as politically, we cannot any longer avoid ruling ourselves except reasonably, humanistically, and autonomously.

We hesitate to do so because we harbor fears: The prospect of freedom produces the experience of dread. What Kierkegaard has shown in relation to the freedom of the Christian faith is as true of the political autonomy of a society: There is no way of forecasting to what extent the adoption of autonomous political governance would incidentally secure safety. It is certain that it would not secure the feeling of safety: As in every other respect, freedom of autonomy in international relations, quite as much as in the Christian's *con-fidencial* relation with God, must be paid for in the coin of anxiety, insecurity and unpredictability—yet not with any tax on happiness, exultation, serenity, or joy.

If the West adopted the course of autonomy now it would choose heroically—as heroically as the mystic chooses just before the dawn of the dark night of the soul. The Church, too, in its collectivity has a mystic vocation, and there is no reason to think that the Holy People of God might not be required now and then to be heroic. History has inexorably and perhaps providentially brought the whole world to a juncture where it is faced with a challenge to which Christian citizens, as citizens and as Christians, must respond with a radical resolve to pursue and purify social and political justice, domestically and internationally, ecclesiastically and secularly, spiritually and temporally, irrespective of consequence.

Moreover, to seek justice à outrance, passionately and

"foolishly," as the very purpose of civil society and without any of the wisdom of the worldly wise, may well be not only reasonable but also prudent and safe. For though we are called to no less arduous and grandiose a task than the reorientation of human history, one may suspect that, considering our history, to reorient its course may be an eminently sane thing to do. It may, indeed, be the only source of long-range safety for our world. If so, one cannot at this point do less than to hint once again how that fraternity of persons professionally committed to a universal faith could easily be one of the most powerful agencies in such a reorientation of political history and one of the major forces in fashioning the civilization of a world that is already emerging as catholic in nature. To attempt less than this would be to fall short of the intrinsic requirements of the world situation in which we find ourselves today.

The conditions that have made international justice indispensable to the continuation of human life demand a somewhat broader conception of the right order among human beings than was possible at a time when, for instance, international justice and some type of war were not altogether incompatible. If today there cannot be just wars it is because the conditions in which we live demand the full recognition of the unity of the human family. Justice today cannot obtain among nations unless it takes place within the unity of the human race; the concept of political justice itself must be recast in order to mean not an approximation to an ideal reality, but the concretization of human fraternity.

Henceforth we can only be guided in international politics by the widest loyalty to the whole of mankind. We have become one world. What we need to do for our own good, collectively and severally, is to recognize this truth and to act upon it. This is the political vocation of the Christian citizen in our time.

That brings us finally face to face with the crucial problem of a Christian political philosophy: the basis of the relation of Church and State—or more precisely, of Church and World. Christian thought and practice have alternated between identifying and separating Church and world and, loosely speaking, the best compromise that we have developed to date is that of distinguishing between them without either separating or uniting. This solution may improve upon the solutions worked out by the medieval and by the modern periods of history, but in common with them it assumes a doctrine of the basic relation of the Church to cultural manifestations—of which political society is but one instance. Should this basic relation be one of association, whether by marriage, by intussusception, by friendship, or by mortal combat? Caesaropapism shares a common foundation with theocracy—their dispute rages upon a flat battleground. But grace and nature, whether individually or collectively, as in Church and State, do not share a common level of metaphysical reality along which they can interact and react, struggle inimically or harmoniously co-operate. It may be that the Christian faith's basic relation to cultural forms, without some determinate set of which it cannot possibly exist, is found in its role as transformer and redeemer of such forms.

The fact that this collective Christian faith, which is the Church, cannot exist without cultural forms, any more than the individual person's faith could exist without humanity, does not mean that such forms are acquired only by means of that process which anthropologists call acculturation. In the history of Christianity certain cultural forms previously extant and established, namely, the Greek and Roman,[3] were appropriated and transformed by acculturation. By adopting them, hallowing and baptizing them, Christianity acquired a Hellenic complex. But now it has wrung them dry: In virtue of its very success in developing and transforming these cultural forms they have become inadequate for the continued life and development of the Christian faith.[4] The Christian crisis of this age, thus, is definable in terms of the inadequacies of the Hellenic complex.

Moreover, there would be little point, even if it were possible, in turning to other extant cultural forms. The time has come, therefore, for Christianity to create its own cultural forms. No doubt, this creation, required by the development of our history, demands by its very nature continuity with tradition: There is no material out of which to create the Christian cultural forms of the future except our

[3] In all basic respects, particularly those of ideology, these forms can be reduced to the Greek. Let us, therefore, say Hellenic.

[4] John XXIII's opening address to the Second Vatican Council proposed that "the Church should never depart from the sacred patrimony of truth received from the Fathers; but at the same time she must ever look to the present, to new conditions and new forms of life introduced into the modern world, which have opened new avenues to the Catholic apostolate . . . Our duty is not only to guard this precious treasure, as if we were concerned only with antiquity, but to dedicate ourselves with an earnest will and *without fear* to that work which our era demands of us . . . One thing is the substance of the ancient doctrine of the *depositum fidei*, and another is the way in which it is presented . . ." [italics mine]. The question may be controverted whether this means no more than the use of new words, and nothing but new words, to recast the same truth, or whether it also means the recasting of the same truth in new cultural forms of which new words are only a secondary and perhaps even trivial aspect.

past and our history. But the continuity of this creative process with the past should not in the slightest detract from its being a process or from its being creative.

Perhaps, then there are good reasons and legitimate bases for Christianity's participation in the public life of the city. If so, then it may be possible to suggest that it is not only insofar as the Christian citizen is an individual Christian and an individual citizen that the thermonuclear age offers him a political vocation. It may be that to make peace, to work toward the making of an unprecedented world without war and, thus, to begin to create a united, catholic world under the sponsorship of the Catholic faith, is the political vocation offered by history to collective *ecclesiastical* Christianity in our time.

Finally, in this connection, an immediately practical remark.

I have tried to show in my account of the Cuban revolution that though it is as unnecessary as it is impossible to try to allot the guilt among the parties responsible for the Cuban tragedy, it may be important to understand the various roles played by the different protagonists. In a sense, as we have seen, it could be said that the decisive role may have been played by the Catholic Church. But within the whole Cuban Church it seems to me that the most decisive role, at least in what pertains to lack of initiative, was played by Catholic laymen. And within the laity it was the Catholic intellectuals that failed most completely of all.

We have seen that there were exceptions. But these intellectuals were just that, exceptions—and they, too, capitulated in the end. They began their work too late, in January 1, 1959, they gave up too soon, on August 7, 1960, and they gave up once for all. I know of not a single Cuban

Catholic layman today who has any proposal or hope that
does not hinge upon the improbable return of Cuba to
some, ill-defined, stage of the past. If the future of the
Cuban Church depended upon them the Cuban Church
would be doomed.

Although Cuban Catholic intellectuals are, on the whole,
quite liberal, a streak of authoritarianism was not altogether
absent from them, and this was enough to compromise
their advisory role to the Cuban hierarchy. Despite what I
judge to have been the exceedingly good dispositions and
receptivity of the Cuban bishops toward them, in the end
it was the suspicions of the hierarchy that stilled the argumentation of the intellectuals and not the other way about.
I do not refer to the fact that the laymen were ready to submit to the hierarchy's decision regardless of their own
opinions on the matter. I refer to the possibility that in
their very advisory capacity they may have allowed themselves to be convinced by the authority of the hierarchy
rather than by the lucidity of their own logic. If so, however understandably in view of the majoritarian pressures,
they failed to discharge the obligations which, precisely as
intellectuals, they owed to their bishops. Though as faithful
they were required to obey the bishops' commands, as advisors they ought not eventually or at any time to have said
to the episcopate what the episcopate wanted to hear, but
only what they themselves, and they alone, thought was
correct.

Now, I have tried to show that the world problem of the
Universal Church is not essentially different from that of
the Cuban Church, except that it is considerably more
complex. It involves the whole temporal order, not only or
even primarily (though perhaps most urgently) the polit-

ical. It is not only the things that are Caesar's that need the revaluation that only Christian respect for them can provide: It is the whole range of the things of nature and the things of man that must be revalued by the Christian's veneration and love of them. Christianity cannot hate the world or contemn the times. We already believe that, but our fears and our delusions of persecution prevent us from following through even in our own minds.

The Christian layman and most especially the lay intellectual is confronted with essentially the same temptation to which the Cubans succumbed. It often seems as if those who belong in these categories cannot do without excessive encouragement and reassurance or without unqualified agreement. How often does the layman think of undertaking a project or of offering a reflection or a proposal for general consideration, without first having asked the bishop's encouragement, endorsement, and support? It is one thing to consult the hierarchy and to be disposed to obey the ordinary. It is another thing to condition Catholic action and thought upon the exclusive initiative and the necessary encouragement and impulse of the pastors of the Church. The bishop should be allowed the last word, but he cannot be reasonably expected always to utter the first—or to be the first to recognize a good idea when he sees one. It may be that the hierarchy's first function is not to inspire, to lead, to take the initiative, but to oversee. If the overseers do more, they do what one might wish. But their unilateral responsibility does not absolve the faithful from its own.

Without in the least detracting from the fact that the first responsibility for initiative and leadership devolves upon the pastorate, the responsibility of the laity under contemporary conditions is, in a sense, rather greater than anyone else's—

and this applies with particular force to lay intellectuals. The onus of the reformation or, rather, self-realization, of the Catholic Church is very predominantly upon them. As for encouragement, the Second Vatican Council has already offered all the leadership and encouragement that one might desire at this point in history. For this reason it is difficult to sympathize with those Catholics who complain about reactionary bishops. Such complaints may be more justified among the clergy though perhaps even they might ask themselves whether their fears are not sometimes exaggerated and, above all, a little premature. Some of them do not wait to be censured before they desist. Though there may be bishops so conservative as actually to stifle initiative, one doubts if any of them would actually persecute Christian responsibility. Rarely does one hear of a bishop in North America who lacks respect for the fundamental freedom of thought and enquiry of the Catholic intellect. On the other hand, one frequently meets Catholics whose effectiveness is hampered by a superstition to the contrary effect. Freedom of Catholic thought and expression is not in danger today from flaming faggots on the town square, but from dry rot in university halls.

It would be self-contradictory in a Catholic Church, which precisely as Catholic and as Church is the depositary of the Christian faith, if the burden for the realization of the mission of the Church to anoint, to consecrate the world in actual existence and not merely in vows, did not fall upon all the faithful. Yet, we tend to think of the Church in the third person, as they or as she. Well, the Church is never they. And the metaphoric motherhood of the Church refers only to the reality that she is the carrier and reproducer of supernatural life, the bearer of faith: she is by her collectivity and society the nurse of our belief. But the ontological reality is that it is not something or someone else: We are the Church.

Christian intellectuals, however, have a special responsibility in regard to that mission, since the self-realization of Christianity can be brought about only through self-consciousness and this in turn is a matter of reflection, of knowledge, of taking thought. We do not need so much new exhortations to practice justice as we do, for instance, a more accurate, more extensive, more intelligent, more faithful, and truer appreciation of the history of the Church by the generality of Christians. What is the point of knowing the catechism's definition of faith if we do not suspect either faith's historical or its social dimension? We do not need so much an exclusive conviction that grace is caused by a sensible efficacious sign as we need to realize more fully that the sacraments have an essentially worshipful, liturgical function—or as we need, even more basically, imaginative studies of the relations of nature and grace in which it is not taken for granted that nature must be understood by the Christian as the *phusis* of the Greeks.

It is easy to forego these things, or to make them less effective or less public, if we rationalize inactivity or reduced effectiveness with the excuse that a bishop might not approve. No doubt, on judgment day we shall be judged, faithful and pastor alike, on whether we discharged all our responsibilities, including that of obedience. It is doubtful whether a bishop may be excused because he thought it safer to forbid all thinking in order to ensure the non-existence of error. Nor is the layman likely to be excused on the grounds that, having abdicated his freedom, conscience, and responsibility, he ought to be rewarded for having done nothing at all. It is surely not for nothing that talent has come to mean principally intellectual endowment. Catholic intellectuals who are not ready to make their talent fructify can always choose any equally noble, but less arduous, less responsible, way of Christian life.

THE THEOLOGY OF COUNTERREVOLUTION

The Catholic Church in Cuba did not develop its counterrevolutionary conscience over a few months nor exclusively by heeding its bishops, especially since the later's pronouncements lagged behind the common Catholic opinion and thus served rather to confirm and justify than to lead and inform. Nevertheless, theirs was the official stand of the Church. Therefore, it may be important to determine exactly what they taught; to approve or disapprove their posture is ultimately to agree or disagree with their theological stand.

Msgr. Pérez Serantes' pastoral of May, 1960, was more important for its being the first, and for the dispositions it communicated rather than for its specific teaching, which was scant. It is worth noting that it took issue with Cuba's establishment of diplomatic relations with Russia, because only three months later, in the collective letter of August 7, more important issues having since come up the bishops tried to make light of the question of mere diplomatic relations. The bulk of the letter is devoted to a summary explanation of the doctrine of *Divini Redemptoris*, listing and describing the evils of communism. The letter does not say that, in point of fact, those evils were accruing to Cuba:

It is difficult to judge from the wording of the document whether it was meant as a warning or as an insinuation.

What is unequivocal in the letter is Msgr. Pérez' teaching concerning the predominant feeling and attitude that the Catholic must have regarding communism, namely, fear, suspicion, and the uncompromising disposition to extirpate it: For example, Catholics, the letter says, must not "be misled by the cunning communism displays in extending the hand that with such cleverness knows how to toast Catholics, because all of this is actually nothing more than a well-planned strategy for the achievement of an easy conquest over the unwary."[1] Msgr. Pérez also teaches that whoever thinks otherwise is either foolish or guilty: "It is easy to discover communism everywhere and in all places, either standing erect or cowering. Nevertheless, even among our own there are some who—heedless, innocent[2] or extremely cautious—persist in denying it and even resent that not everyone thinks as they do."

Msgr. Pérez distinguishes between communism and communists, and charity must be the only rule regarding the latter. But, as he explained, "there cannot be on our part consessions[sic] in matters of principle," implying, as one may suppose, that in other matters accommodation was possible. On the other hand, since the very existence of communism in Cuba was, obviously, not a matter on which accommodation was possible, it is difficult to see what sort of concessions he may have had in mind.[3] Msgr. Pérez

[1] Text in translation reproduced in Catholic Mind, LXI, 1153 (January–February, 1961). The quotations following refer to the same source.

[2] This seems to be a mistranslation of inocente, i.e., naïve.

[3] According to what seems to be the teaching of John XXIII material co-operation with communists is permissible. Indeed, the Pope

recommends, among other spiritual measures to be adopted by Catholics to combat communism, a more assiduous study of the catechism in every Catholic home.

In contrast, the collective pastoral of August 7 was briefer and milder in tone, but its importance, since it had been subscribed to by all Cuban bishops, was much greater. The document's style is quite removed from that of Msgr. Pérez' and its argumentation is subtle and well thought out. The starting point is simple: the Cuban hierarchy chose this moment to give its approval to the social program of the revolution:

A more equitable distribution of wealth has always been and continues to be an essential point of the Catholic social doctrine. Hence the Church always accepts with the greatest sympathy whatever measures may contribute to raising the standard of living of the humble; and this is what the Church has done lately in this country, as has been shown in the statements that several among the undersigned bishops have repeatedly issued.

Indeed, it was the occasion of great satisfaction for the Church when, more than a year ago, it was stated that agrarian reform was being planned . . . She heard with hopeful delight vast industrialization plans bruited about . . . She saw with pleasure that there were persons in power concerned with the adoption of measures [favoring] . . . the needier classes; and she rejoiced when schools and hospitals multiplied . . . She approvingly looked upon the building . . . of low-cost housing; and she noted with patriotic joy that an energetic effort was made to render the public administration honest, to eradicate the vice of gambling, and to eliminate [discrimination against] many of our brethren by reason of the color of their skin.

Those social reforms which, while respecting the legitimate

---

has urged co-operation in space exploration and research between the United States and Russia. See G&M, December 24, 1962. The reconciliation of co-operation with communists with earlier prohibitions has been studied by Marcello Gentili, "Condizioni del dialogo fra Cattolici e Marxisti," Nuova Presenza, V, 5 (Primavera, 1962), pp. 57–73.

rights of all citizens, tend to better the economic, cultural and social condition of the lowly, thus, have today and always shall have the most decided moral support of the Church.[4]

A predictable adversative proposition was immediately to follow. Before we consider it let us observe that the bishops found it possible to juxtapose without comment or explanation what the Church always does and what the Cuban hierarchy had done "lately." Had they been able to say, "and that is what the Church has always done in this country," it would not have been extraordinary if they had tried to cover themselves with the moral authority of the Universal Church. Since they had to admit otherwise, it would have been wiser to do so forthrightly. The rhetoric they chose to follow robbed whatever truth and cogency their subsequent remarks may have had of much of their credibility. This was not at all what Angel del Cerro had recommended concerning the recognition of past mistakes: This was glossing them over very lightly. It could be seen in no other way than as an attempt to put on a mantle of moral ascendancy which, by their own grudging admission, they were not entitled to wear. It did not occur to them, it seems, that only absolute candor, sincerity, and humility would have restored their moral authority in the eyes of the Cuban people and the government.

Equally sophistic was the bishops' attempt to argue that

[4] The English translations published in the United States departed from the original at several points. *Catholic Mind*, LIX, 1155 (May–June, 1961), rendered part of the foregoing as follows: "and thus she has done recently in our country, as has been seen in the declarations her bishops have issued over and over again." This bald statement would not have gone unchallenged in Cuba, where everyone knew the exact extent of the hierarchy's acceptance of Castro's social measures: that is why in the original the expression is left vague. My translation is from the Spanish text of the actual leaflets distributed in Cuban churches at the time.

they were entitled to voice their criticism of the government with moral authority because some of them had previously voiced their recognition of the government's accomplishment. We should remember that the government had needed their support; that every one of the accomplishments they now praised had been used at home and abroad in order to tax the government with the charge of communism; that land reform had been the origin of the dispute with the United States; that the social measures they praised had been the result of "the excess of state control in economic and social life" which Msgr. Boza had written against. The government had direly needed the backing of the bishops and it received very little of it—much too late and only from a few. To use that small base now as if it were a pedestal was to appear obviously insincere. In sum, their case might have been stronger had they not tried to begin their indictment with a however: The hollowness of their foundation revealed only a conscience uneasy, but not quite contrite.

"However," they continued, "we would be remiss in our duty to speak the truth to our faithful and to the people of Cuba in general if . . . we did not also let them know . . . our principal preoccupations and fears. We could point to certain respects in which the social measures previously mentioned have not been executed with all the respect due to the rights of all the citizens . . . but we believe it would be better to restrict ourselves to a problem of extraordinary gravity . . . and that is the growing advance of Communism in our Fatherland." The apophasis was unfortunate: It adhered to the strictest truth: but this was probably not the best time to remind the government that justice applies equally to the rich and to the poor.

Communism, in the bishops' own words, was their pre-occupation and their fear:

> In the last few months the Cuban Government has established close commercial, cultural and diplomatic relations with the governments of the principal Communist countries and, particularly, with the Soviet Union. We would have nothing to say[5] from the pastoral point of view concerning the strictly commercial or economic aspects of these *rapprochements*, but we are profoundly disturbed by the fact that, therefore, there have been newspapermen, government officials, labor leaders and even some high Government figures who have repeatedly and warmly praised the ways of life that prevail in those nations, and have even suggested . . . the existence of coincidences and analogies, in objectives and procedures, between the social revolutions of those countries and the Cuban revolution.

Once again, ambiguity was introduced into the statement as to whether the bishops did or did not object to commercial, cultural, and diplomatic relations with Russia. Perhaps they felt that they could not flatly contradict Msgr. Pérez, who only three months earlier had strongly objected to them. Perhaps they also felt, at the same time, that they could not very well build a case upon such relations when every other Western country maintained them, including, of course, the United States. As for America, the complete absence of reference to it after all the events of the previous months could not appear to anyone except as a studied omission. The Cuban problem, in fact, was not definable exclusively in terms of Russia and communism.

Of course, it was undeniable that there were "coinci-

---

[5] The original reads: "*nada tendríamos que decir.*" *Catholic Mind* rendered this in the indicative mood: "we have nothing to say," which made it sound more reasonable. The mistranslation was encouraged by the fact that the condition upon which the hypothetical mood of the original Spanish was supposed to rest is never stated or otherwise made clear in the letter.

dences and analogies" between the Cuban and communist revolutions. But there were also differences and divergences which may have deserved some attention. The hierarchy, evidently, thought otherwise.

Thus, it may be an important question whether or not the exclusiveness of the bishops' concern with the danger of communism was made possible only by abstracting from the reality and gravity of real and grave problems which at that very time threatened the viability of the revolution. This was an abstraction which the government, charged as it was with the welfare of its citizens, could not possibly have made without a radical betrayal of itself. The hierarchy did not explain or suggest either in this pastoral or elsewhere how the social reforms—of which it said it approved in principle—could be translated into action under the regnant conditions, principally opposition by the United States, without some sort of backing from "the Communist countries and, particularly, the Soviet Union." Could one have reformed Cuba and pleased the United States at the same time? If this was possible no one suggested concretely how.

"Let no one think, therefore," the pastoral concluded, "that he may come and ask Catholics, on behalf of a poorly understood civic unity, that we still our opposition to such doctrines, because we could not agree to it without betraying our most fundamental principles. The absolute majority of the Cuban people, who are Catholic, is against atheistic and materialistic Communism, and they could be led towards a Communist regime only through deceit or coercion." Here, again the question of lasting significance for the Universal Church is not whether the Cuban bishops' appeal to a democratic majority rule was any more credible than was their assertion that the people of Cuba were in their absolute majority Catholic. Nor is it whether the bishops, intentionally or not, failed to discriminate between a request that they still their opposition, which was never made, and a request that their opposition be not unconditional. The question of deeper Christian import is whether the stilling of one's unconditional opposition to the doctrines of communism is a betrayal of fundamental Christian principles. No doubt, under certain conditions it is clearly such a betrayal. It is not self-evident, however, that it is so under all conditions, nor, specifically, under the conditions that obtained in Cuba at the time.

It has been stated above that neither diplomacy nor the understanding of human relations was the Cuban bishops' forte. This was especially true of Msgr. Pérez, particularly on the occasion of his second pastoral letter of early October.[6] Its object was to deal with the charge of disloyalty predictably preferred against the hierarchy in reaction to their pastoral of August 7. Msgr. Pérez complained that:

Today [in Cuba] he is considered . . . a traitor who allows himself the luxury of combatting or of openly making known his opposition to marxist directives, indoctrination and methods. This reaches such an extreme that, according to some, only Communists and their adherents have the right to dictate the line of conduct binding upon all.

We know that a traitor is he who breaks his bonds of fidelity and loyalty. By delivering his Master, Judas became a traitor, and he remains the prototype of treason.

This being established, who would dare with a semblance of reasonableness to label as a traitor to his fatherland him who

[6] The pastoral was dated September 24, 1960, but it was not read and distributed immediately. It had reached most congregations toward the second week in October. It was printed in *Ecclesia* on October 13. The version used here is my translation from *Fidel Castro Parle*, pp. 167–71.

detests atheistic and materialist Communism, him who remaining faithful to his conscience and to his sworn faith does not kneel and even refuses to bow in front of the pseudo-redeemers of the people, him who, in brief, is not disposed to trade Rome for Moscow?

Who could arrogate to himself the right to affirm that he is a traitor to his Fatherland to whom all that can be reproached is to have loved it with his whole soul, to have dared to say that his convictions are not at all points the same as those of the enemies of God, the enemies of freedom and of human rights, the communists and their accomplices?

As a defense, however, this argument was not very effective. Castro had not called the bishops traitors on the grounds that they loved Cuba with their whole souls; they were entitled, of course, to protest that they did so love her. And Castro's accusation of disloyalty was not grounded on the fact that the Cuban bishops held or voiced convictions that were "not at all points the same as those of . . . the Communists" but, rather, on the bishops' demand that the government shape its foreign and domestic policies in accordance with those convictions and, even more, in their opposing the government for not acceding to the demand even at the cost of foreign and domestic failure. That was the real charge: It could not be ignored forever.

To deal with it Msgr. Pérez had to devise a more sophisticated defense than he had put up in this document—at this point he simply began to establish its foundations. If the betrayal of Christ by Judas is the prototype of political treason, the accusation leveled at the Cuban bishops could be true only if they were heterodox. He who detests atheism, who keeps the Christian faith, etc., and who, in brief, does not "trade Rome for Moscow" cannot be a traitor to his country. "Can those citizens be called traitors to their Fatherland who remain faithful and loyal to the state or to

legitimately established institutions?" The answer, by definition, is no. The Christian's civic and political obligations
are determined by loyalty to Rome.

Having, therefore, not merely identified Russia and
communism with anti-Christianity, but also any collaboration with them as a betrayal of Christianity, Msgr. Pérez
had but one step to take in order to round out his doctrine
—and he now proceeded to take it. "We are not ashamed
to affirm—indeed, it would seem to us cowardly not to do
so—that between the Americans and the Russians we
would choose without the slightest hesitation." It was no
longer, therefore, merely a question of refusing to choose
the Russian side. Since not choosing the American side was
to be construed as the equivalent of choosing the Russian
side, the Christian's disposition, if not his act, must be to
choose the American side.[7] And to choose the American
side even against one's own country is not treason, for
treason is essentially disloyalty to God. Thus, the counterrevolution was both patriotic and pleasing to God.

[7] The difference between the negative stand, opposing Cuba's
policy toward Russia, and the "positive" conclusion, namely, opposing Cuba's policy toward the United States, is not very important:
the bishops never meant by the first to exclude the second, and they
never meant the second except as a function of the first. The difference served only to make the hierarchy's opposition to Castro all
the more clear cut and determined. Ramón Casas has told me of
having been present at several "bishops' conferences in which it was
always insisted upon the need to avoid associating names of countries or personalities or establishing comparisons between the United
States and Russia." It is true that only two bishops, Msgr. Pérez
Serantes and Boza Masvidal, ever made these comparisons in official
documents. This simply shows that these two were willing to follow
their premises in public through to their logical conclusion. I fail to
see what merit there would have been in not making the comparisons explicit. The condemnation of August 7 clearly implies the alleged need for Cuban Catholics to choose between Moscow and
Washington.

So far the Cuban hierarchy's case against the Cuban government had been cast, strictly speaking, only in "preoccupations and fears." The earlier direct accusations of Msgr. Pérez Serantes had been patently emotional. The hierarchy needed, in effect, a White Paper on its policy. This is what Msgr. Boza set out to provide in an article that appeared in *La Quincena's* issue of October 30, 1960, and which addressed itself directly to the question: "Is the social revolution at present being effected in Cuba a Christian one?"[8] His conclusion would be that since the revolution was demonstrably Marxist in nature it was therefore not compatible with Christianity.

Msgr. Boza first lists many things which, at least in the abstract, are compatible with Christianty: "Is it Christian to seek the betterment of the lot of the little people? Yes, it is Christian. Is it Christian to eliminate racial discrimination . . . to promote a just distribution of the wealth . . . to seek that the advantages of education and culture may benefit all and that they be not the privilege of the rich . . . [etc]? Yes, it is Christian. All this is Christian on condition that it be founded upon a Christian conception of life and applied, as it can be done, through just means and without prejudice to any legitimate interest." Thus, even more prominently than the August collective pastoral, Msgr. Boza's article takes a stand on the principle of justice for all, even the rich. And yet, it is certain that Msgr. Boza did not take such a stand by reason of any baser motive than an inflexible devotion to the idea of justice. The imputations of confederacy with either American imperialism or Cuban plutocracy are simply false in what pertains to motivation.

[8] The version used here is my translation from *Fidel Castro Parle*, pp. 171–4.

Only a community of interest and material objectives made it appear so. What moved Msgr. Boza was simply the fact that justice does apply equally to poor and rich alike. What apparently did not occur to him is that unlike Plato's *Republic*, in which the idea of justice impartially rules human existents in virtue of its logical necessities, in the Christian society the actual reality of social justice is sufficiently existential to confuse the logician: It is not the same thing to affirm that a just social order should obtain provided it does not transgress the legitimate interests of the rich, and to affirm that a just social order must obtain, though due care ought to be exercised not to fall into the same excesses that once had been committed by the rich. Msgr. Boza's Christian sense of justice prompts him to affirm the first; his sense of justice is sufficiently Hellenic to enable him to affirm the first instead of the second.

It was only when the question was whether the revolution showed its Marxist ideology by promoting class struggle that Msgr. Boza thought to distinguish between the injustice committed by the rich against the poor and that committed by the poor against the rich—though even then he did not unambiguously state whether in fact the Cuban rich had been unjust to the Cuban poor or whether this was only a pretext conveniently adduced by the government to justify its policies. Finding fault with the revolution for not "basing itself upon the love of neighbor [but] upon hatred and the class struggle," Msgr. Boza explained: "to oppose the poor to the rich under the pretext that at one time the rich abused the poor is not to act according to justice: it is to carry injustice to the opposite extreme." It is difficult to interpret Msgr. Boza's insistence on justice for all only at this juncture of Cuban history except as meaning that the exploitation of the poor by the rich may be unjust, but is not dangerous to the faith, whereas the exploitation of the rich by the poor is not only unjust, but also of the essence of revolutionary socialism.

In any case, Msgr. Boza's main concern was not so much to explain what sort of revolution he would have favored as it was to examine precisely "what was wanting in this social revolution . . . if it should not be opposed to Christian principles." He lists these defects *seriatim*. They are six.

"In the first place," he charged, the revolution "does not have a spiritualist conception of life. It began by deleting every mention of God in the Constitution,[9] in which no others are considered important but material necessities and our earthly life." The implication is apparently that it pertains to the state as such to help provide the necessities of our supernatural life. This is, of course, a tenable position within Catholic orthodoxy: it may be redundant to explain that it is neither the only tenable nor necessarily the correct one.

The second point has been mentioned already: The Cuban revolution encouraged class struggle (of this charge it was obviously guilty), whereas "Christian charity embraces one's neighbor wholly, even one's enemies." Even more correct was Msgr. Boza's indictment on the next score: "this social revolution is wanting in recognition of the dignity of the human person and the freedom of the children of God, who has given every man the right to think, write, act and to try his initiative without any other limitation than the respect of the moral law and the liberty of another." But

[9] This would refer, I take it, to the *Ley Fundamental*, the only constitution for the framing of which the revolution (though not Castro personally) was responsible. It is inexact that the name of God was deleted; it had never been inserted.

the paradox is that for all the revolution's demagogy and intolerance, up to the moment when these words were written liberty of thought, political action, and expression had not been curtailed by the government—whereas the hierarchy's and other Catholics' complaint had been from the beginning that such rights should be denied to the communists. And Msgr. Boza's words appeared in a journal whose freedom he himself had suppressed.

Msgr. Boza continued: "the individual has become a mere cog in the machinery of the state. One is subjected to a threatening and constant psychological pressure to impose upon one a uniform way of thinking and action, without the possibility of resisting, or failing to conform, given the total control of the means of expression and the sanctions which threaten him who had the audacity to make his opposition known." We have seen that by this time Castro had shown considerable and ever increasing intolerance, that the revolution as a whole had become similarly intolerant, and that the Cuban people almost universally were extremely intolerant of each other on all sides and at all levels. But it is difficult to find any reason why in this respect any exception should be made of Cuban Catholics or the Cuban hierarchy or of Msgr. Boza in particular. In this respect, too, as it once had been in the field of battle, the contribution of the Catholic segment of the society to the revolutionary process was out of all proportion to its meager size.

In the fourth place, according to Msgr. Boza, "this social revolution does not respect the natural right of property." We have seen above the sense in which this charge too was basically correct regarding the administration of land reforms. Msgr. Boza, on the other hand, seemed to express himself as if in the Christian faith the right to property were generally thought to be absolute rather than relative to a stewardship. At any rate, Msgr. Boza's fifth point was that "this revolution is wanting in respect for the reputation and good name of others." Again, the truth of the bare statement cannot be denied. And Msgr. Boza continued with a laudable sentiment: "in a discussion it is not one's adversary, but his arguments, that should be destroyed." On the other hand, the revolution, and Castro personally, were also entitled to their good reputation and their good name. What might not have been the effect upon the course of history if only a few months earlier, in January, February, March, and April, 1960, the Cuban Church had spoken collectively and stated precisely, accurately, truthfully, minutely, and extensively, what was and was not true about the allegations that were being freely made at all levels and from all quarters by the United States?

Msgr. Boza, moreover, did not apparently feel that to argue to guilt by association was an analogously unfair procedure, for in the very next sentence he declared: "systematically to discredit one's enemy, publicly to trample under foot his reputation, to overwhelm him with insult and infamy, well-founded or not, all this puts in relief typically Communist methods and is wholly contrary to the teaching of the Gospel." Msgr. Boza seemed to take for granted that the revolution was incapable of committing its own sins.

Finally, Msgr. Boza reached his last point: "the United States and the Western nations are systematically attacked,[10] while a friendship too intimate to be fortuitous is secured with the Soviet Union and the socialist countries."

[10] It is unnecessary to confirm that this was true when the United States was involved. For other Western nations, however, the statement was incorrect.

Msgr. Boza then granted, for the first time, that "it is normal to have commercial and diplomatic relations with all countries, but an intimate friendship such as is manifested by continuous voyages and by an ever closer mutual understanding and collaboration cannot exist except between countries that share the same way of thinking and which experience the same aspirations."

And, thus, the conclusion was reached: "I may possibly have omitted to point out numerous facts, but those which I have shown are enough to prove that the characteristics of our social revolution are quite evidently Marxist." By his own words, Msgr. Boza chose to rest his case upon the foregoing evidence. His peroration closed the article:

> A few days ago I read in *Revolución* an article in which the Christian social doctrine was criticized on the grounds that it formulates beautiful theories which are never put into practice. However, this does not depend upon the Church. The role of the Church is to teach those doctrines, as she has done and as she continues to do, albeit every day with fewer means at her disposal. But the Church does not have the power to apply that doctrine. It pertains to the government to put them into practice if it so desires. Let it be so done and it will immediately enjoy the support of all Catholics.

It matters little that a few months earlier only the most decided opposition of most Catholics had met the revolution's social reforms and that, therefore, Msgr. Boza's reassurance was as empty as the hope of Castro's return at this date to his earlier "humanism" would have been vain. From the point of view of the Universal Church it may be more important to note that Msgr. Boza's doctrine directly implies the identification of the Church with the hierarchy and the clergy to the exclusion of the faithful. As pastors of the Church, of course, one of the essential functions of the hierarchy is to teach, and the purity and credibility of such teaching is best maintaind by a prudent separation of the sacred government from the profane. But this is not the same as to make the Christian social doctrine into a theory or a philosophy, an ideological monument which Christians as such are not charged to bring into existence and, relegating such a role specifically to that which is not the Church, namely, the government or to those who may be Christians but who are to act (if it were possible) precisely insofar as they are not members of the Church. Msgr. Boza's teaching, in effect, far from constituting an adequate answer to *Revolución's* argument served only to confirm its truth.

Msgr. Pérez Serantes' third pastoral letter issued only two weeks later, on November 13, was especially remarkable in that it pursued to further conclusions the theme of the choice which imposed itself upon the Christian and upon the Cuban revolution before it could become acceptable to the Cuban hierarchy. The first part of the letter was devoted mainly to another description of the evils of communism and to listing the reasons why its doctrine is incompatible with the Christian faith—but it did also include some remarks of a personal nature against "a well-known and sadly famous statesman of these latitudes . . . an arrogant man . . . of no great talent."[11] Msgr. Pérez also noted that "Communism prefers to work on the minds of people who are destitute of everything, especially those who, amidst so much poverty, are weakened by the rough and constant struggle of life." On the other hand, he said, the spread of communism also depends upon other causes, including

[11] The text used here is the translation of *Catholic Mind*, LIX, 1155 (May–June, 1961).

"inept and thoughtless" government leaders (this was an understated allusion to the traditional style of Cuban political life in Batista's time), as well as "many capitalists who, like the others, follow their own interest, without fulfilling the serious obligations they have contracted with the people. They lack paternal feeling, which no ruler ought to lack." In view of Msgr. Pérez' own use of the term it would be neither inexact nor irrelevant to one's dating of his doctrine to assert that one of his fundamental sociopolitical assumptions was the concept of paternalistic relations between upper and lower classes and between ruler and ruled.

"What recourse," then, did society have "to stop the triumphal march of Communism, with its . . . fascinating and cajoling promises . . . of all material things . . . ?" Msgr. Pérez considered the suggestion often made that "Communism has not swept the whole world away because of the generosity of the American people who, in the last fifteen years have contributed the fabulous sum of $365 billion to obtain world security . . . [and who] have mounted guard on the world frontiers of Communism." How shall we evaluate this explanation? Msgr. Pérez stipulated: "all this appears to be true, and honor must be given to those who deserve it." However, this was not enough. What was required above all was the weapon of Christian ideology, for "ideas are not destroyed by salvos of cannon, nor can they be bought with gold." But did this mean that to feed the hungry and to clothe the naked was unimportant? By no means: "Material bread, yes; may no one lack it." But it should be understood that "the military, as well as the economic programs are provisional measures that can curtail the invasion [of communism] for a short period of time and give us a little longer to find a permanent solution."

It would have been incorrect to say that, according to Msgr. Pérez, Christianity had little to do with social justice. It had much to do with social order, not in the sense that Christianity ought to inspire the order of society but, rather, in the sense that social order descended to society from the Christian doctrine. His position could not have been construed except as assuming that one must first establish a Christian order which, by definition is just, rather than empirically, experimentally, and existentially aiming in the first place at that just order which even communism endeavored to bring about. That was because states derive their justice from above. Consequently he now could come to the point: "even in the United States, if it were not for the strong religious ferment, particularly Catholic, in the mass of the nation, what would become of such a powerful country, today so firm and disciplined in its humanistic, Christian ideology, a country of such close cohesion and firm purpose?"

Msgr. Pérez had been slowly developing this doctrine over a period of six months in order to erect upon it his defense of the Church's position. For the main purpose of this letter is of course, to complete his refutation of the accusation for *lèse patrie* leveled against the Church. What justified Catholics "between the Americans and the Soviets" to choose the first who were attacking Cuba, over the second who had only helped her? The justification lay in the subordination of both Cuba and the United States to the ends of the Church: being civil societies they existed to serve God. The United States no more than Cuba can rise above the earthly, natural, political order unless it participates in the life of the Church. The same subservience of civil society to the Church that justifies, on the one hand, the opposition of the Church to the Cuban government, legitimizes, on the other, the utilization of the United States by the Church to implement that opposition. Strictly speaking, therefore, in this view, it cannot be said that the Church takes the side of the United States against Cuba, for both the United States and Cuba are of accidental importance to the real conflict, which essentially belongs to the supernatural order:

> The struggle has not exactly started between Washington and Moscow, the two formidable military powers that meet each other face to face with death-dealing arms such as the world has never seen or dreamed of before. If it were thus, and Washington were not flanked by Christians, the battle could be considered lost. The battle is really going on between Rome and Moscow, and Rome could lose it only if the Christians were to cease being the vigorous leavening of the dough. Moscow could only win this battle sooner or later if its opponents, *the forces of Rome and its closest allies* [italics mine] were to lay down their arms, the Decalogue, the sacraments and prayer . . . [or] to desert the ranks of Christ.

This is, therefore, a development of the much simpler stand of a month earlier, in which the Christian was asked to choose "without the slightest hesitation" between the United States and Russia—Cuba not figuring in the matter at all. Msgr. Pérez no longer asked Cuban Catholics, formally speaking, to side with the United States. Rather, he taught that siding with the United States is permissible without disloyalty to Cuba insofar as Christianity permits the United States to become her ally against the enemy of man. However, though ally is Msgr. Pérez' own word, it might not be as apt a term as spouse. For alliance implies a symmetry which matrimony does not. The Cuban Church officiated at the forced marriage of the cause of Christianity with the cause of the Cuban policy of the United States.

We have also seen that a certain Catholic segment, though of ever diminishing numbers, remained of the opinion that the Church was imposing a false choice upon her members and upon the revolution. As the pastorals became increasingly counterrevolutionary in tone and content the dissatisfaction of these Catholics began to take a more active form. In places the practice arose of interrupting the reading of the pastorals by repeated singing of the national anthem until the reading stopped and Mass went on. The reading of the complete letter of November 13 was prevented in this manner in Msgr. Pérez' own cathedral of Santiago. For that reason Msgr. Pérez issued a fourth pastoral letter a week later, on November 21, directed specifically to the recalcitrants. It is not of special importance for an understanding of the Cuban Church's theology of counterrevolution, but it does illustrate rather well a certain conception of the relations between bishop and faithful. It read, in part:

> During the last few months, in several cities such as Havana, Camagüey, Manzanillo, Bayamo and in Santiago itself, a veritable deputation of neo-Catholics and their sympathizers appears to have received a call, of impossibly divine origin, to that rare apostolate which consists in interfering with the internal activities of our churches, so as to regulate them in their own fashion, their reformers' ardor having even reached to the violent hindering of the reading of ecclesiastic documents such as have always been read and are being read in Catholic Churches the world over.
>
> To achieve this harebrained purpose these Christians of new stamp have not hesitated during the celebration of Holy Mass to have provoked aforethought events that are from every point

of view reprehensible, thereby making it plain that they do not attend such places for the reasons, that every good Catholic does, and that they care little or nothing for the Cross or for the Crucified, nor for anything of what is done or venerated in our temples, where they vociferate as if they were in mid-street.

These shameful and unusual events culminated last Sunday 13th, in a semi-field battle after the evening Mass in our Cathedral . . . if we were not well acquainted with the procedures and slogans of our most eminent chauvinists and their flatterers our surprise would be boundless as we hear that for these lamentable occurrences it is the victims, no less, who are accused of provoking such outrages as the traditional Catholics have always detested, who have always seen with horror the profanation of their temples. These proceedings are the culmination of, as well as an elegant way of indulging in, the howling, if not as at another time, "Christians! To the lions!" at least, in the current fashion, "To the wall! To the wall!" which at bottom is the same and equally unjust.

In any event, let these pseudo-teachers of all knowledge know that those Catholics who follow the ancient usage continue to go to their churches, as always, to listen as readily to an Epistle of St. Paul as to a Pastoral from their own Bishop as to instructions from their own Pastor. But if any meddler sneaks in, or if anyone, whoever he may be, does not wish to listen to the reading of the day, or if he simply does not feel at home in the house of God, the recourse is always open to him of withdrawing as quietly as he came in.[12]

Of course, there is not much doubt that Msgr. Pérez was quite correct in objecting to the unsheeplike behavior of his flock, and he was doubtlessly entitled to suggest what was the correct procedure for dissidents. Many withdrew not only from churches, but altogether from the Church. It cannot be denied—however little it may affect their culpability—that they did so at his invitation. Naturally, the pro-revolutionary Catholics exhibited nothing more clearly than their own intolerance by the sort of behavior

[12] My translation of the text reproduced in La Quincena, November 30, 1960.

which, in effect, not merely discharged their conscience and invited others to follow, but which actually imposed a point of view upon their fellow Catholics. They did not think of resorting, for instance, to an ostentatious but quiet, withdrawal from the Church at the appropriate moment; that sort of thing would have been effective precisely to the same degree as the proportion of the congregation that it comprised. That was exactly what they feared, for they were a minority. But perhaps they, too, should have been disposed to fail rather than to make prevail at all costs the judgment of their conscience upon others—even if they were right. It seems, on the other hand, that in Msgr. Pérez' mind his guardianship of the faith consisted rather in the custody of true propositions rather than in his cultivation and care of the true belief actually found in the faithful. Nothing else can explain his readiness to dispense with his own flock. In the episcopal and clerical tradition in which he was formed, many Catholics indeed had taken this sort of advice: They had gone and they have not come back.

Perhaps, on the other hand, the bishops counted (correctly, as events were to prove) on a strong stand against Catholic dissidents which would bring most of them into line. For instance, Con la Cruz y con la Patria became ineffective, through the bishops' disapproval, though also partly because as Castro drifted towards communism its position became increasingly weakened by the very object of its defense. Among the clergy, the few remaining "neo-Catholics" were effectively and almost without exception silenced. The lay Catholic organizations found it necessary to choose definitely and without qualifications: They "closed ranks." Thus, the same issue of La Quincena that carried Msgr. Pérez' pastoral of November 21, carried a statement, also dated November 21, subscribed to by all the national Catholic lay organizations, endorsing Msgr. Boza's position.

It is certain, at any rate, that Msgr. Pérez remained determined to stand fast bound to his duty as he conceived it:

> We Catholics do not forget the fate that may befall us with the passage of time. We know, because it has been written by the finger of God, that upon our heads always hang calumny, persecution, insult, abuse and even death itself for no reason other than hatred of Christ . . . Wherever it has been a question of striking Christians there has always been agreement between Annas and Caiphas, between the Herods and the Pilates, between the Jews . . . and the pagans . . . But there shall be nothing to separate us from the love of Christ, neither tribulation, nor anguish, nor nakedness, nor hunger nor death, as St. Paul teaches us.

This was not Msgr. Pérez' last word upon the subject of the revolution,[13] but later documents do not substantially add to what he had said to this point. The final document in the Catholic case, the collective open letter of the hierarchy to Fidel Castro dated December 4, 1960, has been mentioned already, as well as Castro's reply of December 16. There was nothing else that either side needed to say. The battle of words had ended. The stage of physical violence was about to begin.

[13] A fifth pastoral, dated December 24, 1960, expands somewhat upon his pessimistic estimate of human action as contrasted with divine intervention in human affairs through the agency of the Church. By this time all communication media had been denied to the Church, and the pastoral received little circulation except in the form of typewritten copies.